CONQUEST
AND
CONSCIENCE:
the 1840s

# CONQUEST
AND
# CONSCIENCE:
the 1840s

BY ROBERT SOBEL

Illustrated

THOMAS Y. CROWELL COMPANY · NEW YORK · ESTABLISHED 1834

DESIGNED BY JUDITH WORACEK BARRY

*Manufactured in the United States of America*

L.C. CARD 79-143484

ISBN 0-690-20939-8

1   2   3   4   5   6   7   8   9   10

BY THE AUTHOR
*The Origins of Interventionism*
*The Big Board: A History of the New York Stock Market*
*Panic on Wall Street: A History of America's Financial Disasters*
*The Great Bull Market: Wall Street in the 1920s*
*The Curbstone Brokers: The Origins of the American Stock Exchange*
*Scorpions in a Bottle*

# CONTENTS

## 1 / TO A NEW WORLD                                                  1

A critical decade begins with change and challenge in a young nation. Political maturity evolves with new ideas in the social order. An agricultural economy begins to feel the influence of industry and invention. A deluge of new people arrive at the Promised Land, escaping poverty and famine, and seeking a new life of greater liberty.

## 2 / THE WESTERN MAGNET                                              27

Frontiers roll back further and further from coastal communities. The prairies blossom with wheat and corn. "Manifest Destiny" lures the covered wagons across the heartlands of a new continent. Natural resources draw the pioneers as the West retreats across the vast hinterland drained by the Missouri-Mississippi basin.

## 3 / THE INSTITUTIONAL CHALLENGE                                     51

Democracy meets the test of new ideas. New philosophies perk to the boiling point in political, religious, and economic discussions. A Millerite pastor computes the end of the world and makes an appointment with Heaven. He picks the wrong calendar. The communes of New England, New York, New Jersey, and Pennsylvania try self-management in finance, husbandry, and shelter. They borrow from ideas of European Utopians such as Fourier. Utopian designs fail to make a lasting impression on the Yankee horizon.

## 4 / NOSTRUMS AND ENTERTAINMENTS 75

Brain-strain of phrenology, with its informative lumps on the skull and the spiritualistic mumbo-jumbo of things that "go bump in the night," encourages a number of pseudosciences. Spiritualists draw huge crowds to their performances. P. T. Barnum becomes one of the greatest entertainment entrepreneurs in history.

## 5 / THE BUSINESS OF INFORMATION 99

The commercial world finds an urgent need for light in the dark corners of trade. The umbrella of bankruptcy is a convenient haven for the rainy day in the market place. Country traders have difficult relations with wholesalers and jobbers in coastal cities. Grantors of credit seek proper identification of out-of-town buyers and look for help from Thomas Wren Ward of Baring Brothers, Sheldon P. Church of Merchants Vigilance Association, and the Tappan Brothers with their ample spread of credit correspondents in fourteen states.

## 6 / THE BUSINESS OF BANKING 125

Demise of the Bank of the United States disrupts the whole banking community. Lack of stability in state-chartered banks due to organizational difficulties and bad management. Free banking methods compete with charter banks with limited success. Massachusetts introduces the Suffolk System. Banking dollars at shifting daily discount turn dollar profits into mercantile loss. Albert Gallatin offers a plan to take chaos out of the counting house.

## 7 / THE BUSINESS OF TRANSPORTATION 145

Westward Ho. Hoofs, heels, wheels, keels, and barges move inland via overland trails, turnpikes, canals, and mountain climbing locks which haul finished goods east and raw materials west. Financial watering of canal stocks leaves dry beds for investors at home and abroad. The "Iron Horse," with greater speed, improved roadbeds, and better-quality steel, puts mule power into slow decline.

## 8 / THE BUSINESS OF SLAVERY 171

Human chattels are of importance in the economic life of the nation. Writers, preachers, and legislators argue justification for slavery. The issue is debated by the crass and the sensitive, tongues mixed with religious indignation, demagogic fervors, and economic sophistry. The labels of Free States and Slave States become painful political issue. The nation expands on a barter basis: one for you, and one for me. Slavery as a profitable form of labor is questioned.

## 9 / THE DISTAFF REVOLT 191

The slavery question provokes claims of inferior status of women. Abolitionists take up the battle cry of women seeking equality with men at legal, social, and financial levels. Harriet Martineau believes American women to be more moral than European women. The liberation topic broadens to include "the evils of demon rum." The greater the number of topics, the more evident are the splinters of dissent.

## 10 / SECTIONALISM: THE POLITICAL DILEMMA 215

Jacksonian Democracy is replaced by political chaos. Bitterness of debate leaves little room for the moderates. Words and arteries harden in discussion. The game of political geography is played across the maps by Webster and Clay. The slavery issue overshadows all others of significance in national life. Tactics lead strong men to back weak candidates as opportunity suggests. Tippecanoe for a month, and Tyler for four years after.

## 11 / ONWARD TO MEXICO 239

"Manifest Destiny" is the political imperative. President Polk seeks the "cause célèbre" by which to cross the border into Mexico. Polk chooses "Conquest over Conscience" despite serious objections in Congress. Fortune favors Polk a second time. He buys a bargain from the British at the 49th parallel. "Manifest Destiny" completes the square of Maine to Florida to California to Oregon.

## 12 / AN UNCERTAIN PEACE 263

The large land acquisitions resulting from the Mexican War create extreme political tensions. Congress attempts to compromise the issue of slavery in the new lands. Splinter parties weaken the nation as it moves closer to an irrepressible civil conflict.

# FOREWORD

WHY SHOULD DUN & BRADSTREET INVITE DR. ROBERT
Sobel to write, and Thomas Y. Crowell to publish, a book
that turns an intensive light on a thin slice of the nineteenth
century?

There are several answers. Probably the most important reason is that every decade has its personality and a
significance of major or minor importance. The 1840s appeal
to us because they were a decade of new concepts, wild
prophecies, daring ideas, and transitions in the social and
political order, all of which had a strong influence on business and the manner in which trade was conducted. The
needs of commerce in an expanding country called for innovations, one of which—perhaps the most meaningful, at
least, to us—was the founding of The Mercantile Agency,
now better known as Dun & Bradstreet.

We commissioned Dr. Sobel, historian and research
scholar with a personal interest in mid-nineteenth-century
social and political tensions, to recall the significant trends

that paralleled and influenced the evolution of business. He has examined regional motivations and the manner in which business opinion at home and abroad was influenced, on the one hand, by antislavery businessmen, many of whom favored high tariffs to protect industry, and, on the other, by pro-slavery southerners, most of whom supported free trade with its benefit to the cotton market. Dr. Sobel has also drawn ·heavily on the 1840s press, which used plenty of paper and ink exploring the novelties of religion and political systems and the vagaries of culture and custom but could not obscure the activities and momentum of business in a period when it was seeking a formula for self-management.

We are pleased, too, that Thomas Y. Crowell, pioneer American publisher with a birth date of 1834, has put *Conquest and Conscience* into print and between boards for present reading and future reference. We are reminded that Dun & Bradstreet came into being as The Mercantile Agency seven years after the Thomas Y. Crowell Company was born. The term *mercantile agency* eventually found its way into dictionaries as a generic term for a company performing credit-reporting services, a definition still carried in dictionaries but no longer used as such by businessmen. Change is constant in word values, but principles are stubborn in their maintenance of meaning. The sensitive eye of the credit reporter was everywhere observing the vitality of trade and the shifts in the needs and moods of the credit seeker and credit grantor.

Our story here is limited, of course, to ten eventful years marked by the fast pulse of the people generally; by the speculative urge of inland merchants, city bankers, and promoters of canals, plank roads, and railroads; and by the development of the vast resources of mines, timberlands, and fisheries. *Conquest and Conscience* revives for us the excitement crowded into an eventful decade, especially the circumstances in which Lewis Tappan converted a personal and painful difficulty into a general business benefit.

Tappan's vision of an impartial and centralized reservoir of credit information was a gift of major importance to the business community—apparent to some business leaders of the 1840s, but not fully comprehended in scope for the following three decades. It was not until the 1870s, after a generation of service to business, that the utility of credit reporting and legal recognition of its function were established. Lewis Tappan's description of credit reporting "for the promotion and protection of trade" had been defined seven years earlier in the Senate of the United States when Daniel Webster stated in oft-quoted rhetoric:

Commercial credit is the creation of modern times, and belongs, in its highest perfection, only to the most enlightened and best governed nations....Credit is the vital air of the system of modern commerce. It has done more, a thousand times more, to enrich nations, than all the mines of all the world. It has excited labor, stimulated manufacturers, pushed commerce over every sea, and brought every nation, every kingdom, and every small tribe among the races of men to be known to all the rest. It has raised armies, equipped navies, and triumphing over the gross power of mere numbers, it has established national superiority on the foundation of intelligence, wealth, and well-directed industry.

As Dr. Sobel points out, the 1840s are identified as a pivotal decade, marked by significant changes from established customs in daily life. A celebrated artist, Samuel F. B. Morse, invented telegraphy. His first message, "What hath God wrought?", signaled a major step in communication among men separated by great spaces. Road-building, rail-laying, and canal digging sent their echoes over rivers, hills, and prairies.

A chapter in this book deals briefly with the stress of slavery on the economy as well as on the conscience of the people. The social aspects of slavery in themselves, during the 1840s, would demand many chapters, but our purpose is to consider primarily the business of the period.

The 1840s was a decade of extremes in political and economic philosophy that ranged from the ridiculous to something less than the sublime. However, the period was also one of educational adventure, with more than sixty colleges and universities making their appearance. Capitalism met the paternalistic challenge of the socialistic communes and survived. The Yankee mind moved even further away from the European tradition of class distinctions and the conflicts engendered by varying languages and nationalities. The concept of Manifest Destiny turned Yankee eyes westward from the Atlantic coast. The urge for space, coupled with the inborn spirit of adventure, led to the eventual challenge to the Hispanic domain and influence on the Pacific.

*Conquest and Conscience* mirrors a constant tug-of-war. Risk-taking generally outweighed prudence, and virtue often hid behind self-justification when opportunity beckoned. The face of the 1840s had its beauty marks and also its blemishes. And there is no need to boast about, or to excuse, the way it looked.

The picture of the times and its business people comes into sharp focus when we read the credit reports by Lewis Tappan's scriveners of the 1840s. Twenty-five hundred report ledgers with approximately two million handwritten histories of American enterprises in all categories are now in the files of Baker Library at Harvard University. The reports served as a catalyst, bringing buyer and seller together to their mutual benefit. They reflect not only the spirit of business of the times, but strongly indicate the philosophy that would evolve in business during the next 130 years. Samples of these credit reports written in the 1840s, as well as liberal quotations from them, are given in this volume, especially in the appendix which has been added to Dr. Sobel's text.

Management, approaching the complex society of the last quarter of the twentieth century, can look through a rearview mirror and appreciate how the concept of business in the 1840s was influenced by contemporary events. It can observe how necessity devised a means of self-restraint in a decade when precedent was scarce and mutual understanding was imperative to both sides of the marketplace. Yes, the 1840s was a decade of struggle between the urges of conquest and the demands of conscience, a decade of differing moral judgments, and a decade of many events to recall with pride.

It is my hope that *Conquest and Conscience* will be the first of a sequence of over-the-shoulder looks at the decades that followed the 1840s and the significant economic and social trends of these ten-year steps in the progress of our nation's business.

Hamilton B. Mitchell

PRESIDENT

manifestations and ramifications was the leading domestic problem of the period, and toward the end of the decade the women's rights movement was born. The nation engaged in a war that at first divided it, and these divisions might have proven serious had not the war ended quickly. There followed a union of the antiwar and antislavery movements, which at first tried to find voice in conventional politics and then sought other means, at times violent, to attain their objectives. The decade began with economic depression and feelings of optimism and ended with economic prosperity and feelings of pessimism.

No attempt will be made in these pages to point out the similarities between the 1840s and our own times. Yet, through the words of the people of that decade and the accounts of their activities and thoughts, the reader will surely find them. This does not mean, however, that the author believes these parallels should be taken too literally, for history does not repeat itself. One function of this work is to indicate that problems which appear unique and new have antecedents and roots in the past, and that some of these may be found in the 1840s. Such knowledge can enhance our perspective and understanding, but it cannot provide a guide for those who would foresee the future.

*Robert Sobel*
NEW COLLEGE OF HOFSTRA
June 1971

CONQUEST
AND
CONSCIENCE:
the 1840s

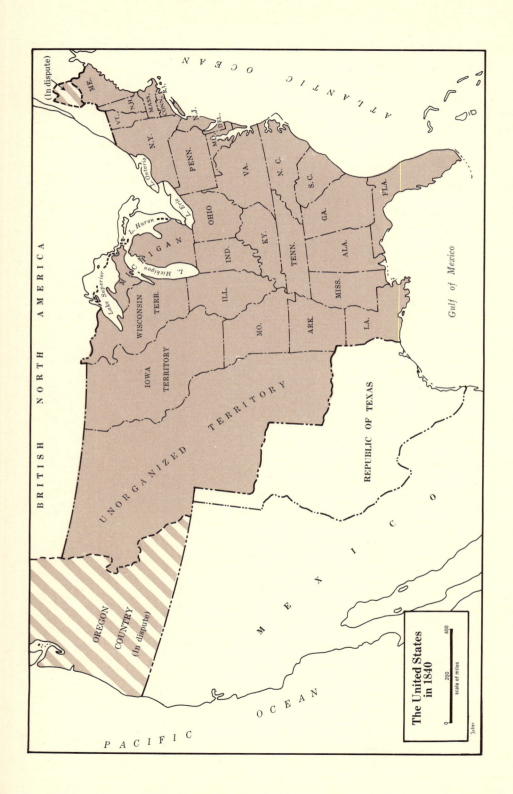

The United States
in 1840

scale of miles

0    200    400

Juber

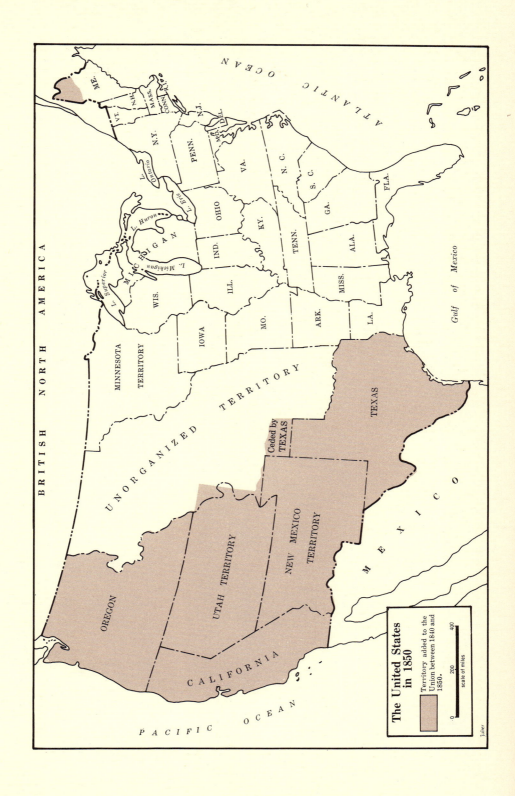

ATLANTIC OCEAN

BRITISH NORTH AMERICA

ME.

N.H.
VT.
MASS.
CONN. R.I.

N.Y.
N.J.
PENN.
MD. DEL.
VA.
N. C.
S. C.
GA.
FLA.

L. Ontario
L. Erie
L. Huron
L. Superior
L. Michigan
MICHIGAN

OHIO
KY.
TENN.
IND.
ILL.
WIS.
ALA.
MISS.
LA.

IOWA
MO.
ARK.

MINNESOTA TERRITORY

UNORGANIZED TERRITORY

Gulf of Mexico

TEXAS

Ceded by TEXAS

NEW MEXICO TERRITORY

UTAH TERRITORY

OREGON

CALIFORNIA

MEXICO

PACIFIC OCEAN

**The United States in 1850**

Territory added to the Union between 1840 and 1850.

0  200  400
scale of miles

Jules

# 1/TO A NEW WORLD

EVEN PRIOR TO INDEPENDENCE THE UNITED STATES had been a land of diverse peoples, many of whom had been drawn to its shores by idealism and ambition. America may have appeared raw and uncivilized to Europe's aristocracy and fascinating to its intellectuals, but to the common peoples of the old continent it seemed a promised land. Such individuals listened eagerly to tales of opportunity in America, and many took the ocean voyage to see for themselves whether or not they were true or exaggerated. To those who remained at home the United States remained the golden land, now made even more popular by letters and messages from their more adventurous relatives and friends who had made the Great Crossing.

One evening in the mid-nineteenth century a Dublin audience gathered to witness the Irish premiere of *Rip Van Winkle,* a dramatization of the Washington Irving story that had recently enjoyed moderate success in New York. American works were usually popular in Ireland, but the audience's response to one line in this play surpassed the actors' fondest expectations. Rip awakens from his sleep and returns to his native village to inquire about his family and friends. During this scene a young man asks him his opinion of George Washington. When Rip naively answers, "Who is he?" the astonished youth replies, "What! Did you never hear of the immortal George Washington, the Father of his Country?" These words evoked an immediate reaction from the spectators. According to a contemporary newspaper,

the whole audience from the pit to the gallery seemed to rise, and with shouting, huzzaing, clapping of hands, and stamping of feet, made the very building shake. These deafening plaudits continued for some time, and wound up with three distinct rounds.

Deeply moved, the actor who portrayed Rip turned to the audience and exclaimed, "God bless old Ireland!" Now even greater cheers shook the hall, and the play could not resume until a brief intermission had calmed the emotionally charged atmosphere of the theater.

Nowhere in the world were Americans more popular in this period than in Ireland. At a time when the French considered Americans either noble savages or barbarians, and the British believed that what was good in America was due to the nation's English heritage while the wilderness had undermined and eroded the rest, the Irish thought the United States the hope of the world.

The Irish had good reason to hold the nation in such regard. Almost every Irish family in the mid-1850s had relatives in America. Thus, the Dublin audience saluted the adopted land of its brothers, sisters, sons, and daughters when it cheered the *Rip Van Winkle* production. A generation later, their children would give the same kind of applause to another play about Rip Van Winkle—this one the version by Dion Boucicault, who himself had left Ireland during the "Hungry Forties" to find a new life in America, where he became the nation's most popular playwright.

Immigrants swelled America's population at a sensitive period. The 1840s was a time of transition between the Age of Jackson and the first clear alarms of the coming Civil War; the decade drew upon earlier issues and anticipated those of the future.

The great battles of the Jacksonian era still raged in the 1840s, but even those who had rejected Andrew Jackson's "mobocracy" realized that the movement to elevate the common man would not die. Prior to Jackson the nation's presidents had been individuals of wide education and social status; though some Europeans might consider Thomas Jefferson, James Madison, and John Quincy Adams the products of a radical society, these men were clearly "natural aristocrats," who had the talent and sophistication to rule an erratic and impetuous people. The same could not be said of presidents like William Henry Harrison and Zachary Taylor, who, though able enough in some ways, were roughhewn in manners and limited in political vision when compared with their predecessors. It was as though the Americans, having proven a nation could survive without a monarch, were determined to demonstrate that the man of typical range of talent was capable of filling the highest post in the land.

America's enchantment with the common man drew many observers to the country in the 1840s. They traveled to all parts of the nation, returned home, and wrote of what they had seen and heard so that others, equally curious but unable or unwilling to make the trip, could learn of events in what was still called "the New World." Never before or since have so many travel books on the United States been written and sold. Indeed, such works are the most important single source for an understanding of the nation during that time. They were read not only by Europe's intellectuals and middle class, but by their American counterparts, who were even more curious to discover who they were and where informed people thought they were going.

The poor of Europe did not read these books, if indeed they could read at all. But through the often exaggerated letters and tales of friends and relatives, they learned of the democratic nature of America. Many determined to cross the Atlantic to escape the remnants of feudal restrictions and live in a land where, in the words of one Scots immigrant, "the air is more free."

Circumstances on both sides of the Atlantic produced mass migrations in the 1840s. As the decade began, the worldwide depression which had started in 1837 persisted. The United States recovered by 1844, but the decline continued in Europe for several years. Ireland was particularly hard hit in the 1840s, and then suffered an even more severe blow in the form of the potato blight of 1845–1849. In desperation, many left for the United States and Canada. "The Irish on their arrival in America cannot believe their own eyes," wrote an English noble in the mid-1840s. "They feel as though under a spell. They do not dare to describe to their friends in Europe the streams of milk and honey that flow through this promised land. One such newcomer wrote his family that he had meat three times a week, when in fact he had it three times a day. When asked why he [didn't tell the truth] to his correspondents, he replied, 'Why is it? It is because they wouldn't believe me if I did.' "

The lure of business also drew people to America in the 1840s. Tales of rapidly growing railroads opening new commercial opportunities for individuals with a little capital and much daring enticed thousands to the United States.

*Landing from an emigrant ship.*
(THE GRANGER COLLECTION)

There were fortunes to be made in factoring, stock-jobbing, dry goods, cotton, manufacturing, and exports, and as had been the case since the seventeenth century, Englishmen with more boldness than capital came to America to make their fortunes. Many failed, for hard work and good intentions were not sufficient to earn a fortune in the rough American business arena, but some did rise to the top, and their success encouraged others to measure opportunity against ingenuity and the blind rush of capital.

Political as well as economic distress brought people to America. Toward the end of the decade Europe underwent a series of upheavals known as the Revolutions of 1848. Essentially middle class and liberal, the revolutions aimed to create constitutional governments, establish popular elections, and increase economic opportunity in all parts of the continent. In effect, Europe's middle class, which had achieved economic power earlier in the century, attempted to win political power as well in 1848. But the movement failed. Although several central European and Italian governments were overthrown and King Louis Philippe's France was replaced by a new republic, the kind of political transformation dreamed of in February 1848 did not take place. Nowhere was the failure more evident than in the Germanys, where the middle class was not only rebuffed but also persecuted. Unable to change their government in Europe, many Germans and other disappointed revolutionaries came to America.

Finally, gold was discovered in California in 1848. Word of nuggets as big as a man's head, rolling down streams almost begging to be taken, spread to Europe soon

6

after the first finds at Sutter's Mill. Immediately Europeans of all classes tried to obtain transatlantic passage. Only a small fraction of those who set out for California in 1849–1850 reached their goal, and of those who did, few managed to find sufficient gold to make the trip worthwhile. But the gold fever did give an added fillip to the immigration figures, and the decade ended on an upswing.

A few statistics provide a quantitative framework for the human story. In 1830 there were 12.9 million Ameri-

*Sutter's Mill.*

(CULVER PICTURES, INC.)

cans; in 1840 there were 17.1 million; and in 1850, 23.2 million. Thus, in only two decades the nation's population almost doubled.

Natural increase continued to provide the largest number of new Americans in this period, but immigration had become increasingly important. In the 1820s only about one out of every twenty additional Americans came from overseas or Canada. In contrast, immigrants accounted for one fifth of the increase in the 1830s and for three tenths of the nation's population growth in the 1840s. The peak year in this two-decade period was 1850, when 370,000 foreigners came to America. Since the population increased 630,000 from 1849 to 1850, almost 59 percent of the yearly increment was the result of immigration. This was the highest ratio of immigration to population in American history.

Immigration statistics and those relating to national origin are necessarily approximations, and there are undoubtedly errors in the figures. For example, the records indicate that 656,145 Irish and 385,431 Germans came to America between 1840 and 1850. But these figures certainly underestimate the scope of Irish and German migration, because many persons from these nations sailed to the United States via British ports and were mistakenly counted as Englishmen. Moreover, the decade's total of 1,427,337 immigrants does not include Canadians and Mexicans who arrived at other than official entry points; nor does it take into consideration those immigrants who returned to Europe after brief stays in America. Nevertheless, these statistics do give an idea of the scope of immigration to America. Its acceleration during the 1840s is perhaps best illustrated by noting that the number of Irish who arrived in the United States in 1849 was only slightly smaller than the *total* immigration of the years 1840 and 1841 combined.

To gain profits as well as to aid the immigrants, several American authors wrote, printed, and distributed advice to those coming to America. *The Emigrant's Guide,* first published in 1832, remained a favorite in the 1840s, when it was joined by the *American Guidebook,* the *Emigrant's Handbook, Information for Emigrants: North America,* and *Travellers Guide and Emigrants Directory.* Some of the new works were quite successful. J. H. Colton, a New York businessman-turned-writer, published *Emigrant's Handbook: or directory and guide for persons emigrating to the United States of America, especially to those settling in the Great Western Valley,* and it sold very well in Germany in 1848. Patrick O'Kelly's *Advice and Guide to Emigrants going to the United States of America,* first published in Dublin in 1834, went through many editions in the 1840s, and it was a popular farewell gift for those leaving Ireland.

The books were quite similar; they offered worthwhile advice and repeated unfounded tales of wealth and opportunity. Almost all were overly optimistic regarding America and exaggerated the possibilities of success, wages, and profits. Francis J. Grund, a strongly pro-American Austrian who spent ten years in America before writing his *The Americans in their Moral, Social, and Political Relations,* proffered counsel that was sounder than most, while at the same time reflecting the views of a middle-class European toward the United States.

of the immigrants. Robert Whyte, who left Dublin on a brig bound for Quebec on May 12, 1847, kept a vivid journal of the voyage. On June 1 he noted that some of the steerage passengers seemed quite ill, and that one had consumption. Ordinarily such a man would have been kept off the ship by the required medical examination in port, but there was no guarantee that the man examined was the passenger who boarded, or "that the person with the ticket was the person named on it, or that the real owner was not down with typhus and being represented by some conniving friend."

Although the law required that each passenger be allotted seven pounds of food per week, cooking facilities were inadequate, so that most of the time half-rotten meat was eaten raw. The situation caused numerous diseases, the most common of which was dysentery. Such was the case on Whyte's vessel. On June 7 fever broke out, and 110 passengers became deathly ill. To protect the rest, the sick were quarantined in "the unventilated hold of the small brig, without a doctor, medicines or even water." When the healthy immigrants demanded better treatment for their fellows, the mate responded by firing a shotgun over their heads, warning that he would take aim next time. Before the voyage ended, more fever victims were added to the list. To make matters worse, the ship was becalmed, and the captain was forced to halve the water ration. Whyte was unable to sleep the night of June 27 because of the "moaning and raving from the hold," where the feverish immigrants called for water. The stench was also unbearable. A Canadian doctor, who had visited many such ships, wrote, "I have seen a stream of foul air issuing from the hatches as dense and as palpable as seen on a foggy day from a dung heap."

The ship entered the St. Lawrence estuary on July 14. All the water except half a cask was gone, and this the crew guarded for its own use. When the ship finally anchored almost two weeks later there was scarcely a healthy person aboard. And yet another week passed before the sick and dead were taken off. "Hundreds were literally flung on the beach, left amid the mud and stones to crawl on the dry land as they could." Shocked by these events, Whyte spoke to Quebec officials and learned that such voyages were not uncommon; indeed, his ship was in better shape than some. The *Larch,* which in 1847 sailed with 440 passengers, lost 108 at sea, and another 150 were in critical condition when the ship docked. Of the 476 passengers on the *Virginius,* 158 died on board and another 106 had to be hospitalized.

All this was common knowledge, although the details were often unknown; even the guidebooks admitted the voyage was hazardous. But the desire to leave an intolerable situation in Europe, coupled with dreams of a golden future in America, was so strong that many took the risk. And the survivors did not seem to blame the captain and crew for their misfortunes. Whyte reported that one immigrant, after burying his wife and placing two shovels in the form of a cross over her grave, said, "By that cross, Mary, I swear to avenge your death. As soon as I earn the price of my passage home I'll go back and shoot the man that murdered you—and that's the landlord."

Most Irish immigrants sailed on the Cunarders, the

ships Samuel Cunard had constructed after he received the British transatlantic mail contract in 1833. At first the Cunarders docked only in Boston. In 1840 that city's population numbered 93,000 persons, and since a sizable proportion was already Irish, a strong Irish-American community developed in the Hub City. After 1847, every other Cunard ship landed in New York City. New York's Irish populace outnumbered Boston's, but since the city itself was also more than three times larger, the newcomers had a more difficult time making their presence and needs felt.

Those foreigners who visited both cities usually preferred Boston. "The city is a beautiful one, and cannot fail, I should imagine, to impress all strangers very favorably," wrote Charles Dickens, and another English visitor, Lady Emmeline Wortley, thought "Boston is a very handsome, very large, and very clean town." But such judgments reflected the writers' sentiments and prejudices as much as the actual conditions in the cities. Lady Emmeline, for example, noted that "the town reminds me of an English village in many respects"; Dickens was impressed by the tone Harvard University gave Boston. He was not alone in this belief. Charles Lyell, the noted geologist, found the intellectual life there stimulating, and that of New York considerably inferior; Francis and Theresa Pulszky, two foreign guests, noted that "Boston and its society had a peculiar character, different from all other cities of the world. It is the only one where knowledge and scholarship have the lead of the society." Since most of the visitors were upper class, had intellectual interests, favored abolitionism, appreciated the arts and letters, and were intrigued with the new religious and philosophical movements in the nation, their preferences are understandable. Boston was the home of the nation's leading philosophers; many abolitionists lived there; and the city had a more aristocratic tone than New York. Even Dickens, who considered himself a champion of the common people, preferred Boston for these reasons; he also found much to admire in the city's charitable institutions. But neither he nor most other upper-class visitors dwelt at length on the wretched conditions of immigrants in Boston. The immigrants themselves did not write of this, but indicated discontent in a more eloquent manner; after 1847 a greater number chose New York as a port of debarkation than Boston. In the 1840s Boston was a place where intellectuals could find a common home, while New York was the proletariat and business capital of the nation.

In the 1840s New York City, with specific reference to Manhattan Island, was a filthy, harsh, dangerous place. Pigs, which were the city's scavengers until mid-decade, roamed the streets at will, as did thousands of dogs, who assisted in their work. The pigs were docile enough, but the dogs at times turned vicious, and in 1842 the city's newspapers contained stories of children being killed by a dog pack on Broadway. Cattle were driven through the city's streets to markets on the West Side. In 1844 an enraged bull gored a man to death on Hester Street. But animals were a minor threat in New York compared with the gangs that owned the city's streets. In the Five Points district on the West Side the Forty Thieves, Shirt Tails, and Plug Uglies ruled unchallenged. In 1840 police entered the area in teams; by 1847 they refused to go in at all,

*Scene at the Irish Emigrant Office on Ann Street, New York.*
(THE BETTMANN ARCHIVE)

since the gangs had bested them in almost every encounter. The same was true of the East River section, where the Daybreak Boys, Swamp Angels, and Hookers were in control.

Few upper-class visitors mentioned the gangs or the city's brutality, for their hosts would hardly take them to areas where these were in evidence. Dickens was one of the few to venture to the immigrant quarters, where he saw slum conditions as bad as any he had witnessed in Britain. He saw garbage piled four feet high in the streets, prostitutes at every turn, and thieves at work in locations where police were absent.

Foreign visitors often thought it interesting that the Irish, who had been farmers at home, tended to remain in

16

the. urban areas of America. Dickens ascribed this to the need for cheap, unskilled labor in the cities and to the fact that the Irish, being the lowest on the social and economic ladder, were able to find menial jobs there. "Who else would dig, and delve, and drudge, and do domestic work, and make canals and roads, and execute great lines of internal improvement?" he asked. J. S. Buckingham, an English journalist and politician who visited America in 1837 and published his memoirs of the country four years later, thought the Irish gathered in cities because they were habitually drunk, and cheap gin and other alcoholic beverages were easily obtained in New York and Boston. But Buckingham was not only strongly anti-Irish, he was also a temperance worker. The earl of Carlisle, who was a more disinterested observer, remarked on the sobriety of the Boston Irish, and contrasted them favorably with the more rowdy New Yorkers.

Some writers, Ebenezer Davies and the American editor E. L. Godkin among them, thought the Irish concentration in the cities was part of a Catholic plot to take over the nation. A segment of the press echoed this strain for the next century. Thomas Grattan, who served as British consul in Boston from 1839 to 1846, and who was one of the most perceptive observers of Americans in the period, thought the anti-Irish sentiments were a heritage from Britain. Since the British and Irish were always at odds, and the American middle class looked to Britain for guidance in social and intellectual matters, it was natural for many Americans to hate the Irish. American anti-Catholicism may have had more immediate roots in domestic politics, but at least one English visitor to the United States expressed violent anti-Irish feelings:

The Irish servants and porters were the nuisance of the United States. Despised by the Americans, themselves despising the blacks; with their bellies full for the first time in their lives; insolent in their looks; extortionate in their demands; oaths in their mouths; free from all restraint of a neighborhood or parish priest; beggars upon horseback.

Like almost all immigrant groups, the Irish clashed repeatedly with the free Negroes. They recognized the urban blacks as competitors for jobs and believed that the Negroes represented an immediate threat to their efforts to rise on the social ladder. Indeed, the Irish fear and distrust of the Negroes was so great that it blinded them to the fact that the blacks were a people even more oppressed than themselves. Dickens made the following observation of a Negro tenement area:

The match flickers for a moment, and shows great mounds of dusky rags upon the ground.... Then the mounds of rags are seen to be astir, and rise slowly up, and the floor is covered with heaps of negro women .... They have a charcoal fire within; there is a smell of singeing clothes, or flesh, so close they gather round the brazier; and vapours issue that blind and suffocate .... Where dogs would howl to lie, women and boys slink off to sleep, forcing the dislodged rats to move away in quest of better lodgings.

None of the European visitors to America in the 1840s considered the possibility of a union of the poor against the wealthy; such notions were two decades in the future. Some Americans did touch upon the idea, but none developed it to any great extent. The reason for this was an aspect of

*Charles Dickens.*

19

American life that struck all who came to study the land and its people: the absence of a rigid class or caste system. Europeans complained that Americans were too money-conscious, but they also noted that money in America was the universal class solvent. In Europe a poor man who had obtained a large amount of capital was merely a wealthy parvenu; in America he was a member of the bourgeoisie. In America there were classless railroad carriages, classless restaurants, and classless theater stalls—indeed, at a distance it was not possible to know whether a person was a member of the upper or middle class.

The immigrants were aware of the possibility of social mobility in America. Upon arrival in the United States men often found work as waiters or canal laborers. Immigrant women often became maids, cooks, and domestics. Foreigners, both men and women, received lower salaries than their native counterparts, and often competed with Negroes for work. But most hoped that their lowly jobs would eventually lead to better opportunities. Unfortunately, this proved true for only a small minority.

Most immigrants in the cities were law-abiding. They saw wealth all around them, and occasionally a friend would get a good job, open a small business, go west and obtain a farm, or in some other way enter the middle class. The remote possibility that this, too, might happen to them made the immigrants hate those who, like themselves, were trying to rise higher, and not the men above them. Oftentimes immigrants who had arrived only a year before went to the piers to see the ships dock and to watch newcomers walk in a daze from the gangplank. Their clothes would be ragged and their faces pinched. The "old-timers" would reflect that this was what they had looked like a year earlier, and consider their meager progress impressive. Perhaps they also thought that since the newly arrived foreigners formed the bottom of the social heap, they themselves got a boost up. Thus, the factory worker viewed the foreman not as a class enemy, but as a man who had a job he wanted. His fellow-worker was not a comrade in arms, but a person competing for his job. In bad times he joined unions whose goals were to prevent new immigration to America, which might threaten his position. In good times he looked to the small unions to obtain wage increases that would make his life easier. Never did he see the union as a means of over-throwing the established social order. Harriet Martineau, who visited America prior to the panic of 1837, wrote of well-dressed clerks, well-fed newsboys, and a generally happy people. She noted that New Orleans stevedores, by threatening to strike during a particularly busy period, ob-tained two large wage increases in a month. Americans were indeed materialistic, she observed, but their material-ism was more than a manifestation of greed, for through acquired wealth Americans proved their worth.

Newly arrived immigrants learned this lesson even before they could speak English. Within weeks they be-came "Yankees," and wrote home of the wonders of their new country. Their reports were so favorable that when foreign visitors wrote and spoke of starvation in some American cities during the depression that followed the panic of 1837, they were believed in America, but not in Europe. Buckingham stated that "instances of death, from destruction and want, are much more numerous than I had thought possible in a country like this," but found that few of his English readers would accept this. The Irish and others continued to come, and even if they suffered and never achieved much more than they had at home, the chance of success in America was still far better than in any place they had left behind.

Like the Irish, the German immigrants hoped for a better life in the United States, but unlike their counterparts from Ireland, many Germans found their way to the Midwest. Some provided a cheap source of labor for such cities as Cincinnati. Many more became farmers, and one English visitor, who complained that he had walked through New York without hearing a word of "civilized English," noted that "the states of the plains area are as much a part of Germany as is the Palatinate."

The Germans went to the Midwest for understandable historic and economic reasons. In the first place, there were many Germans in that part of the country prior to 1840. American cotton ships, bound from New Orleans to continental ports in the early part of the century, would bring back German, French, and Dutch immigrants on the return voyage; once they reached New Orleans it was not a difficult trip to St. Louis, Cincinnati, or even Chicago. Since land was less expensive in the Midwest than in the East, the farmers who came from Germany prior to 1840 often continued their agricultural pursuits in the United States. Many Germans who left their homeland early in the 1840s were assisted by relatives already in the Midwest, and they went to that region to join them. Middle-class Germans who came for political reasons had sufficient funds to make the journey on their own, and unlike the Irish, they did not remain in the eastern cities. In the 1840s Germans established communities—many of which retained the language and customs of their native country—throughout the Midwest.

On the other hand, the Germans had a language problem, while the Irish did not. As a result, they could barely communicate with their native neighbors in their wilderness farm communities, even though the older settlers often admired their efforts. When the Germans learned English and adapted some of their native customs to the American soil, they became readily assimilated with the older English and Scots settlers in the region. Such was not the case with the Irish, who were distrusted for their religion, stigmatized as drunkards, and disliked by many Anglo-Americans who retained Old Country attitudes. Philip Hone, a former New York mayor and a diarist, wrote in 1836 that

there arrived at this port during the month of May, 15,825 passengers. All Europe is coming across the ocean; all that part at least who cannot make a living at home; and what shall we do with them? They increase our taxes, eat our bread, and encumber our streets, and not one in twenty is competent to keep himself.

This observation was an exaggeration to be sure, but it illustrated a common American view of the urban immigrants. There was no similar reaction to the midwestern Germans in this period.

In the 1840s it was commonplace to say that the United States was a young nation, and so it was when compared with the nations of Europe. But it was something else; America in the nineteenth century was also the *oldest* new nation, for the world was changing quickly even then, and the United States was aware of these changes and reacted to them rapidly. The middle and upper class European visitors to the United States did not say so, but their journals indicate a recognition of this fact. They came not only to see how a people tried to rule themselves, but to witness what might happen in Europe in the next generation or later.

When they arrived they saw people living in the same conditions as they had left behind, and this might have led them to believe that the United States was becoming the refuse heap of western civilization. In 1850 more than one of every eight Americans was foreign-born; in the Northeast the ratio was one of every seven. Harsh critics of America thought the immigrants would overwhelm the natives and turn the nation into a huge slum. After all, how many destitute, uneducated, and uprooted people could even the United States absorb before suffering a decline? Others, more sympathetic to both America and the immigrants, noted that the newcomers were making significant contributions to their adopted country, that many were accepting American ways, and that most appeared invigorated by the institutions of their new homes. One of these observers, Francis Grund, even recognized that the immigrants' antisocial behavior was caused not by their "innate nature," as some believed, or "racial characteristics," as the New York *Herald* wrote, but by wretched poverty. Grund wrote:

The Irish in Boston are a remarkably orderly people. They are *not* given to intemperance; but on the contrary, willing to aid in its suppression. If the annals of prisons and houses of correction furnish a larger number of Irish than American names, it must be remembered that, in all countries, the greatest number of culprits is furnished by the poorer and least educated classes, and that as strangers, unacquainted with the peculiar police regulations of the towns, they are more apt to trespass against the laws, and make themselves liable to punishment, than those who have been brought up under its influence, and with whom obedience to it has become a habit.

But even Grund did not consider whether Europe's misfits were not indeed the *best* kind of citizens the nation could have. A person who left a backward, agrarian nation in which his family had lived for centuries, or a country wracked by political upheaval, who endured a dangerous transatlantic voyage and took up residence in an urban, commercial, raw country, where he was surrounded by strangers, was well endowed with ambition, energy, and daring.

In Europe such an individual would have had to find his place in a fixed society. In America the society was fluid, and the immigrant, bound by neither antique ties nor obsolete conventions, had at least the possibility of improving himself. Knowing this, the immigrant thus took a major step in his Americanization. Furthermore, he was part of the giant sweep westward that changed the face of the globe in the mid-nineteenth century. For as Europeans crossed the Atlantic to seek a new world, so many native Americans, equally restless, traversed the continent to satisfy their dreams and ambitions.

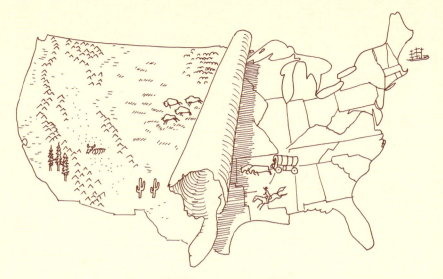

# 2/THE WESTERN MAGNET

IN THE NINETEENTH CENTURY CIVILIZATION MOVED westward. While immigrants crossed the Atlantic to come to the United States, many Americans from the more settled eastern states traveled to the western territories and newer states—relocations that were often as dangerous as ocean voyages. Census officials might define the frontier as the area where there were fewer than two people per square mile, but to easterners it was a much more romantic place. It was the West, the place that historian Frederick Jackson Turner would later call the arena "between civilization and savagery."

Just as Europeans in the 1840s would ask New Yorkers about their contacts with the Indians, New Yorkers believed that Indians still roamed Indiana and that Chicago was a wild, cowboy-ridden town long after it had become one of the nation's major cities. The attitude of Europe vis-à-vis America was comparable to that of the East vis-à-vis the West, and this was so not only for regions but for individuals. On the one hand, Europeans looked upon immigrants as brave and daring men, while on the other they thought only misfits and criminals would prefer the savage New World to the safety and comforts of the old. Similarly, easterners viewed those who went west as adventuresome but foolish. In 1846 the New York *Herald* quoted with approval the words of President Timothy Dwight of Yale, which four decades earlier had summed up the negative views easterners held of those who ventured west.

All countries contain restless inhabitants; men impatient of labor; men who contract debts without intending to pay them; who had rather talk than work; whose vanity persuades them that they are wise, and prevents them from knowing that they are fools; who are delighted with innovation; who think places of power and profit due their peculiar merits; who feel that every change from good order and established society will be beneficial to themselves; who have nothing to lose, and therefore expect to be gainers by every scramble; and who, of course, spend life in disturbing others, with the hope of gaining something for themselves. Under despotic governments they are awed into quiet; but in every free community they create, to a greater or less extent, continual turmoil; and have often overturned the peace, liberty, and happiness, of their fellow-citizens.

Not all observers shared Dwight's pessimism. Alexis de Tocqueville, the French nobleman who visited America in the 1830s, had a different view of the West. His famous *Democracy in America,* published in 1835, is the most perceptive study of the Americans written in this period. Several of its paragraphs indicate Tocqueville's belief that the West was the cutting edge of American democracy.

It is in the West that one can see democracy in its most extreme form. In these states, in some sense improvisations of fortune, the inhabitants have arrived only yesterday in the land where they dwell. They hardly know one another, and each man is ignorant of his nearest neighbor's history. So in that part of the American continent the population escapes the influence not only of great names and great wealth but also of the natural aristocracy of education and probity. No man there enjoys the influence and respect due to a whole life spent publicly in doing good. There are inhabitants already in the new states of the West, but not as yet a society.

The West of which Tocqueville wrote was the "Old West," or the Northwest Territory, which by 1837 was considered "settled." Emigrants from the East were the principal occupants of this land, and since considerable capital and long preparations were required for the trip from the Atlantic seaboard to the Midwest, most settlers made the journey in short jumps of two or three hundred miles. Thus, a New Yorker might aim for Pennsylvania, a Pennsylvania farmer for Ohio, and an Ohio settler for Indiana or Illinois. The exceptions to this pattern were southerners who went up the Mississippi and later the Missouri, and the Germans who landed in New Orleans and then went upriver. But for the most part, settlement proceeded along rivers that ran from west to east, and not from north to south.

At one time historians believed that the West was a "safety valve" for the East, allowing impatient young men to realize their dreams in areas where they would not come up against an established order, and thereby sparing the nation possible social upheavals and civil war. More recent studies have shown this was not the case. Few urban workers went west, since they lacked the skills and interests for

*Customhouse on the Plaza in San Francisco, built by the Mexicans in
1844 — a typical early California structure. After the American
occupation of California the customhouse was used as an office
building.*

that kind of life. Nor did great migrations take place during depressions; discontent was high during such periods,
but cash reserves were low. Instead, families went westward in good times, and more often than not they were
experienced farmers and knew generally what to expect

when they got to Indiana and Illinois. The western settlers of the pre-1840s era were rarely intellectuals, rebels, or dreamers. These types could not have survived the dangers and difficulties of the raw frontier, where pragmatic cooperation, not idealistic individualism, was necessary for success.

By the 1840s a pattern of settlement was set and seemed to work satisfactorily. Speculators acquired public lands and encouraged families to buy farms. In most cases western banks, owned or controlled by the speculators, provided the settlers with their mortgages. The government, for its part, cooperated by moving the Indians to lands located farther west and establishing forts along the frontier. The panic of 1837 ended this phase abruptly, for the depression hit the West harder than any other section of the nation and many of its key land banks failed. Land sales fell off at once, and prices for farm products went into a bad slump. Western farmers lost their meager capital, their markets were weak, and prices for their products evaporated. During the five-year depression thousands saw their entire life's work go under the auctioneer's hammer.

The West recovered from the depression in 1842, but the former pattern of settlement did not revive. Indian removal was an early casualty of the panic. The Democrats, who under the leadership of Presidents Andrew Jackson and Martin Van Buren had pursued that policy, were turned out of office in the 1840 elections and replaced by the Whigs, who had far less interest in the program. In addition, the western banks and land speculators never recovered from the disaster.

This did not mean the nation's drive to the Pacific was ended. Indeed, if anything, the movement accelerated. Until the 1840s Americans were content to nibble away at the Indian frontier, slowly pushing westward, and replacing Indian lodges with small farms. After 1840 the nation prepared to play the game of continental hopscotch, to bypass much of the Louisiana Purchase territory, and to establish states on the Pacific coast. This movement was a reflection of the concept usually known as Manifest Destiny, the term coming from an article that John O'Sullivan, the editor of the strongly anti-British, intensely patriotic New York *Morning News,* wrote for the *United States Magazine and Democratic Review* of August 1845. In this article O'Sullivan called for war against both Britain and Mexico so that the nation would have more "growing room."

Noting that the nation's population had increased from 4 million during Washington's administration to more than 20 million in 1845, O'Sullivan argued that the nation would burst its seams unless more land were made available. Only the extension of the United States to the Pacific coast would relieve this pressure; there was no other solution to the problem, and no force on earth could prevent the western drive. "Our manifest destiny," he said, "is to overspread the continent allotted by Providence for the free development of our yearly multiplying millions." Four months later, in a *Morning News* editorial, O'Sullivan wrote of "our manifest destiny to overspread and to possess the whole of the continent which Providence has given us for the development of the great experiment of liberty and federated self-government entrusted to us."

But Manifest Destiny was more complicated than O'Sullivan indicated. As he saw it, the United States had to remove the influence of the Mexicans from the Southwest and the Old World British from the Northwest to allow the vital Americans to seize, develop, and make bloom the garden of the West. If this had been all there was to the movement, it might have excited a few eastern intellectuals and then died, as did many other similar programs. But this was not the case. Manifest Destiny had much broader support: easterners wanting a larger safety valve, imperialists dreaming of an American empire in the West, an assortment of pro- and anti-slavery men, practical politicians, would-be immigrants to the new lands, and a varied collection of religious and social experimenters all had a common interest in populating the trans-Mississippi West.

One of the groups interested in Manifest Destiny was led by young men who had not been old enough to participate in the Jacksonian reform movement of the 1830s, and who considered the drive for social and political equality in the 1840s either completed or irrelevant. As the nation turned its attention increasingly to the slavery issue during the latter decade, these men argued that slavery was unimportant when compared to the challenges of the West. Instead of worrying about the slaves, they urged, Americans should concern themselves with national needs and an imperial destiny. Should they do this, North and South could unite in a crusade to bring American civilization to the Pacific instead of destroying each other in what the group considered a fruitless exercise of little consequence.

33

The group even had a name: Young America. According to the *Boston Times* of December 11, 1844:

The spirit of Young America . . . will not be satisfied with what has been attained, but plumes its young wings for a higher and more glorious flight. The hopes of America, the hopes of Humanity must rest on this spirit . . . . The steam is up, the young overpowering spirit of the Country will press onward. It will be as easy to stay the swelling of the ocean with a grain of sand upon its shore, as to stop the advancement of this truly democratic and omnipotent spirit of the age.

To this, the *United States Journal* of May 3, 1845, added:

There is a new spirit abroad in the land, young, reckless, vigorous, and omnipotent . . . . It sprang from the warm sympathies and high hopes of youthful life, and will dare to take antiquity by the beard and tear the cloak from hoary-headed hypocrisy. Too young to be corrupt . . . it is Young America, awakened to a sense of her own intellectual greatness by her soaring spirit. It stands in strength, the voice of the majority . . . .

Whether or not Young America attracted a major portion of the population is not known, but the movement did number in its ranks some of the most articulate and promising of the new crop of political leaders. Stephen Douglas of Illinois was only thirty-two years old in 1845, yet he had already established himself as a bright star in the House of Representatives. His colleague from Illinois, John Wentworth, was only thirty, and he was serving his second term in the House of Representatives. The journalist O'Sullivan was thirty-two years old in 1845, and Walt Whitman, who at that time favored the United States' expansion, was

*Brigham Young.*

twenty-six. All spoke in glowing terms of the West; all were strongly anti-British, since Britain's control of the Oregon territory seemed the major barrier to the Pacific destiny; all were martial in tone and spirit, eager for a new war to prove America's worth.

Young America adopted Manifest Destiny as its slogan and the West as its utopia. Its leaders called upon Americans to go to the Pacific coast and establish America's claim for once and for all. To encourage such migration, Young America writers published leaflets and guidebooks not unlike those given Europe's would-be immigrants. "It is frequently asked why are those western people so peculiarly colossal in their notions of things and the prospects of our nation," said the Albany *Argus,* a leading Young America newspaper. The answer was obvious:

Does not this inspiration spring from their extraordinary country? Their mighty rivers, their vast sea-like lakes, their noble and boundless prairies, and their magnificent forests afford objects which fill the mind to its utmost capacity and dilate the heart with greatness. To live in such a splendid country ... expands a man's view of everything in this world ....

While Young America was interested in the potential of the entire West, an alliance of small farmers and merchants concerned itself with a specific area of settlement and commerce. Since the time of Zebulon Pike's 1806–1807 expedition to the Southwest, Americans had been intrigued by the commercial possibilities of the region. New Mexico, Chihuahua, and California were nominally part of Mexico, but the central government had poor control north of the Rio Grande, offered the inhabitants of the Southwest few manufactured goods, and could not transport goods from Mexico's southern states to Santa Fe as cheaply as Americans could bring them from Independence,

Missouri. In 1821 a businessman, William Becknell, organized the first important trade with Santa Fe. Becknell and those who followed took silks, hardware, woolen goods, and luxury items to Santa Fe, where they were sold for hard cash (usually Mexican silver) and then redistributed throughout northern Mexico.

The trip was expensive. Since mules were cheaper in Santa Fe than in Independence, Missouri traders bought their pack animals in the Southwest. But there were few other Mexican goods for the return trip to Independence. The traders never gave up the search for a profitable Mexican import, but the items were not to be found.

The Santa Fe traders had other problems. The Indians, particularly the Comanches, waylaid many wagon trains, making the trip as dangerous as it was profitable. Moreover, the Mexicans, realizing how lucrative the commerce had become, began in 1839 to impose a charge of $500 on each wagon entering Santa Fe. This added expense encouraged the traders to use larger wagons and to establish friendlier relations with local officials. Corruption quickly dominated the system, and by the 1840s an "understanding" had been reached: the fee was divided into three parts, one for the government, one for the customs official, and the last retained by the trader.

Despite Indians, corruption, the lack of an import commodity, and other problems, the Santa Fe trade was lucrative, returning a gross profit of from 10 to 40 percent, depending on the trade goods, size of wagons, and other variables. In the two decades after Becknell's first wagons arrived at Santa Fe, the trade averaged $130,000 a year and it rose irregularly—reaching $450,000 in 1841. Troubles with Mexico led to a disruption of commerce in 1843–1844, but then it quickly recovered and in 1846 was estimated at $1,752,000. And when the southwest territory came into the possession of the United States as an aftermath of the Mexican War, the Santa Fe trade became a major business for Missouri merchants and manufacturers.

The Southwest also attracted settlers, although not many before the 1840s. In 1840 there were fewer than 350 Americans in California, and most of them were trappers and sailors. A few were boosters of the area. Thomas Larkin, later the American consul in Monterey and the town's leading merchant, urged his countrymen to migrate to California and also functioned as a United States government undercover agent promoting annexation to the United States. More famous was John Sutter, a Swiss farmer who had arrived in California in 1839, acquired Mexican citizenship and a large land grant, and created his own little

*The Mormon exodus from Nauvoo.*
(CULVER PICTURES, INC.)

38

kingdom in the Sacramento Valley. Not only had Sutter the most profitable farms in California, but he organized his own army and issued his own coins. Like Larkin he encouraged others to come to California, but he made it clear that he meant to protect his own interests against any who might threaten them.

Prior to the 1837 panic approximately thirty Americans a year migrated to California; even fewer went in the late 1830s. Then, in 1841, John Bidwell led thirty-two persons to California, and in the following years the numbers increased. By 1845 more than 250 venturesome souls a year were going to California, and the total of Americans in the region was estimated at 700. As the American population grew the movement for annexation of California to the United States also gained momentum.

In 1841 Commodore Thomas ap Catesby Jones, commander of the American Pacific squadron, was given secret orders to seize Monterey in case of war between the United States and Mexico. Jones did not wait for such an emergency. Instead, when he heard rumors of a possible British design on California, he landed at Monterey in October 1842, overran the town, and raised the American flag. Jones quickly realized his mistake and withdrew, and Mexico received an official American apology. But both nations knew that the Jones expedition was a portent of the future. Mexico had already seen how a few Americans in Texas had defeated them and achieved independence; California appeared to be following the same script.

The Bidwell party of 1841 had come to California via the Oregon Trail, which was followed to the present

Wyoming-Idaho border, at which point most of the wagon train continued westward, while Bidwell pushed to the south. In the early 1840s the Santa Fe Trail was a commercial route sometimes used by settlers; the Oregon Trail was the main highway for western-bound farmers. And Oregon proved to be a greater magnet than California.

In some respects Oregon was a more attractive area. Unlike the situation in California, the United States had a territorial claim to Oregon, based on the Lewis and Clark expedition of Jefferson's administration and John Jacob Astor's subsequent creation of Astoria, a fur empire in the Columbia Valley. The British claim went back even further, to Robert Gray's explorations of the Columbia River in 1792 and George Vancouver's descriptions of the area, written in 1798. But Americans resettling in Oregon had more reason to hope for eventual annexation to the United States than did those who went to California.

Oregon also had drawbacks. The Oregon Trail was three times as long as the Santa Fe, was more open to Indian attack, wound through rugged territory that was impassable several months of the year, and took settlers to a country that seemed more threatening and difficult to tame than California. In the late 1830s and early 1840s California's destiny seemed to be agriculture, while Oregon was trapper country. This posed special problems for would-be farmers in Oregon. They knew only too well that in addition to fighting the elements and the Indians, and defending themselves against the British, they would have to contend with an unfriendly and powerful group of trappers. Despite this, Oregon attracted more than 3,000

American farmers in 1845, or twelve times the number that went to California.

Oregon was a larger American settlement than California for a variety of reasons, the most important of which were better organization and leadership coupled with religious zeal. In the 1820s Hall Kelley, a Boston schoolteacher, became obsessed with the idea of founding a settlement in Oregon. A reading of the Lewis and Clark journals fired his imagination, and he wrote brochures and pamphlets extolling the virtues of a land he had never seen. "No portion of the globe presents a more fruitful soil, or a milder climate, or equal facilities for carrying into effect the great purposes of a free and enlightened nation," he said, comparing Oregon to the Garden of Eden.

Kelley was never able to create the large Oregon settlement he planned, but in 1832 he headed a small party bound for Oregon by way of New Orleans, Veracruz, and San Diego. He lost his group along the way, and by the time he arrived in Vancouver he was sick and penniless. Soon afterward Kelley returned to Boston, where he spent the rest of his life propagandizing on behalf of Oregon.

The Kelley expedition was a failure, but Kelley's books and articles encouraged others to make the trip. The most important of them was Nathaniel Wyeth, a leading New England ice merchant, who made two unsuccessful overland trips to Oregon in 1832 and 1834. Wyeth had hoped to open Oregon to American commerce and reap large profits, while at the same time fulfilling his romantic dreams for the area, but after 1834 he abandoned his plan, returned to the ice business, and recouped his fortune.

Wyeth's efforts were watched carefully by leaders of the Methodist Church and the American Board of Commissioners for Foreign Missions, which included the Presbyterian, Congregational, and Dutch Reformed churches. In the 1820s and 1830s these religious groups mounted major campaigns to Christianize the western Indians. Indeed, a small group of Methodists led by Jason Lee traveled with the Wyeth expedition of 1834 and remained in Vancouver after Wyeth returned home. Lee established a small colony in the Willamette Valley and urged others in New England to join it. He himself returned to Boston in 1838 to plead for assistance, and the church was so impressed with the colony that Lee returned to Oregon with another party of pioneers interested in farms and conversions.

The American Board also sent a mission to Oregon in 1834, but its leader, Samuel Parker, was too old and ill to continue past St. Louis. Dr. Marcus Whitman joined the expedition there and in time took charge of the group; Reverend Henry Spaulding took over responsibility for the religious work. Whitman was able to establish three settlements near present-day Walla Walla, Lewiston, and Spokane, but none was very successful. Whitman quarreled with Spaulding constantly, the Indians refused to accept the Spaulding version of Christianity, and the death rate was high. A similar mission, led by Catholics under the Jesuit Jean De Smet, also failed to meet expectations. The Whitman party remained as farmers, but the American Board mission was burned by the Indians in 1847, marking the effectual end of the religious experiment.

As early as 1840, Whitman came to realize that if

Oregon were to attract Americans, missionary work would have to be secondary to farming. In articles for the *Christian Advocate* and other magazines and newspapers he called farmers to "come to Oregon, where the land is rich and opportunities beckon." His words were seconded by John C. Frémont, an army officer who made two expeditions to the Far West in 1842 and 1843.

Frémont was a young, dashing, and romantic figure, whose explorations captured the imagination of the nation. But Frémont also made practical contributions. He mapped the western areas, described the best routes to Oregon and California, and gave good advice on how would-be settlers

*Tabernacle camp built by the Mormons on their arrival in Utah.*
(THE GRANGER COLLECTION)

should prepare for the trip. The report of his first expedition was a "best seller" in 1844. Published under Frémont's name (though actually written by his wife, Jessie, the daughter of the pro-western and Jacksonian senator Thomas Hart Benton of Missouri), the book made "the Pathfinder of the West" a national hero and a much-discussed presidential possibility. But Frémont's advocacy of the South Pass route to both Oregon and California led many unsuspecting settlers to their deaths. Snaking through the High Sierras, the Pass was a death trap for those who ventured through in the early winter. In 1846 the most famous tragedy of the South Pass occurred when the party led by George and Jacob Donner became snowbound at the present-day Donner Lake. Unable to move, the Donner party resorted to murder and cannibalism before rescuers came to the assistance of the few survivors. News of the Donner atrocity shocked the nation, but did not prevent others from following to the promised lands of Oregon and California.

At almost the same time the Donner party looked westward to California, the Mormons set out for a haven in the wilderness. The great trek of the Mormons to Salt Lake closely parallels the decision of the Pilgrims to come to America. Like the Pilgrims, the Mormons were a despised religious minority, persecuted in their old homes, and like them their search for a refuge was long and dangerous. Of all the groups that went west in the 1840s, the Mormons were the best organized, best led, and best prepared for the trip. Religious zeal motivated their exodus, but it could not have succeeded without excellent management.

The faith's founder was Joseph Smith, the son of a Vermont farmer, who in the mid-1820s spoke of visions and revelations. This was not unusual at the time, or for that matter throughout the first half of the nineteenth century, which was an age of revivalism and emotionalism in religion. In 1827, in Palmyra, New York, Smith claimed to have dug up a series of golden plates and a pair of eyeglasses containing the magic stones Urim and Thummim. With the eyeglasses Smith was able to read the inscriptions on the plates and learned of the wanderings of some lost tribes of Israel who had come to America. The plates also recorded how in the New World the evil Lamanites had destroyed the good Nephites a thousand years before Columbus, so that only two Nephites—the prophet Mormon and his son Moroni—survived. The plates were the work of Mormon and Moroni. They described the history of the Nephites, their destruction, and their mission to reconquer America, "the promised land," from the Lamanites. Smith thought the Lamanites were the Indians, an interpretation that fit in well with the general anti-Indian sentiments of the 1820s. He also felt it was his mission to spread the faith, organize and proselytize, and take the converts to a new land.

Smith and some early converts sold a translation of the Book of Mormon door to door, and although the enterprise was not very successful they were able to form a church in 1830. In 1831 the Latter Day Saints, as they called themselves, moved to Kirtland, Ohio, where they constructed a temple and continued their conversion efforts. The most important of the new converts was Brigham Young, who

45

like Smith was of Vermont parentage and had been raised in New York. Although Young was never personally close to Smith, the two men complemented each other. Smith was a visionary and a mystic, while Young was a brilliant proselytizer, had a genius for organization, and was able to give the movement a practical aspect it had previously lacked. As one historian put it, "Young played St. Paul to Smith's Jesus."

The Mormons had difficulties in Kirtland. Their neighbors accused them of immorality, polygamy, and conspiracy, and internal dissension plagued the movement as rival prophets appeared to challenge Smith's revelations. Some Mormon groups left Kirtland and established their own communities in Missouri, in the vicinity of Independence. This area the Mormons called Zion, but the region proved inhospitable. Persecution, business failures in the wake of the 1837 panic, and the pledge of the Missouri governor in 1839 to either drive the Mormons from the state or exterminate them forced Smith to gather as many of his flock as he could and move once again—this time to Nauvoo, Illinois.

The Mormons consolidated both their membership and theology at Nauvoo. Smith held that the individual must work hard, abstain from alcohol, coffee, tea, and tobacco, and center his life around the Church. A Mormon had to prosper to demonstrate his worth, but all property rightfully belonged to the Church and was allowed the individual only in a form of trust. The Church was directed by a Council of Twelve Apostles, but all males were considered priests and were expected to work for converts. Finally, the

46

*Brigham's shanties at Provo City, Utah.*

Mormons were family-oriented. Plural marriages were not only permitted; they were encouraged. But only a small minority of Mormon males had more than one wife, and polygamy was never central to the religion. It was, however, its most obvious feature to outsiders, and Smith and his followers were constantly accused of immorality.

The Mormons prospered at Nauvoo. In 1844 Smith ran for the United States presidency, at a time when Nauvoo had a population of 15,000 and was the largest city in the state. But the Mormons were never accepted in Nauvoo. Fear of their power, intolerance, and personal antagonism against some of the religion's leaders led to Smith's arrest on charges of inciting a riot in 1844. Smith and his brother were placed in a jail in Carthage, but before they could be tried, a mob shot them to death.

Smith's death led to dissension in the Council, as several members claimed leadership. In the end Young, who had spent much of his time abroad spreading the faith, arrived to win the post. Nevertheless, factionalism continued to plague the religion, and the defeated claimants led their followers into splinter groups. To consolidate his power and to escape his neighbors' intolerance, Young decided to move the community farther west. He had read Frémont's reports, in which the soldier wrote of the Great Salt Lake, an area of plentiful water and of "good soil and good grass, adapted to civilized settlements." Lansford Hastings, in *The Emigrants' Guide to Oregon and California,* a favorite of the time, also spoke well of the Salt Lake region. Young decided to go there, although he did not tell his followers of his plans until later. Promising the citizens of Nauvoo that the Mormons would leave the following spring in return for immunity from further persecution, he set about organizing his great march.

About 15,000 Mormons left Nauvoo in 1846 in a well-organized wagon train that was three hundred miles long. The train was divided into "hundreds" or "fifties," each with its own captain, and further subdivided into "tens," led by a lieutenant. A hierarchy of command, with Young at its apex, was established, and worked well during the long journey. Young ordered his officers to remain as far from established communities as possible, and to send out men to work for local farmers in order to obtain food for the families. "If you do these things," he said, "faith will abide in your hearts; and the angels of God will go with you, even as they went with the children of Israel when Moses led them from the land of Egypt."

Given the excellent spirits of the Mormons and their fine leadership, the journey's first leg was completed without difficulties. "We were happy and contented," wrote one Mormon, "and the songs of Zion resounded from wagon to wagon, reverberating through the woods while the echoes returned from the distant hills." The company rested during the winter near present-day Omaha, and then moved on the following spring. The lead group, consisting of 143 men, three women, and two children, commanded by Young himself, blazed the path, while the others followed. At one point Young ran into Elder Samuel Bannan, a Mormon who had gone to California by sea the year before, and he urged them to turn back, or at least follow him to California. Young refused the offer. "God has made the choice—not Brigham Young," he said, and continued toward the Salt Lake.

The lead groups reached their destination in July 1847, and by the coming of winter about 1,800 were living on the shores of the lake. The winter was harsh, and some died. Since the summer crops had failed, the food ration was only a handful of grain and whatever weeds could be found. "I used to eat thistle stalks until my stomach would be as full as a cow's," wrote one pioneer. The following spring other Mormons trickled into the area, while the men planted the fields and prayed for a good harvest. Late frosts killed part of the crop, and in June swarms of locusts or black crickets descended upon the fields to attack the rest. Thousands of seagulls filled the sky and swooped down to devour the insects, thus saving a meager part of the crop from destruction. The seagulls were therefore responsible for sustaining the pioneers through the following winter, and the Mormons considered them a sign of God's support. By then the rest of the settlers had arrived, and the desert Zion was secure. Young called the settlement Deseret. It was the most successful utopian community in an age when such experiments were common.

People went to the West in the 1840s to realize visions of Utopia or to seek profits, often both. Some, like the Oregonians and Mormons, came at first to create new religious communities or to proselytize and then remained to prosper economically; others, like the Americans in California, came for economic reasons and, once arrived, became infected with visions of statehood. In this they resembled the Irish and German immigrants who poured into the eastern cities and midwestern farms. America was a nation of immigrants in the 1840s, and the pioneers in Salt Lake, Oregon, and California were no less strangers in the land than were the masses of the eastern ghettos and the settlers of the midwestern prairies.

# 3/THE INSTITUTIONAL CHALLENGE

MORMONISM'S SPECTACULAR EARLY HISTORY EXEMPLI-
fied the rejection of old, established institutions and the
quest for new ones during the 1840s. But not all those who
rejected established institutions felt it necessary to make the
western trek. Indeed, most remained in their old sections,
hoping to remake them through example and persuasion.
Never before had such a variety of utopian movements,
novel schools of philosophy, and young organizations dedi-
cated to drastic change attracted so many people. Many
movements were highly structured, disciplined, and complicated, demanding of their followers complete acceptance of
a creed. But at the same time, the nation was still infatu-
ated with the goals of individualism and pure democracy it
had inherited from the Jacksonian era. Thus, a paradox developed as the highly individualistic American people, who
believed fervently in democracy, joined organizations that
demanded strong discipline. The contradiction did not seem
to bother many persons at the time, but in the end it caused

most groups to splinter, disappear, or relinquish one or the other of their ideals.

Several old, almost forgotten movements gained new life in this period, while newer organizations found their membership rising dramatically. Although phrenology, hydropathy, astrology, and spiritualism faded by the end of the decade, they eventually reappeared and again found a limited audience. Other concerns, most notably the temperance, women's rights, and peace crusades, became major forces in American life. The abolitionist movement, which grew rapidly and then divided into factions, helped spark the bloodiest war and the greatest social change in the nation's history.

Had the existing institutions been able to adapt themselves to new ideas, the nation might have avoided much of the turmoil of the next quarter century. For example, had either major party been able to incorporate abolitionism into its fabric, the excesses of the abolitionists might have been muted, while at the same time many of their goals could have been realized in a more peaceful manner. Instead, the Democrats and Whigs divided over the issue of human bondage and then tried to ignore it. The reaction of the political parties mirrored that of the national government. When the slavery debates became heated in 1836, Congress adopted the "gag rule," which forbade discussion of antislavery and which remained in force for nine years. But the abolitionists refused to let the issue die; unable to influence the parties or obtain consideration of their ideas in Congress, they became more radical as time went on, and less responsible.

The same was true of religion. Many of the new sects, including Mormonism, had much in common with Calvinist theology and values. But the Calvinist churches rejected the new ideas and those who held them, and the splintering of religions proceeded. And in so doing, the new religions became increasingly radical. Perhaps this fragmentation and radicalization would have happened in any event, for the individualists of the 1840s tended to discard anything that was old and established. Abolitionist Theodore Parker, for example, dismissed the nation's business structure, saying, "All is the reflection of this most powerful class. The truths that are told are for them, and the lies." As he saw it, business was incapable of reform, and would have to undergo a drastic change if it were to be "socially useful." Ralph Waldo Emerson, the famous philosopher, also had harsh words to say against what he called "the system."

I content myself with the fact that the general system of our trade (apart from the blacker traits, which, I hope, are exceptions denounced and unshared by all reputable men), is a system of selfishness; is not dictated by the high sentiments of human nature; is not measured by the exact law of reciprocity, much less by the sentiments of love and heroism, but is a system of distrust, of concealment, of superior keenness, not of giving but of taking advantage.

Henry Thoreau, the most eloquent and perceptive critic of existing institutions, thought that "everywhere a man goes, men will pursue and paw him with their dirty institutions, and, if they can, constrain him to belong to their desperate odd-fellow society." Thoreau rejected almost every organized form of human activity. Of railroads he said, "We do not ride on the railroad; it rides upon us," and he considered post offices unnecessary, since "there are very few important communications made through it." "I never read anything memorable in a newspaper," he said, and so they, too, could be abandoned. The political state, of course, was the worst of all: "I was never molested by any person but those who represented the State."

On the other hand, Thoreau, Emerson, and Parker could not find a substitute for the state. Their only solution was a vague, undefined, utopian anarchism that by its very nature was incapable of benefiting large numbers of people. They and others like them would join many *ad hoc* organizations and movements, most of which were opposed to one or several aspects of the existing society, but they rarely developed programs to take the place of the old institutions.

At the base of the utopians' philosophy was the idea that man was essentially good, but that evil organizations corrupted him. Remove the evil, and the natural good would shine through. Consistent with these beliefs, most utopians called for an end to slavery without completely understanding the problems that might follow; Parker wanted to end commerce without offering an alternative to business; and Thoreau demanded the cessation of all organized activities that limited freedom without considering that men could make little happen of either a good or an evil nature without common goals and organizations to carry them out.

The individualists of the 1840s frequently squabbled among themselves and viewed with contempt the lower classes who were breaking the old order. In 1840

Emerson attended a convention of the Friends of Universal Reform, most of whom represented new organizations. He wrote of them:

If the assembly was disorderly, it was picturesque. Madmen, madwomen, men with beards, Dunkers, Muggletonians, Come-outers, Groaners, Agrarians, Seventh-Day Baptists, Quakers, Abolitionists, Calvinists, Unitarians, and Philosophers—all came successively to the top, and seized their moment, if not their hour, wherein to chide, or pray, or preach, or protest.

Because they lacked programs, organization, and unity, and indeed disdained such matters, the individualistic radicals of the 1840s were largely ineffectual. They were able on occasion to remake their own lives, but had little influence elsewhere. Their ranks included many of the finest intellects of the decade as well as a large number of discontented lower-class citizens, but neither group knew what the other was doing, or showed any inclination to find out. The intellectuals loved humanity in the abstract but had little use for their inferiors in practice, while the lower-class reformers, for their part, were unaware of the ideas emanating from the more rarefied circles of Boston and New York. Neither group had much contact with the immigrants, or understood the land-hungry westerners. They hated the businessman and loved the slave, but their writings show that they did not understand either business practices or slave life. The intellectuals wrote many books, pamphlets, and newspapers to publicize their causes; the lower-class reformers staged protest rallies in the larger cities. But neither organized an effective new political party, or impressed its ideas on the existing Democratic and Whig

*An outdoor "camp meeting."*
(THE GRANGER COLLECTION)

parties. In time some of the reformers' ideas were accepted by the middle class, and then some effects were felt. But such was not the case in the 1840s.

In addition to class differentiations, the movements of the 1840s can be categorized according to the impact their leaders hoped to have on society and according to their methods of operation. On the one side were the religious and social reformers who abandoned what they considered an evil or corrupt society, went into the wilderness, and attempted to set an example from which others might profit. On the other were reformers and radicals who worked within society, hoping to change it peacefully if possible, but willing to use violence if necessary. And a third group, the faddists, believed they had found the key to happiness, health, sexual prowess, and they eagerly spread the word to others.

Of the many religious leaders who preached against the evils of materialism in America, William Miller was perhaps the most intriguing. An itinerant preacher in upstate New York, Miller in 1822 calculated that the world would come to an end in 1843. For a while he kept this idea to himself, but then he was invited to discuss the matter at local Baptist and Methodist churches in New York and northern New England. These areas, where revivalism and spiritual sects flourished, were known as the "burned-over district" because the region's ministers so often sparked the fires of religion.

Miller soon won an eager audience and many converts. In 1833 he formally joined the Baptist Church, became a minister, and openly heralded the coming of Judgment Day. Millerite tabernacles were constructed throughout northern New England, upper New York, and into the Midwest; Miller led huge revival meetings, and despite extensive preparations, the huge crowds that gathered to hear him were never adequately accommodated. Miller was an effective speaker. "Behold, the heavens grow black with clouds," he would say; "the sun has veiled himself; the moon, pale and forsaken, hangs in middle air; the hail descends; the seven thunders utter loud their voices; the lightnings send their vivid gleams and sulphurous flames abroad; and the great city of the nations falls to rise no more forever and forever!" Few who flocked to the camp meetings could fail to be swayed by such words, uttered in a calm, matter-of-fact voice. Miller had no doubts, and neither did his followers. "The clouds have burst asunder; the heavens appear; the great white throne is in sight! Amazement fills the Universe with awe!! He comes!—He comes!—Behold the Savior comes!—Lift up your heads, ye saints! He comes! He comes!"

As the glorious year approached, the nation's dry goods stores reported shortages of muslin because Millerites were purchasing the approved fabric to make gowns and prepare to greet Jesus. Miller did not predict what date He would arrive, so the faithful had to be ready on January 1. A few Baptist ministers took their flocks to hilltops to watch for the Second Coming. But their enthusiasm was not shared by the Methodist Bishop of Vermont and other major Church leaders, who denounced Miller as a well-meaning fool. This action caused a split in the Baptist Church; a large number left the older church and joined Millerite congregations.

When 1843 ended without the expected cataclysm, Miller returned to his charts to discover what was wrong. Emerging from his home, he told his assembled followers that there had been a slight miscalculation. "The time as I have calculated it is now filled up," he said, "and I expect every moment to see the Savior descend from heaven." He predicted that the Coming would take place in March 1844. April arrived, and still no Savior appeared. Undaunted, Miller announced a new date, October 22, based on the Jewish belief that a new heaven and earth would commence "on the tenth day of the seventh month."

On the evening of October 22, 1844, Millerites gathered on hilltops throughout the nation. They wore white gowns and did not bring food, since there would be no further need for nourishment. After a futile vigil they straggled back to their homes the next morning, tired and dirty; some were led away insane. Although a few Millerite churches remained, the movement quickly evaporated. Miller himself died heartbroken in 1849, but his leading disciple, Joshua Himes, lived till 1895, and was buried according to instructions on a hilltop, so as to be close to God when He descended.

The 1840s witnessed the growth of old religious sects and the birth of new ones. Most were not as spectacular as the Millerites, but they lasted longer. The Ephrata Cloister, the Rappites, the Bethel and Aurora communities, all prospered, while the Community of True Inspiration, more commonly known as the Amana Society, was begun by German immigrants who had fled Europe in 1842 for religious and economic reasons. All, like the Millerites, were related in one way or another to older European-originated religions.

Another group, basically American in origin but with some European roots, was begun by New England philosophers or their followers, and sought new ways of life instead of elaborating upon old themes. Unwilling to await a transformation of human nature, abandoning hope of having their ideas accepted by the broad mass of Americans, these people were determined to create their perfect world in the wilderness.

Like the religious utopians, the philosophers based their

model communities on ideological rather than practical considerations, and these came from the twin roots of Unitarianism and Transcendentalism. Of the two, Unitarianism was the older, having had its origins in the ideas and works of William Ellery Channing, a New England minister who put forth the original tenets of Unitarianism. Channing's teachings emphasized God's love and the dignity of the individual, not the Calvinist beliefs of predestination and strict observance of the divine law. By the mid-1830s many of the Congregational churches in New England accepted Channing's ideas, but the older doctrines held sway in backwoods communities. In the early 1840s Channing moved further from rigid Calvinist teachings. "The adoration of goodness—this is religion," he told a Boston audience, and more radical Unitarians entirely denied the importance of ritual. Theodore Parker, speaking in a South Boston church in 1841, called on the worshippers to "let the full heart pour forth," and announced his disbelief in the miracles of the New Testament. To him Jesus was not the Son of God but a great teacher, from whom all men could learn the lessons of goodness. Channing stressed the spirit of religion rather than the forms; Parker denied the very basis of Calvinist theology. A third Unitarian leader, Edward Everett Hale, moved even further away from traditional religions. He glorified man, not God.

When I see that no man has ever been able to show where Christ's divinity ended and where the powers and qualities which he showed in common with the perfect man began, I cannot but believe that the nature of man, when carried to this perfection, is more beautiful, more spiritual, more divine, than, without this exhibition, there was reason to suppose.... When I find that man's nature is assumed by a being who is entitled to style himself the Son of God, I find strong proof of the dignity of man's nature.

Whereas the Calvinists looked to God in order to find man, the Unitarians studied man to find God. Henry Ward Beecher completed the utter rejection of Christian orthodoxy when he claimed there was no religion in the Bible. "Religion is *in the man,* or it is not anywhere," he said. "The great truth which God is driving through our times, as with a chariot of fire, is the *importance of man.*"

The Unitarians eliminated absolutism and divine law from their religion. But what replaced them? Free will and individual conscience appeared to be the answer, but these concepts were too nebulous to a generation that sought guidance of one sort or another. The Unitarians still clung to the idea that individual man could experience some kind of supernatural revelation, by which God would make his presence felt. The problem was how to determine whether the revelation was genuine or completely understood. Inspiration was an acceptable explanation for the lower classes and uneducated farmers who followed Miller and others like him, but the Boston intellectuals who embraced Unitarianism demanded more. Transcendentalism provided their rationale.

The Transcendentalists, who flourished in and around Boston in the 1840s, held that God did not communicate directly with man, but instead dwelt within each person, and it was the individual's responsibility to find Him through inspiration and study. Such a man trusted his instincts, which transcended tradition, set beliefs, and old ideals. Ralph Waldo Emerson, the movement's most famous leader, defined the belief as extreme individualism, and thought the individual would be able to find God within himself. Such a person, said Emerson, believes "in the perpetual openness of the human mind to the new influx of light and power; he believes in inspiration and ecstasy."

This belief sat well with reformers of the 1840s. It implied that all men had the spark of God within them, and so was democratic and Christian. It also tacitly assumed that those who had succeeded in their quest for the inner God could speak on a variety of subjects with moral rectitude. While the Jacksonians spoke of the Bank of the United States as the tool of the wealthy to crush the poor, the Transcendentalists denounced as immoral the denial of women's rights, slavery, low wages, and other pressing problems of their time. They had seen the light, and would provide a torch for others to follow. Transcendentalism was, indeed, a fitting philosophy for the times, the location, and the men.

Transcendentalists found common cause with such Europeans as the utopian socialists. One of the most prominent of these, Charles Fourier, had devised a plan for a perfect community, in which free will working for a common cause would solve all major problems. American Transcendentalists seized this program as a practical method of demonstrating their ideas, and from it came a series of utopian communities.

In 1841 members of the Transcendentalist Society

established Brook Farm, which was led by a Unitarian minister and Transcendentalist, George Ripley, and located a few miles from Boston. All who participated in the experiment were expected to work at manual occupations and received one dollar for each ten-hour day of labor. The rest of the time was set aside for contemplation, discussion, and pursuit of the arts. Stockholders were entitled to schooling for their children and little else, except that which their own labors brought them. Each subscriber owned property at Brook Farm and was required to spend a major portion of the year in residence. The government of the Farm was modeled after the New England town meeting, and all who wished were given the opportunity to air their viewpoints. Ripley was enthusiastic about the project, which he saw as a great experiment that, if successful, would prove a beacon for the nation. Its main objective, he wrote, was

... to ensure a more natural union between intellectual and manual labor than now exists; to combine the thinker and the worker, as far as possible in the same individual; to guarantee the highest mental freedom, by providing all with labor adapted to their tastes and talents, and securing to them the fruits of their industry; to do away with the necessity of menial service by opening the benefits of education and the profits of labor to all; and thus to prepare a society of liberal, intelligent, and cultivated persons, whose relations with each other would permit a more wholesome and simple life than can be led amidst the pressure of our competitive institutions.

The Farm never lacked eager applicants, and Boston's leading Transcendentalists generally spent part of each year there. It was also a major tourist stop, as the idle and curious went to see how it operated. The Farm's schools were particularly impressive and were the most successful aspect of the project; many of the ideas developed there influenced educational philosophers for a century. But the Farm itself did not live up to Ripley's expectations. Boston's philosophers made poor farmers; physical labor was not only alien to most Transcendentalists; it was distasteful. Others objected to the stringent organization necessary to run a successful community. Ripley himself spent only part of the year there, preferring the intellectual stimulation of Boston to the idyllic life at Brook Farm.

The original design failed, because of a lack of interest

*An early communal society: the Shakers.*
(THE GRANGER COLLECTION)

64

and ability. In 1845 Brook Farm became a Fourierist phalanx, in which all property was held in common. After this change the members tried to be entirely self-sufficient, producing household supplies and crockery as well as grain and fruit, but these ventures met with disaster. Brook Farm was finally sold in 1849, and its price—$19,150—barely paid its outstanding debts.

But even after the experiment ended, Transcendentalists and their friends remembered the Farm longingly, forgetting that while it was in operation they had failed to make a complete commitment to that kind of life. In his *Blithedale Romance,* Nathaniel Hawthorne exhibited this tendency in discussing his memories.

Often in these years that are darkening around me, I remember our beautiful scheme of a noble and unselfish life, and how fair in that first summer appeared the prospect that it might endure for generations, and be perfected, as the ages rolled by, into the system of a people and a world. Were my former associates now there—were there only three or four of those true-hearted men still laboring in the sun—I sometimes fancy that I should direct my world-weary footsteps thitherward, and entreat them to receive me for old friendship's sake. More and more I feel we struck upon what ought to be the truth. Posterity may dig it up and profit by it.

Bronson Alcott, father of the novelist Louisa May Alcott, was also the mystical parent of the Transcendentalist utopia called Fruitlands, which he started with Charles Lane, an English philosopher, in 1842. Using Lane's money, the Transcendentalists purchased a ninety-acre farm some fifty miles from Concord, which soon attracted interested Bostonians. Since Lane had provided the capital, he set the community's tone. Like Brook Farm, Fruitlands combined physical labor with philosophizing. Inasmuch as Lane was a strict vegetarian, no meat was allowed; the members lived off a diet of potatoes, fruit, and vegetables. The brochure offered a fair description of life at Fruitlands.

We rise with early dawn, begin the day with cold bathing, succeeded by a music lesson, then a chaste repast. Each one finds occupation till the meridian meal, when usually some interesting and deep-searching conversation gives rest to the body and development to the mind. Occupation . . . engages us out of doors or within, until the evening meal—when we again assemble in social communion, prolonged generally until sunset when we resort to sweet repose for the next day's activity.

The members tended to ignore agriculture for philosophy, and consequently Fruitlands was a dismal economic failure. Furthermore, the usual philosophical infighting of the Transcendentalists plagued the community. Alcott and Lane were continually squabbling, leading the few utopians with agricultural ability to leave in disgust in 1843. Then, in January 1844, Lane announced that he, too, was departing to take up residence in a Shaker community. Shortly afterward Alcott fell ill and left for Boston, marking the end of Fruitlands. But years later Alcott's daughter, Louisa May, wrote nostalgically of the experiment.

"Ah, me! my happy dream. How much I leave behind that never can be mine again," said Abel [Bronson Alcott], looking back at the lost Paradise, lying white and chill in its shroud of snow . . . . "Poor Fruitlands! The name was as great a failure as the rest," continued Abel, with a sigh, as a frost-bitten apple fell from a leafless bough at his feet.

Emerson, too, bemoaned the failure of Fruitlands and Brook Farm. He later noted that some of the nation's leading artists and writers owed their inspiration to stays there. "Letters were always flying, not only from house to house, but from room to room," he said. "It was a perpetual picnic, a French Revolution in small, an Age of Reason in a patty-pan." Unfortunately such a state of affairs does not make for a successful farm.

The inability to combine intellectual prowess with physical labor was a major cause of the failures. Significant, too, was the philosopher's implied belief that anyone could be a successful farmer. The difficulties of preparing fields, sowing seed, harvesting crops, milking cows, and other innumerable agricultural chores were only casually realized. Moreover, the need for cooperation, accepted in the abstract, was too often forgotten by the highly individualistic Transcendentalists and their allies.

The history of a third community, Hopedale, near Milford, Massachusetts, may be summed up in three representative quotations. Channing, one of its founders, wrote in 1840:

I have for a very long time dreamed of an association, in which the members, instead of preying on one another and seeking to put one another down, after the fashion of the world, should live together as brothers, seeking one another's elevation and spiritual growth. But the materials for such a community I have not seen.

Hopedale provided the opportunity for such a community, and the utopians flocked there to fulfill Channing's dream. In its charter one reads of the need for both individualism and assent.

Each individual is left to judge for him or herself with entire freedom, what abstract doctrines are taught, and also what external religious rights are enjoined in the religion of Christ.... In such matters all the members are free, with mutual love and toleration, to follow their own highest convictions of truth and religious duty.... But in practical Christianity this Church is precise and direct. There its essentials are specific. It insists on supreme love to God and man.

The members could not live up to these ideals, and in 1853 Adin Ballou, one of its guiding forces, left. Soon afterward the rest followed his example. Writing of the failure, Ballou said:

It is my deliberate and solemn conviction that the predominating cause of the failure ... was a moral and spiritual, not a financial one—a deficiency among its members of those graces and powers of character which are requisite to the realization of the Christian ideal of human society.

To this Ballou appended the hope that "the work of Social Reform is by no means abandoned; it is only suspended till the world is fitted by intellectual growth and spiritual elevation to take it up again and prosecute it to successful results." But Ballou did not say how this change would be effected, nor did he realize that in such a world utopia would be everywhere, and there would be no need for special communities. A cynical critic might have noted that the Boston intellectuals, who could not make a success of their small villages and farms, might be the worst guide possible for the larger and broader world outside.

A few utopian communities fared better. One of these, the Sylvania Phalanx, was established in 1842 in northern

Pennsylvania, and was supported by several prominent New York intellectuals. Publisher Horace Greeley served as its treasurer. The Sylvania settlement attracted more than a hundred people, most of them working-class families from New York and Albany, and since the entire holding was more than 2,300 acres, success at first seemed possible. But the settlers knew little about farming, and the land was not suitable for agriculture. The "purchase committee" had been comprised of a medical doctor, a cooper, and a landscape painter. They were all good, decent men, but none knew anything about farming. They selected the land for its low price, not its fertility. Only four acres produced crops—the rest of the land was covered by dense forest that defied cultivation. Sylvania marketed a total of eleven bushels of grain its first year, and conditions did not improve. The experiment failed within a short time, and Greeley alone lost $5,000. Years later, however, when a private company purchased Sylvania for its timber resources, the lumberers made substantial profits from the acreage.

The North American Phalanx was still another effort to establish an American utopia. Founded in 1843 by such major figures as Albert Brisbane, father of the celebrated editorial writer Arthur Brisbane; Horace Greeley, William Ellery Channing, and George Ripley, it was widely heralded as a major experiment in communal living. Great care was taken to select a proper site. One was found in Monmouth County, New Jersey, not far from Red Bank. Known previously as the Van Mater Farm, it was now officially renamed the North American Phalanx, but was better known as Red Bank. The land was good, transportation was available, and the community was solvent. In September 1843 the first families arrived and began construction of the buildings.

Life at Red Bank was simple. Each settler was permitted to work at any task that interested him, and to do as much or little as he desired. For his labor he received wages,

*William Ellery Channing.*
(THE NEW YORK PUBLIC LIBRARY)

70

which varied according to the attractiveness of the work. Artistic endeavors might fetch a penny an hour, while "necessary but repulsive work" paid as much as ten cents an hour. The members paid rents and were charged for food, but both were inexpensive and could be financed through a few hours of work per day. Red Bank seemed a model of its type, a successful utopia.

Many of the members were unsatisfied, however. They soon discovered that community life required them to relinquish a portion of their individuality. This was difficult for most Americans, but more so for intellectuals than anyone else. There was trouble in paradise. Fredrika Bremer, who visited Red Bank in its prime, noted that all had gone according to plan, but that she would not want to live there. As an individualist, she preferred to be "on the bleakest granite mountain of Sweden, alone by myself, and live on bread, and water, and potatoes . . . than in a Phalanstry on the most fertile soil, in the midst of associate brethren and sisters!"

In 1852 the value of the Red Bank property was $80,000, against liabilities of $20,000, and the original $8,000 investment had been redeemed. The Phalanx was an economic success, but the experiment in communal living was a failure. When a mill was burned to the ground in 1854 the members met to consider Greeley's offer of a loan to build a new one. Instead of discussing the mill, someone took the opportunity to suggest abandoning the community and dissolving the Phalanx. To the surprise of most, the motion carried, and Red Bank closed its doors. The land was sold, paradoxically, at a large profit.

Red Bank demonstrates that Ballou's sentiments regarding Hopedale could be applied to other phalanxes as well. It was not financial losses that caused the experiments to be abandoned, but the members' unwillingness to live for extended periods in communes. In theory the members admired the beauties of communal life; in practice they rejected them. Then, too, pure utopia proved to be dismaying. After attaining all their goals, the members were more bored than elated. Finally, Red Bank lacked a strong leader, a man who might have inspired the inhabitants and set them on new paths.

One of the few philosophical utopians who realized that strong leadership was necessary was John Humphrey Noyes, the founder of Perfectionism. After several religious experiences in the 1830s, Noyes proclaimed, "I do not pretend to be perfection in externals, I claim only purity of heart and the answer of a good conscience toward God." After carefully studying the experiences of the Transcendentalists and reading the works of European utopians, Noyes gained firsthand knowledge of the possibilities and pitfalls of community life by extensive visits to Red Bank. He called it the "test-experiment on which Fourierism practically staked its all in this country." Heartened by Red Bank's early success, Noyes decided to start his own community, based on an inner light. Noyes' experiment, known as the Oneida Community, was established in Madison County, New York, in 1848.

Like the other utopian settlements, Oneida was founded in the belief that hard work and philosophy could be combined. Unlike them, it had a leader who knew how to press its members into action, organize work gangs, and manage books. Noyes encouraged vegetarianism but did not insist upon it; he permitted a degree of religious and philosophical debate, but did not allow it to interfere with the running of the community. Noyes discouraged competition and excess zeal in work, but he harshly criticized those who did not do their share of the labor. His most novel idea, communal marriage, was based more on a belief in sexual equality and freedom than on licentiousness, although his neighbors, like those of Joseph Smith and Brigham Young, believed the community was wicked and depraved. One local joke was that the bedroom partitions at Oneida were set on hinges so as to be more easily moved to accommodate changing partners. However, in practice, the communal marriages worked as well at Oneida as polygamy did at Deseret.

The Oneida Community not only survived, it flourished. By 1879—thirty-one years after its founding—Noyes recommended the abandonment of communal marriage because of outside pressures. The following year Oneida changed its charter and the community became a joint-stock company, Oneida Community, Ltd. Shares in the company were distributed among the inhabitants, and many eventually became quite wealthy.

Oneida never became a model for the world, but its business practices were admired and adopted by nearby companies and rival concerns. Perhaps without realizing it, Noyes learned the lesson that eluded the Transcendentalists: few copy from failure; many imitate success.

The utopians of the 1840s set out to change the world

through example, and to accomplish this they organized communities. They failed to convince the majority of Americans that their course was correct, or that their analysis of the nation's ills was reasonable. On the other hand, the management techniques pioneered at the communities would intrigue businessmen of later generations. Ironically, the utopians, who had hoped the world would accept their ethic, instead offered a laboratory for the businessmen of the future, who, worrying about the "loss of community" in the modern corporation, would seek alternative methods of organization.

# 4/NOSTRUMS AND ENTERTAINMENTS

*December 29, 1836* . . . . Walked down to college with Chittenden and then to Clinton Hall, to see Mr. Fowler the phrenologist there and have my bumps examined. Bought a kind of chart with all the bumps registered. On the whole, impressed in favor of phrenological science by Mr. Fowler's statements; indeed, I have always believed in it, in some degree . . . .

So wrote George Templeton Strong, at the time a nineteen-year-old student at Columbia College in New York. Strong was interested in all aspects of life, and kept a diary from 1835 to 1875. This book reveals glimpses of a person of education, intelligence, and high social position reacting to the major issues of the time. Even then, in 1836, Strong was an avowed skeptic and freely criticized much that he saw in politics. Because of this, his interest in phrenology and his belief in its potential are intriguing.

It was not at all unusual for men of great learning who prided themselves on their scientific training to embrace phrenology and other pseudosciences in the late

1830s and 1840s; just as businessmen were at the time vaguely interested in the phalanxes, so they were curious as to the claims of dealers in mystical and magical "sciences." At a time when new issues and causes constantly challenged outworn ways, men like Strong might join dozens of reform movements, dabble in the occult, and listen attentively to unusual plans to change the world. They proclaimed their belief in programs which, if carried out, would have destroyed them, and considered themselves enlightened for doing so. This was the age of Emerson, Thoreau, Polk, Poe, Webster, Brigham Young, and Clay, but a more representative figure for the mass of Americans was Phineas T. Barnum; it was the age of showmanship and bunkum.

Orson Fowler—who examined Strong's head—was one of the most popular American-born phrenologists. Soon after graduating from Amherst in 1834 he took the title of professor, proclaimed himself a leading practitioner of phrenology, and embarked on a lecture tour for which he received $40 an evening. Fowler faced stiff competition, so he decided to popularize both the study and himself by publishing magazines and books on the subject. His company, Fowler and Wells, soon became one of the nation's most successful publishers. Its *American Phrenological Journal* and *Phrenology Proved, Illustrated, and Applied* found an eager audience. Fowler and Wells also published a do-it-yourself handbook, complete with charts and instructions, for those unwilling or unable to consult a specialist directly. Fowler's popularity reached its peak in 1844 with the publication of *Religion Natural and Revealed; or, the Natural Theology and Moral Bearings of Phrenology* ...

*compared with those Enjoined in the Scriptures,* which went through ten editions in four years and would have been found to be a best seller had the appropriate tabulations been made at the time. In this book Fowler claimed that the ancient study of phrenology was the science and philosophy of the future.

Its roots run deep into the nature of man. Its branches yield all manner of delicious fruits, for the healing of the nations, and the renovation of mankind. Its moral truths are food to the hungry, a cooling beverage to the thirsty soul, a foundation to those whom the tides of error are sweeping onward to destruction, and a feast of reason, with a flow of soul—sight to the blind, feet to the lame, health to the invalid, vitality to the dying, and life to the dead.

Fowler's success encouraged other Americans to become head readers. Meanwhile, leading European phrenologists visited the United States. One of them, George Combe, made a particularly interesting "phrenological visit." He traveled to all the major cities and was received warmly wherever he spoke. Combe stopped in Washington to watch the nation's leaders in action, observe the shapes of their skulls, and report on his findings. He thought John C. Calhoun's head "indicated much self-will and determination; great powers of perseverance; a capacity for details, but little profound judgment." Henry Clay came off better; his head "bespeaks a man greatly above the average in point of mental power, and also practical in his tendencies; and therefore well adapted to the general American mind of the present day." But even Clay was insignificant when compared skull-by-skull with Daniel Webster, who, according to Combe, "like Burke, will be quoted for the depth of principle and wisdom involved in his speeches, when the more fascinating but less profound orations of Mr. Clay have sunk into oblivion." The phrenologist was also able to talk with many leading congressional figures. The aged John Quincy Adams, the product of a more rational age, pronounced Combe a charlatan and quack and phrenology a hoax. But not surprisingly, Webster thought there was much to be said for the study. Most congressmen agreed, and Combe returned the compliment.

The appearance of the members of the Senate is favorable. With few exceptions, their brains, and especially the organs of intellectual facilities, are large, while there is a good average development of the organs of moral sentiments. Collectively, they seem to me to be a highly respectable and gifted body of men.

Nor were the nation's leading intellectuals immune to the lure of phrenology. When John Spurzheim of Germany made a whirlwind tour of the eastern United States the faculties of Yale and Harvard greeted him warmly. Known internationally as the most astute student of the science, Spurzheim was given the kind of reception usually accorded major statesmen. President Jeremiah Day and the entire Yale faculty were on hand to greet him when his train arrived at New Haven, and his name was hastily added to the list of Commencement Day speakers. The faculty even voted to establish a phrenological society at the school, and Spurzheim's books were much in vogue. Not to be outdone, Harvard accorded Spurzheim an equally warm reception. President Josiah Quincy, the distinguished scientist Nathaniel Bowditch, and many other members of the Harvard faculty were on hand when Spurzheim alighted in Boston. The phrenologist delivered the main Commencement Day address at Harvard, spoke before the local Phi Beta Kappa chapter the following day, and ended his tour with a major address at the Boston Athenaeum the third day. All of this was too much for the aged Spurzheim, who died in the city soon afterward. On learning of his death, Professor Karl Follen of Harvard noted, "The Prophet is gone but his Mantle is upon us." The Harvard faculty and many members of the Transcendentalist Club attended Spurzheim's funeral at Mount Auburn Cemetery, the final resting place for many members of Boston's intellectual aristocracy.

Phrenology appealed to those who wished to mix empiricism and spiritualism. Many persons were willing to have their heads examined; each seemed to possess a different set of bumps. Consulting charts and using calipers and complex formulas, the phrenologists pleased those who insisted on mathematical rigidity while at the same time they intrigued those interested in the occult. Not surprisingly, the Transcendentalists took phrenology seriously.

Spiritualism pure and unalloyed was another matter. Although some Transcendentalists went to séances and flirted with the study, most believed it a relic of a superstitious age. They allowed that many might experience God within themselves, but they denied the realm of ghosts, table rappings, and sounds in the night. However, spiritualism did find an audience in the lower and middle classes and, indeed, there were far more mediums at work in America in the 1840s than there were phrenologists.

Joseph Buchanan, who in 1843 published *The Phrenological Portion of Neurology,* and, two years later, *The
Neurological System of Anthropology,* tried to combine the
studies of phrenology and spiritualism. Buchanan held that
the phrenologists were correct in assuming that study of the
skull could tell a man's nature, but argued that the presence
or absence of "nervaura," a substance which emanated from
the nervous system and differed among organs as well as
individuals, determined personality. Those who understood
the nature of, and could control, nervaura had the power to
influence others, predict the future, and uncover secrets. Bu-

*Advertisement for a book on phrenology.*

(THE NEW YORK PUBLIC LIBRARY)

80

chanan demonstrated his technique across the nation. He placed his hand on the skull of his subject, directed his nervaura into the man's body, and sent it to a preselected organ. Then the nervaura returned to Buchanan, telling him everything he wanted to know about the individual. "Psychometry," as Buchanan called his method, amazed his audiences. Theresa Pulszky, a Hungarian visitor, wrote of her encounter with Buchanan and psychometry. She saw Buchanan read a subject's character from touching his head, and then learned he could do the same from feeling an object or seeing handwriting. Eager for a personal demonstration, she and her husband arranged for a private audience.

One evening he brought a young man to us, who, according to the doctor, was endowed with this facility. We tested him by the handwriting of Mazzini, and were really astonished how correctly and minutely he described his character. But the next test struck me more. Mr. Pulszky gave him a paper, and said, in order to mislead him, "it is from a German revolutionary leader," whilst it was Mr. Pulszky's own handwriting. And yet the young man gave so exact a picture of him, as only those could have given who had known him for a long time. One fact was especially striking: "It is a person," said he, "who has more taste and inclination for Art than for Politics. It was an unexpected event which gave to his life a political turn." And in fact this did happen fourteen years past, but no one could possibly know it in America. How to account for this, I do not know.

J. Stanley Grimes, who like Buchanan wedded spiritualism to phrenology, rejected nervaura for "etherium." Grimes claimed that etherium not only had spiritualist purposes, but also connected the planets and communicated "light, heat, electricity, gravitation and mental emo-

*Miss Margaret Fox, Miss Katherine Fox, and Mrs. Leah Fish.*
(THE GRANGER COLLECTION)

tion, from one body to another, and from one mind to another." Other pseudoscientists put forth equally earth-shaking theories. R. H. Collyer's "psychography" employed mental images, which a trained person could use to communicate with a subject at will. Laroy Sunderland was a "phrenopathist," who tried to systematize phrenology and, through his experiments with hypnotism, actually did some important scientific work in the field of autosuggestion. John Wroe and John Reid used their mystical galvanic devices to gain insights, and were the founders of "electro-biology." Roswell Park put forth "pantology," a science he modestly proclaimed as "an exhaustive analysis of human knowledge, in which all the fragments, even of minor importance, find a distinct and proper place." And there were many more, all of whom found an audience.

Most of the more successful spiritualists eschewed phrenology and other pseudosciences to concentrate directly on the mystical experience. Such individuals were scorned by the intellectuals, but they often won large mass followings.

Andrew Jackson Davis at the age of seventeen attended a Grimes lecture and demonstration in Poughkeepsie, New York. Grimes tried to mesmerize Davis but he met with little success, and blamed his failure on the youth's innate stupidity. Nonetheless Davis was fascinated by the concept of etherium, and he embarked on an intense study of spiritualism. Then he began to tell friends of his newly discovered psychic powers. He claimed to be able to read material that was held behind his back and on one occasion proceeded to demonstrate this ability—a truly amazing feat since Davis did not know how to read. Within a short time Davis, aided by a local tailor who served as his agent, took to the lecture circuit. In 1845 he wrote *Lectures on Clairmativeness,* and two years later *The Principles of Nature, Her Divine Revelations.* Since the latter work is over eight hundred pages long, it would appear that Davis also used his powers to learn to read and write. By 1847 Davis hired a new manager, Dr. John Lyon, who was a minor spiritualist and a first-class showman.

In 1847 Lyon took Davis to New York City, one of the major centers of spiritualism in the nation. At first Davis was a failure because the competition, in a city where spiritualism was the reigning fad, was simply too great for him to handle. Davis wanted to leave, but Lyon persisted; if his protégé was ever to become a major figure, it would have to be in New York. Lyon sought out several Universalist ministers and began to promote Davis with great skill. One of the ministers, Reverend William Fishbough, was a good friend of Horace Greeley, the influential editor and publisher who flirted with almost every new idea of the decade. Reverend Fishbough told Greeley of Davis' miraculous powers of understanding the past and predicting the future, and the newspaperman went to see Davis perform. Greatly impressed, Greeley began to promote Davis in the pages of the New York *Tribune.* Within weeks he was the most famous and successful spiritualist in the city.

Not content with this notoriety, Davis branched out into other fields. He started his own religion, a variation upon Christianity. He claimed that the twelve commandments of his faith had been delivered to him by God Him-

self. Davis spoke of the origin of the universe and its ulti-
mate end in ways suggestive of lurid science fiction of today.
Meanwhile he continued to give "readings" to select clients,
lead séances, and write of the need for spiritual regenera-
tion in his journal, *The Univercoelum*. By the end of the
1840s he was the most famous and influential spiritualist
in the nation.

Two followers of Davis were Margaret and Katherine
Fox of Hydesville, New York. Neighbors swore their home
was haunted, but their father, John Fox, discounted the
talk and congratulated himself on obtaining the house for
a low rental because of it. In March of 1848, however, he
first heard strange noises in the night, and then the house
itself began to shake. Mrs. Fox, who knew something of
spiritualism, believed the noise was caused by an unhappy
soul. She began to ask it questions and was answered by
knocks, three for yes, two for no. This "tapping" was a
common way of communicating with spirits. Through the
rapping Mrs. Fox learned that the spirit was that of an
itinerant peddler who had been murdered in the house.
He would not say who committed the deed, but he indicated that his own initials were C. R. Having determined
that the raps were authentic, Mrs. Fox decided to call in a
pair of "experts" in the subject—a neighbor called Ellis
and Mrs. Fox's oldest daughter, Mrs. Leah Fish, who hurried
to Hydesville from Rochester for the consultation. These
two "experts" claimed that the ghost of C. R. was more
at home with the two younger Fox sisters than with Mrs.
Fox. The two sisters had many conversations with the ghost
by means of rapping and became local celebrities. Under

the management of Mrs. Fish the girls began to charge a fee for séances, and many persons, each paying one dollar, witnessed otherworldly exhibitions at the Fox home.

The Foxes might have remained merely local heroes had it not been for Judge John Edmonds, who, in addition to his legal work, was a member of several reform organizations and a believer in ghosts. The judge saw many similarities between the Foxes and Andrew Jackson Davis and thought that they, too, should be brought to the attention of a wider audience. Indeed, he thought they were vastly superior to Davis, for by late 1848 C. R. had introduced them to many other spirits, and they seemed to have the whole otherworld at their command.

Edmonds organized the First Spiritualists of America. Its membership, which included many outstanding intellectuals, was particularly interested in the Fox sisters. They organized weekend trips to Hydesville, and later, when the girls went to live with their sister, they went to Rochester for séances. In this way they came to the attention of the great Phineas T. Barnum.

Realizing that the attractive sisters were a potential gold mine, Barnum spoke with Leah Fish about the possibility of their moving to New York, where he would promote them as a marvel of the universe. Barnum and Mrs. Fish came to an understanding. The sisters went on display at the Barnum Museum, and for two dollars a head the curious were treated to a demonstration of rapping. The sisters became a major attraction at the museum; indeed, the crowds who came to see them often had to stand through their exhibitions. So great was the Foxes' following that not even the revelation that Katherine Fox pro-

*P. T. Barnum with three of his famous attractions: "General Tom Thumb," "Mrs. Tom Thumb," and "Commodore Nutt."*
(THE NEW YORK PUBLIC LIBRARY)

87

duced raps by cracking her smaller joints slackened their business. Horace Greeley, for one, was by now convinced the spirits were real, and could be used to advantage. Soon afterward he announced a standing offer of $100 to any medium who could obtain a leading article from the London *Times* in advance of the steamer, so that the *Tribune* could scoop the opposition press; and when his daughter died, Greeley spent years trying to communicate with her soul in the hereafter.

The Foxes conquered New York, and then set out on a national tour to bring rapping to the other cities. While in Cincinnati they gave a demonstration for the Pulszkys, who seemed to have dabbled in every occult art in the nation. At first they were impressed with the Fox sisters, but they quickly became skeptical.

The manifestations immediately began. The young ladies requested us to put questions. I naturally asked, "Shall we return to Hungary?" Three distinct raps were heard on the table below. The table was uncovered. Miss Fox stood near it, keeping her hand on the edge of the table. I closely watched her movements: the rap did not proceed from her. I asked several other questions of a similar kind, and got just as favorable replies as I could wish. Of course I did not care for them, though one was remarkable. Asking the age of my eldest boy, I was bid to write down a series of different numbers, at the right one the spirit would rap; and this was the case.... Dr. Spaczek, our clever physician, was likewise present. He, too, could not tell in what way the rappings were produced, but he rejoiced at least to get an evident proof that they came not from the spirits of deceased persons. He asked whether his father was in heaven? Three raps answered, "Yes," whilst the father of our friend lives in good health in Poland. The spirits were likewise at a loss to guess how old Mrs. Spaczek was. They added ten years to her actual age. When the Doctor began to protest against these manifest falsehoods, Miss Fox coolly replied, that she and her sister were not responsible for anything the spirits said, as they, in fact, could not tell whether the spirits who manifested themselves were veracious or lying spirits. That there were lying ones amongst them, they had found out by experience.

From the descriptions of the Pulszkys and others, it is clear that rapping sessions were as much entertainments as serious experiments. The same may be said of phrenology and other fad movements of the times. But, on the other hand, the 1840s was a decade in which self-improvement was much prized. Attendance at a séance could be, as the Pulszkys put it, "instructional," while Francis Grund considered the experience "edifying." George Templeton Strong rejected spiritualism, but thought the idea worthy of careful analysis in his diary. Individuals of all social stations went to such otherworldly exercises, congratulating themselves on their interest in contemporary affairs at the same time as they viewed them as shows.

It was an age of shows and showmanship. The era began in May 1840, when the *Great Western* docked in New York and discharged its most important passenger, Fanny Elssler. Miss Elssler was Europe's most famous dancing star and a popular figure of the first order. Opera houses vied for her services; millionaires showered her with gifts; nobles begged for her hand in marriage. Philip Hone, who was ordinarily cool to such celebrities, wrote on her arrival, "She has been anxiously looked for, and will create a sensation. . . ." He later obtained an invitation to one of her parties, and although irritated by the crowd, was most impressed with her beauty and charm. Hone also went to her debut, and of it wrote:

Many and many a night has passed since the walls of the Park have witnessed such a scene. Fanny Elssler, the bright star whose rising in our firmament has been anxiously looked for by the fashionable astronomers since its transit across the ocean was announced, shone forth in all its brilliancy this evening. Her reception was the warmest and most enthusiastic I ever witnessed.

THE SECOND DELUGE.

*Cartoon depicting the first appearance of Jenny Lind in America.*
(THE EDWARD W. C. ARNOLD COLLECTION, LENT BY THE METROPOLITAN MUSEUM OF ART.
PHOTO, COURTESY, MUSEUM OF THE CITY OF NEW YORK)

The great Elssler danced fifteen times in New York City, and could have filled the Park Theatre for years if she had not had to continue on her tour. She traveled throughout the nation for the next two years, but repeatedly played in New York, Boston, and Philadelphia. Although originally fearful of America, she came to love the country, and her willingness to say so made her still more popular. In October she appeared at a benefit for the Bunker Hill monument, after she had offered to make a $1,000 donation or to dance for the fund at an evening performance. When the *New York Journal of Commerce* criticized the way she had made the offer, the paper was mobbed and its offices vandalized. Despite the criticism Miss Elssler danced for the benefit of the fund, and after the performance a group of Harvard students unhitched the horses from her carriage and pulled it through the streets, cheering as they went. The beaming Fanny bowed as she rode in triumph.

Fanny Elssler's Boston farewell of October 1841 crowned her success. In what became a model for future performers, she went to the footlights after what was to have been her last performance and made a short speech.

Ladies and Gentlemen—I am very much bothered. I don't like to leave you now, for the last time, and I am afraid to try your patience by a longer stay. Really, I don't know what to do— (Shouts of Stay! Stay! from all parts of the house.) I have a great mind to stay—shall I? (Yes! Yes! and great cheering.) Now remember, if you get tired of me it's your own fault.

Fanny remained in Boston for additional performances, and then set off to Havana. Early in 1842 she returned to

Europe. The tour was a financial as well as an artistic and popular success. Fanny's New York earnings for her initial fifteen days were approximately $10,000; in Philadelphia she received $500 for each performance. After all expenses and charges were deducted, she showed a profit of $85,000 for the slightly less than two years she had appeared on the American stage.

The Elssler success was not lost on Phineas T. Barnum. He vowed to duplicate, if not better, her record. He would succeed in this ambition by the end of the decade, when he would bring an actress to America whose triumphs would surpass those of Fanny Elssler.

Barnum went to New York in 1834, at the age of twenty-four. Earlier he had edited an abolitionist newspaper in Danbury, Connecticut, and had done odd jobs. Realizing the need for entertainments and possessing a fine sense of showmanship, he opened an exhibition featuring Joice Heth, a Negress whom he passed off successfully as George Washington's 161-year-old nurse. The show's program was simple. Joice sat on a stool, answering questions about her life, the young Washington, and the problems of slavery. Paying customers flocked to Barnum's to hear her tales, and when attendance fell off, Barnum found new attractions. In 1841 he changed direction temporarily and became a salesman for *Sear's Pictorial Illustrations of the Bible.* Barnum was a successful salesman, but when Sear's agents swindled him of his profits he took the opportunity to return to the staging of extravaganzas.

In June 1841 Barnum leased Vauxhall Garden, a run-down theater, which he ran at a small profit, while he

# MECHANICS' HALL!

## NO. 472 BROADWAY, BETWEEN GRAND AND BROOME STREETS.

### OPEN EVERY NIGHT DURING THE WEEK

# CHRISTY'S

G. N. CHRISTY,    W. PORTER,    E. P. CHRISTY    T. VAUGHN,    J. RAYNOR,    E. H. PIERCE

# MINSTRELS

## ORGANIZED, 1842.

### THE OLDEST ESTABLISHED COMPANY IN THE WORLD

The First to Harmonize Negro Melodies, and originators of the present popular style of Ethiopian Entertainments, whose success in this City during the past THREE YEARS, is without Precedent in the annals of Public Amusements in this Great Metropolis; convincing evidence of their Superior Merit and Attractiveness.

## The Company,

### UNDER THE DIRECTION AND MANAGEMENT OF E. P. CHRISTY.

# WENESDAY EV'ING, Sept. 19, 1849,

## PROGRAMME—PART 1.

Medley Overture .......................................................Full Band
Dinah's Wedding Day, from the Opera of Leonora .......................Company
Come with me, my Dinah dear...........................................E. P. Christy
Stop that knocking, introduced with Happy and Light, from the Bohemian Girl .. Company
Julius's Bride.........................................................George Christy
Rosa Lee, or don't be foolish Joe.....................................E. P. Christy
 yrolean Solo, displaying a flexibility and volume of voice truly astonishing and
     hitherto unknown...............................................Christian
Phantom Chorus, or the Darkey's Apparition, from La Sonnambula ............Company
Masquerade Waltz, with Street Organ and Automaton Imitations ...........Company

*Part of the playbill for Christy's Minstrels, one of the entertainment hits of the decade.*

earned additional money doing publicity for other hucksters. Apparently he hoped to turn Vauxhall into a high-toned theater, and was on the verge of accomplishing this when he learned that Scudder's American Museum, one of the most famous showplaces in the city, was for sale. Barnum was interested in buying it, but he lacked sufficient funds. Instead Peale's Museum, a rival concern, purchased Scudder's, intending to finance the museum by issuing stock. Barnum learned of this plan and flooded the newspapers with stories of Peale's insolvency. The potential purchasers rejected the stock, and the deal was about to fall through when the directors of Peale's Museum approached Barnum with an offer: they would name him director of the combined museum if he would call off his newspaper campaign. Barnum accepted, and entered the world of big-time show business. Two years later he bought out the directors and took sole control of the museum.

The Barnum shows of the 1840s were national attractions and they helped make New York a tourist center. Middle-class matrons from Chicago made the trip to New York and took their children to Barnum's as a special treat. Philadelphia's aristocracy came to see the Barnum shows, and so did Boston's intellectuals. Realizing the spirit of the age, Barnum combined entertainment with education. He showed such attractions as a mechanical chess player, a mathematical genius who could do complex sums in his head, and other unusual spectacles "from the far corners of the world, for your edification and amusement." His most popular success was General Tom Thumb, who headed a long line of freaks at Barnum's. He portrayed Tom Thumb as an accomplished individual of great talents. Thumb was proclaimed as

the smallest Man in Miniature in the known world, weighing only fifteen pounds, who has been patronized by all the crowned heads of Europe, and has been seen by over 5,000,000 people. He will be seen on the platform in one of the main halls of the museum in his extraordinary and popular performances, including his Citizen's Dress, in which he will dance the polka and sailor's hornpipe, give representations of Napoleon, Frederick the Great and Grecian Statues. He will also appear in his magnificent Court Dress presented to him by Queen Victoria, and which he wore before all the principal courts of Europe. After which he will appear in his Beautiful Scotch Costume in which he will dance the Highland Fling. The magnificent presents received from Queen Victoria and the principal Crowned Heads of Europe will be exhibited.

Barnum took Tom Thumb to Europe in 1844, and he was a huge success. But in 1857 he admitted that the General was a child:

But had I announced him as only five years of age it would have been impossible to excite the interest or awaken the curiosity of the public.... I had observed the American fancy for European exotics, and if the deception ... has done anything toward checking our disgraceful preference for foreigners I may readily be pardoned for the offense I here acknowledge.

For those who wanted more, Barnum had other attractions, such as huge eggs, boa constrictors, "Miss Elizabeth Simpson, a delicate young Quakeress of 21 years" who was "nearly eight feet high and weighs 337 pounds," and a large wax museum. In 1848 he acquired the Chinese Museum, and there he boasted of showing industrious fleas, educated dogs, jugglers, automations, ventriloquists, living statuary, tableaux, gypsies, albinos, fat boys, giants, dwarfs, rope dancers, caricatures of phrenology, "life Yankees," pantomimes, models of Dublin, Paris, Niagara, Jerusalem, mechanical figures, fancy glass blowing, knitting machines and other triumphs of the mechanical art, dissolving views, and American Indians.

Barnum capped this part of his career and entered upon a new one in 1850, when he brought Jenny Lind to America. It was the Elssler craze all over again, but this time the artist had a manager worthy of her talents. Philip Hone, then approaching seventy, wrote in his diary that "so much has been said, and the trumpet of fame has sounded so loud, in honor of this new importation from the shores of Europe, that nothing else is heard in the streets, nothing seen in the papers, but the advent of the 'Swedish Nightingale.' " Barnum offered a prize of $200 for the best song written by an American in honor of Jenny, and claimed that almost six hundred entries had been submitted. If we are to judge from the newspapers of the time, Jenny Lind was one of the great singers of the age. But afterward, when the ballyhoo was over, sober critics reflected that although she was most personable and sweet, her voice left much to be desired. When opera star Adelina Patti arrived to make her 1859 tour, those who remembered Jenny conceded that without Barnum she would not have made the splash she did.

The same could be said for others, who were not so clearly labeled as entertainers. The phrenologists, spiritualists, utopians, and varied reformers who captured the public imagination could do so only with the aid of agents and newspapers. Although the phrase would not appear for more than a century, the medium was indeed the message in the 1840s. The difference between Barnum and lesser men in the occult fields was that he knew he was a show-man while they thought they were purveyors of Truth. He was also a better businessman than his competitors, a man with a keen affinity with the people who came to see his shows. Barnum's advertising techniques were similar to those of other showmen, but his copy was more sophisti-cated and his messages more appealingly presented. With-out knowing the phrase or developing sampling techniques, Barnum was a master of public relations and the greatest marketer of his time.

# 5/THE BUSINESS OF INFORMATION

THE MONEY QUESTION PROVIDED THE LEITMOTIF FOR
American economic and business history throughout the
nineteenth century. The combination of a growing and
hard-working labor force, abundant natural resources, and
skillful business leadership created the engine for economic
expansion. But the engine could not perform without the
fuel of capital, and after the disestablishment of the Bank
of the United States the means by which it could be created,
controlled, and utilized was absent. Thus, the problem of
raising funds bedeviled many would-be entrepreneurs of the
1840s as did the question of whom to trust with funds
and inventories. In this way money and information were
intertwined, and because of it, the United States became
the first nation to develop the business of business information in a scientific fashion. The more marginal the businessman, the more insecure the banking system, the greater
would be the need for such knowledge.

In 1834 there were 506 banks in the United States

capitalized at $200 million; by 1837 there were 788 with $300 million capital; and in the same period bank-note circulation more than doubled. Notes of dubious value would circulate for close to their face value in areas near the bank; in case of trouble, the holder could rush to the office, demand—and, hopefully, receive—gold for the paper. But what of the holder of a Tennessee bank note who lived in Boston? He would find few merchants, or even bankers, willing to accept the note, and so would have to sell it at a discount, which would fluctuate according to the general tone of business and the bank's reputation. Major "currency exchanges" were found in all the large eastern cities, and the prices for specific bank paper were often quoted in the daily newspapers. The nation's businessmen used these quotations to check on the·condition of distant banks, and this kind of service became especially important when many local and state banks failed in the wake of the 1837 panic.

The rapid development of the corporation as a form of business organization in America was another response to the need for raising capital. So long as small business dominated the scene, individual proprietorships and partnerships sufficed. But in an age when canals and railroads required what were then considered huge sums of money, the selling of shares to the public in these mammoth enterprises was necessary.

While desirable and natural, the corporate form created problems, most of which revolved around the concept of limited liability. Creditors knew that sole proprietors or partners, whose liability for the debts of their businesses was unlimited, would make every effort to avoid failure. Bankruptcy was less a stigma in America than in Europe, but it was still a shameful state, and those who resorted to it did so realizing that insofar as business life was concerned, they might be finished in the community. Such was not the case with a shareholder in a bank, canal, or railroad. Should the enterprise fail, he would lose his investment, nothing more; a bankrupt company was an anonymous thing, and the blemish did not rub off on its shareholders.

Early critics of corporations, then, came to consider them easy paths to bankruptcy, as well as possible vehicles for big-business control of the nation. Throughout the 1820s and 1830s reformers tried to win legislative approval for an end to limited liability, and in some states they succeeded. But where they did, investors refused to finance large undertakings, and business declined. Apparently industrialization was not possible without the attraction of limited liability, but with it, business ethics seemed to be lowered. The paradox was illustrated in 1837, when C. J. Ingersoll of Pennsylvania observed that most of the business failures in that state had been corporations, and to remedy this situation he urged the constitutional convention held that year to enact severe restrictions on their organization and operation. To this, J. M. Scott replied, "Our great canals, many of them have been made by corporations, our bridges have been erected by corporations, and our turnpikes through almost every county in the state, have been made by corporations."

Those corporations of the period not engaged in transportation were more often than not mercantile and in some cases were small manufacturers. The homemade item was far more common in the 1840s than were factory-made goods, and this would remain the case until well into the 1850s. In 1849 the nation had some 123,000 "factories" —some large, most very small—with 957,000 Americans engaged in work there. Thus, the average manufacturing establishment employed eight workers. According to the 1850 census the nation's largest manufacturing activity was the milling of flour and meal, with cotton in second place and lumber in third. As late as 1860 more workers were engaged in the manufacture of boots and shoes (123,000) than in that of iron (49,000) and machinery (41,000) combined.

The typical manufacturer of the 1840s was a man who established a gristmill to serve the wheat farmers; the

*The north side of Reade Street in New York, from Broadway to Church Street, in the heart of the textile industry. Many buildings of this type were faced with cast-iron shells, anchored to the walls.*

owner of a cotton-fabricating operation employing fewer than ten workers; a family shoemaker or blacksmith; or a local lumberjack. This was still an age of agriculture. Of a work force of 5.4 million in 1840, only 790,000 were employed in nonagricultural pursuits. Ten years later only one of every six workers were in occupations that could be classified as manufacturing, and some of these were part-time workers, who spent planting and harvest time on the family farm. Much of the manufacturing consisted of operations geared to supply the farmer with a needed commodity or to process his goods for market. The key figure was not the manufacturer, however, but the merchant.

Residents of a small town knew local merchants by reputation, and word of their integrity usually spread to neighboring towns. But the reputation of a newly formed industrial concern could not be so easily known. Its suppliers and customers needed information regarding its reputation, finances, and general trustworthiness, and in the mid-1830s the only way one could obtain such information was by word of mouth and by personal experience.

The commission merchants were key figures in American business in the late 1830s and 1840s. Operating for the most part in large cities, they would receive goods from Europe on consignment and would enter into similar relations with American firms when domestic businesses became large enough for such operations. Commission agents often sold these goods at auction and for their services usually received about 5 percent of the sale price. In addition, the merchants would extend credit to their customers and expect their suppliers in turn to give them credit. In a large, cash-poor country, with inadequate transportation, credit was vital; without it business would have been impossible. "An American merchant obtains and gives more credit, and has, therefore, a wider range of speculation and action before him, than one possessed of the same capital in any other country," wrote Grund. But this presented many problems as well. He continued:

Again, credit being personal and business done to a much larger amount than is covered by property, it is not sufficient for him to know the fortunes and present means of those whom in the course of his ordinary transactions he is obliged to trust: he must be able to judge of their honesty, their talent for business, and the motives which they may have for fulfilling their engagements. He is thus compelled to study characters, while his own is made the subject of the severest scrutiny; and he becomes as skillful in discovering the personal qualifications of others, as he is solicitous to banish from his own conduct all that can give rise to premature judgments or suspicions.

Toward this end an American writer, Charles Edwards, said in 1839 that a merchant must show "confidence without obstinacy, and constancy of purpose under all circumstances." He must be ambitious so as to "accomplish a name which will give to his bill of exchange the currency of the world, and to his merchandise the best price and the highest consideration." Finally, he must have honor, "an aid and consolation in adversity." But Edwards did not say how the merchant could avoid adversity. Nor did he acknowledge the growing complexity of American business at the time. The nation was expanding rapidly in the 1840s, and would end the decade as a true continental power. How

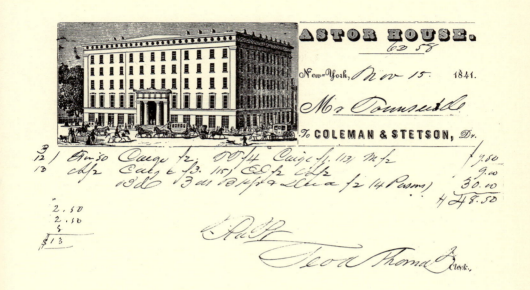

*Bill marked "paid" from the Astor House, New York, dated November 15, 1841, typical of its time.*

was a commission merchant in New York to judge the worth of California customers, their credit worthiness, and their ability to pay? And how could London factors discover the merits of a new firm that had just opened near Pittsburgh? The need for such information was obvious.

Given the growing complexities of the economy, an organization providing credit information would have evolved in time in the best of years. But the panic of 1837 hastened its arrival. The shakiness of many banks, the failures of thousands of small concerns, and the inability of the states to meet their obligations created a business atmosphere in which trust and solvency were greatly prized. Bankruptcy was a difficult procedure, but it now became more common. Many did not bother to file bankruptcy petitions; they simply did not pay their bills. In 1840 sixty-four of the sixty-seven officials in the federal land office had defaulted, a situation which led to an investigation but little in the way of corrective action. One of the investigators, V. M. Garesche, recommended leniency for most offenders. In his report on an Ohio officer, he said:

The man seems really penitent; and I am inclined to think, in common with his friends, that he is honest and has been led away from his duty by the example of his predecessor, and a certain looseness in the code of morality which here does not move in so limited a circle as it does with us at home. Another receiver would probably follow in the footsteps of the two. You will not, therefore, be surprised if I recommend his being retained in preference to another appointment, for he has his hands full now, and will not be disposed to speculate any more .... He has, moreover, pledged his word that, if retained, he will strictly obey the law .... Lenity towards him ... might stimulate him to exertions which severity might perhaps paralyze.

What remained of the nation's credit after the panic of 1837 was shattered in 1841. Early in the year the Bank of the United States of Pennsylvania in Philadelphia, the heir of the Bank of the United States, announced its inability to make gold payments and soon afterward closed its doors. Stock prices collapsed on Wall Street, and a new panic, fueled by bank failures, began. Philip Hone sadly noted that the depression would extend overseas because many Europeans had substantial investments in United States stock. "This enormous loss falls heavily upon the European [stock] holders, who will not in the future be disposed to trust us." Indeed, Europeans did withdraw their funds from America, not only because of the crash, but because of the need for capital to bolster the depressed European economies. Before the crash had ended, British investors alone had lost $130 million. Speaking for them, the London *Times* wrote, "The people of the United States may be fully persuaded that there is a certain class of securities to which no abundance of money, however great, can give value, and that in this class their own securities stand preeminent." The Paris Rothschilds wrote a Jacksonian politician, "You may tell your government that you have seen the man who is at the head of the finances of Europe, and that he has told you that they [the Americans] cannot borrow a dollar, not a dollar."

As the panic deepened, small businessmen demanded a new bankruptcy law that would enable them to purge themselves of their liabilities and make fresh starts. The debate in Congress was spirited. On the one hand, Jacksonians feared the law might provide corporations with an easy method of bilking the public; on the other, they recognized that without legislation the nation's commercial life might remain paralyzed. The law finally passed, and a wave of repudiations followed. Within two years debts worth $450 million affecting one million creditors were wiped out; 2,400 businessmen in Boston alone used the law to escape their debts. Even those few businessmen who remained solvent were looked upon with suspicion, for it was feared that at any moment they, too, would declare bankruptcy. The situation was so critical that the governor of Pennsylvania could recommend the construction of a special one-way railroad to Texas, to be used exclusively by defaulters. Their departure, he thought, might restore Americans' trust in one another. The bankruptcy law remained in effect for two years, being repealed when congressmen learned of the general opposition to its application. In its wake lay the wreckage of thousands of small and large businesses.

The panic and depression made the need for accurate business information more obvious than it previously had been. Trust, good faith, and hearsay might serve when money was cheap and the economy expanding, though even then fortunes were lost through unwise investments and mishandled credit. Now that money was dear and bankruptcy an everyday happening, information as to the activities and habits of one's customers became vital. It was against this background that the business of information grew and became institutionalized in the 1840s.

Fortunately, the foundation had already been set, and not by Americans, but by an English firm. Many European commercial and banking houses had invested in, or were doing business with, American concerns, and more were engaged in the overseas trade, but none had greater or more widespread interests in the United States than Baring Brothers & Co. of London. The Barings acted as agents for the United States government and several state governments in their dealings with European nations and businessmen; their firm was the European correspondent for the Bank of the United States during its existence, and was the most familiar foreign commercial house in New York, Boston, and Philadelphia. The Barings had expanded their American operations after the War of 1812, and during that boom era competed with other European houses for business, usually in the granting of credits and in general banking. Like them, the Barings were aware of the need for information, and sought it eagerly whenever and where-ever it could be found. Should an American merchant or banker of some standing arrive in London, he could be certain of meeting with British counterparts, who would politely but thoroughly pump him for information.

One such individual, Thomas Wren Ward, vacationed in London in 1828. Ward, a retired Boston merchant reputed to know the American commercial scene, met with an old friend, Joshua Bates, who had become a partner at Barings'. Bates introduced Ward to Thomas Baring, who in turn spoke of the impressive American to the firm's senior

*Credit reporter interviewing retail merchant.*

partner, Alexander Baring. At the urging of both Alexander and Ward, Thomas Baring visited America in 1829 to survey new possibilities. Before returning to London, he engaged Ward as Barings' resident agent in the United States, a position he held until 1853.

Ward traveled extensively through the United States, seeking information about merchants and commercial houses and relaying it back to London. He also enlisted others, such as Daniel Webster, to represent the Barings in America, and through his post became a major figure in American business. In his first three years as agent Ward granted commercial credits in excess of $50 million to American merchants, arranged for shipments of goods and collection of accounts, and reported on political events. But his most important service to Barings was his ability to assess the trustworthiness of old and new clients. As such, he became a pioneer in the credit-reporting field.

Ward's reports were both personal and curt. He wrote London that one man, "a merchant from Boston, owns a packet line to Philadelphia and real estate . . . is owner of the *Duncan* with B. F. R. and G. D. C. Has $70,000. Bold but safe." Another report said, "A. D. is rank radical and high Jackson man . . . . Safe enough, but I gave him credit because at the moment he applied, there was some talk in London about the account being changed in Washington. He has influence there for good or evil." Ward was frank to admit his prejudices and preferences. Thus, he judged Thomas D. Curtis of Boston a good risk.

Though a personal friend of mine and his business passing before me, I do not know his property. I feel confident that Curtis and

Baylies have done a very good business and I have seen no bad business of theirs. I think highly of Curtis as to honor and capacity and conclude he may have $25,000 or $30,000 and Baylies $40,000 or $50,000. I have great confidence that they will always keep safe.

Ward's reports were confined for the most part to commercial firms with foreign dealings, and almost all of these were located in the coastal areas. But what of those merchants and businessmen in the interior, who had no direct dealings with foreigners, but rather trafficked with one another and with correspondents in the coastal cities? At a time of tight money and depression, information regarding their activities and worth was extremely important. Just as Ward provided a foundation for the business of information regarding overseas credit, so Sheldon P. Church did the same for the national scene.

Church entered the credit field in 1827, writing reports on customers for large New York dry-goods houses. This was a part-time occupation for Church, whose principal business was saddlery. As economic and business conditions worsened in the late 1830s and the demand for information grew, Church's part-time work expanded. By 1839 he was known as one of the most knowledgeable sources of information in New York.

Sometime late in 1840 or early in 1841 several large New York merchants banded together to form The Merchants Vigilance Association. Their leader was William C. Dusenberry, a prominent businessman and religious leader of the city. The Association had been formed to protect its members against fraudulent buyers and unsound credit

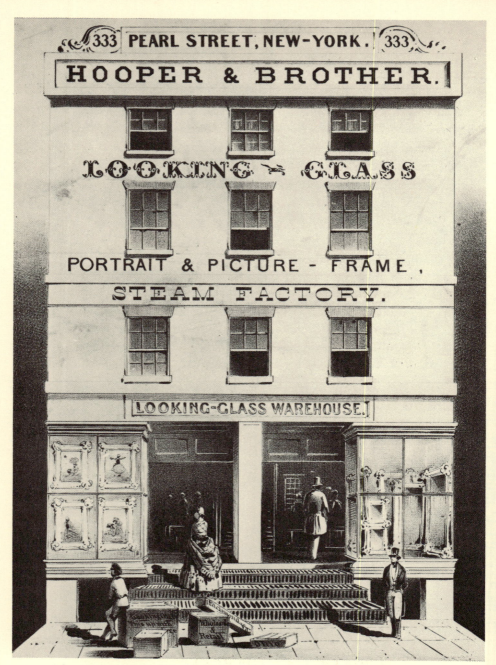

*Advertisement of Hooper & Brother, showing the firm's looking-glass warehouse at 333 Pearl Street, New York, about 1849.*

risks "in the country trade." Those who belonged would pool information regarding customers, which would then be distributed by Dusenberry, who acted as a one-man clearing-house for such matters. More important, however, was the retention of Church as a general agent for the members. Church gave up his other interests to take the post, and then began on his travels throughout the nation. Thus he became America's first full-time credit reporter.

Church's methods of operation were simple. Before going out on the road he would meet with the Association members and learn as much as he could about their customers. He would also be given a list of those to be investigated. Then he would establish an itinerary, which would be given to the members. In November 1844, for example, Church described his route as follows:

After a few days in Petersburgh and Norfolk, I return to Baltimore, and from thence cross the mountains to Wheeling, Va.; then I go through parts of Kentucky, including various towns not visited heretofore; then to St. Louis, thence through Tennessee, North and South Alabama, and Eastern Mississippi, aiming to accomplish thus much in time for spring trade; then through the river counties of Mississippi, then to Florida, and to return through Georgia, the Carolinas and Virginia.

The members would forward additional queries to Church during this trip, and he would pick them up at pre-arranged locations.

Church was a shrewd appraiser of human character as well as financial resources. He wrote his opinions with restraint but did not hesitate to be harshly critical when he felt it necessary. His candor at times involved him in actions for libel. Of a Mr. Thatcher he wrote:

He was formerly in a small business here [in Mississippi] and failed; he was a dissipated loafer for the next few years and has a little shop here and has kept sober but had acquired no standing. I understand he took about $2,500 in drafts on Mobile, and his stock in trade may probably go to pay for them. If such men are safe who shall be called doubtful? I go for right of search, suspecting all strange craft.

The work of the Merchants Vigilance Association and Sheldon Church was important, but limited to a few firms and dependent upon the field work of a single person. Even as Dusenberry organized his group, a second was in operation in New York that would eclipse it and provide a stronger and better organized firm in the business of information. Like the others, it had its beginning in the financial panic.

Arthur Tappan & Co., a large silk house, had suspended business temporarily in 1837, with liabilities of $1.2 million. Other firms had gone under with larger losses, but the Tappan family enjoyed such renown that the suspension of its business caused a great stir all along the East Coast.

There were three Tappan brothers—Benjamin, Arthur, and Lewis. Benjamin was the politician of the family; he served as district judge in Ohio and in 1839 entered the Senate from that state. Arthur and Lewis were successful businessmen and major forces in the abolitionist, women's rights, and temperance crusades. The Tappans closely regulated the lives of their employees. Clerks were expected to work the usual twelve-hour day and be present at morning religious services. In addition, they were expected to re-

# DISSOLUTION.

The Co-partnership heretofore existing between the Subscribers under the name of **G. HATHEWAY & CO.** is this day dissolved.

**EDMUND TABER** is duly authorised to settle the affairs of the late Firm.

GILBERT HATHEWAY,
EDMUND TABER.

☞ The Subscriber having taken the Stock and Stand of the late Firm of G. Hatheway & Co. will continue the wholesale **Dry Goods, Clothing and Commission Business,** at No. 21 North Water Street.

EDMUND TABER.

New-Bedford, 2 mo. 20, 1844.

*New Bedford June 2¶/44*

*Gent.*
*The above notice will apprise you of the dissolution of the late firm of G. Hatheway Co, to whom I have succeeded in the business above referred to,—*

*Please inform me by return mail what are your lowest terms cash for a lot of your sheetings, and oblige*

*Yours Respectfully &C.—*

*Edmund Taber*

*Mess. P. Whitin & Sons*

*Announcement of dissolution and succession of partnerships in 1844.*

frain from alcohol, to belong to an abolitionist society, to be at their homes by ten o'clock every evening, and to stay away from theaters.

Lewis Tappan was an interesting and accomplished figure. After having been a sales agent for several textile firms, he joined Arthur in the silk business. He served as a member of the Committee of the New York Board of Trade, which studied the Commercial Code of France to discover whether some of its ideas might be used in formulating a national bankruptcy law for the United States. With Arthur he founded the *New York Journal of Commerce,* helped found Oberlin College, and in general made his presence felt throughout the nation.

Their 1837 business suspension did not leave the brothers destitute, and within a short time Arthur Tappan & Co. was revived. But their business trouble did impress Lewis with the need for an agency that would collect data regarding a firm's credit and provide this information to subscribers. A. T. Stewart and other leading merchants encouraged Tappan in the project, for they sorely needed credit information.

Tappan was admirably equipped to handle such an operation. As a leading dealer in dry goods, he had an extensive knowledge of business conditions throughout the nation and in particular of businessmen in New York and other cities. Despite his failure, he was considered reliable, honest, and prudent; even conservative businessmen, who tended to believe that those who joined abolitionist organizations were not completely trustworthy, put their faith in him. A. T. Stewart said of Lewis Tappan that he was "a fit and proper person, both from integrity and business shrewdness, to look into [Stewart's own] accounts and make an impartial report of his pecuniary condition, so as to set all doubts at rest." Even before he entered the credit field, Tappan had been consulted about the integrity of various merchants.

On June 1, 1841, Lewis sent an announcement to leading New York merchants "in the country trade," informing them of his intention to form a new company, the Mercantile Agency, which would provide business information for a fee. On July 20 he placed an advertisement to that effect in the *Commercial Advertiser,* and he retired as an active partner at Arthur Tappan & Co. Offices were procured at 7 Dorr's Building at the corner of Hanover and Exchange streets, and were opened on August 1. At the time Lewis said:

This Agency has been established with the concurrence of many experienced merchants in this city and in the country for the purpose of obtaining, in a proper manner, intelligence of the responsibility of merchants visiting the market from different parts of the country to purchase goods from time to time—the same to be imparted with proper limitations and restrictions, to such merchants and others, as may be disposed to patronize The Agency, and become subscribers thereto. The terms, and the plan and greater detail will be made known as above. Merchants interested in such sales are respectfully invited to visit the office.

The Agency prospered; it provided a needed service at a reasonable cost and was available to all, not merely to a small group of insiders. Furthermore, Tappan's staff proved better businessmen and managers than others in the field and soon left many by the wayside. In 1841, for example, the Mercantile Agency took over the files of Warren A. Cleaveland—himself a credit man—and others would follow.

The early Mercantile Agency correspondents were often quite journalistic in their impressions, adding humor to the facts. One of them, who reported on a Lockport, New York, businessman in 1850, wrote:

James Samson is a peddler, aged 30; he comes to Albany to buy his goods, and then peddles them out along the canal from Albany to Buffalo. He is worth $2,000; owns a wooden house at Lockport in his own name; his family reside in it; has a wife and three children, two boys and one girl; boys named Henry and Charles, aged four and six years; girl named Margaret, two years old; no judgement out or mortgage on property; drinks two glasses cider brandy, plain, morning and evening—never more; drinks water after each; chews fine cut; never smokes; good teeth generally; has lost a large double tooth on lower jaw, back, second from throat on left side; has a scar an inch long on his left leg kneecap; cause, cut himself with a hatchet when only three years old; can be found when in Albany at Pete Mason's, 82 State Street; purchases principally jewelry and fancy articles.

Samson's suppliers probably deduced from this description that the peddler was an acceptable credit risk, while the Agency might have surmised the reporter knew him pretty well. Reports of this kind were the norm in the Agency's early days, and they continued to come in even at the turn of the century from reporters who had begun to work for Tappan as young men. By 1900 such detailed descriptions seemed quaint and far too personal, but they were not considered irrelevant in the 1840s and 1850s. Given the distances of the period, the poor transportation, and the memories of the 1837 panic and depression, suppliers wanted to know as much about their customers as they could. They were dealing with not only a purchaser but a human being, and a sense of honor was valuable collateral in the 1840s.

In 1847 Lewis Tappan took on a partner, thirty-year-old Benjamin Douglass, a southerner who was the son of a

*Lewis Tappan.*

119

West India trader. The union of these two men was fortuitous. Tappan was a fine office manager, while Douglass soon proved a perceptive and energetic traveler. The former increasingly devoted his attention to reform movements, and so gave Douglass a free hand in the business. Finally, Tappan was a well-known abolitionist and so was *persona non grata* in the South, while Douglass was pro-southern and was welcomed there. Lewis retired in 1849, and his place at the firm was taken by his brother Arthur. By that time, however, Douglass had become the firm's guiding force. Robert Graham Dun, who joined the Mercantile Agency in 1849 as a clerk, soon exhibited management talent and assumed authority over internal affairs, while Douglass gave his attention to the Agency's expansion in the South and West.

Branches were also established, the first being in Boston in 1843. A second was opened in Philadelphia in 1845, and a third in Baltimore the following year. Cincinnati followed in 1849, and New Orleans in 1851, in time for the Agency's tenth anniversary. By that time the home office employed thirty men who handled correspondence and copied reports by hand into large ledgers. (Examples of these are shown in the appendix.)

A major principle of credit reporting, greatly increasing its value to the business world, was established in 1845 as a result of a libel action filed against the Mercantile Agency by an Ohio plaintiff. At one point in the suit the judge supported the plaintiff's demand that the source of the Agency's information be revealed. Douglass refused, stating that to do so would be to violate a trust. He was

*Advertisement in the* Commercial Register *for John M. Bradstreet & Son, which was founded in Cincinnati in 1849, and moved to New York in 1857.*

sentenced to twenty days in prison for contempt of court but did not reveal the information. This test of security received wide publicity in the press and won general approval among businessmen. Upon his release Douglass was greeted by an enthusiastic group, who praised his defense of a basic credit principle. During a march of supporters on Broadway following his release, Douglass was proposed as a candidate for mayor of New York, but he declined the offer.

The court decision and Douglass' willingness to accept jail rather than reveal sources won him important support. Freeman Hunt, editor of *The Merchants' Magazine,* who earlier had expressed doubts as to the worth of the Agency, now became a supporter of the idea. He summed up the Mercantile Agency system as follows:

The usefulness of the Agency is unquestionable. Without it, the credit system, in a country like ours, with vast distances between seller and buyer, would make mercantile pursuits the most uncertain of all. Its principal advantages are as follows:

It points out to the city merchant solvent, prudent, and thriving customers; cautions him against the doubtful; and apprises him promptly of changes which make it proper to press the collection of his claims.

It traces absconding debtors and fraudulent traders from State to State, exposing their pretences, and rendering it difficult for them to find dupes or victims.

It makes the solvent and punctual trader known in every city, giving him credit, and dispensing altogether with letters of introduction or guarantee.

It prevents delay in the delivery of goods ordered, giving full reports of the purchaser and making further inquiry unnecessary.

It corrects many evils incident to the credit system, and tends to keep commercial business in the hands of men of integrity, means, and experience.

It tends to promote a high standard of mercantile honor, to check speculation and extravagances, to enhance the value of punctuality and good character, and to make it the interest of every trader to be temperate, industrious, economical, and desirous of an unspotted reputation.

America was a growing, changing country in the 1840s. Its businessmen were among the hardest-working entrepreneurs in the nation's history. Their battleground was a difficult one. During the depression of the early 1840s they had to struggle just to survive; after recovery in mid-decade they had to compete fiercely for footholds in the rapidly growing economy. Under such conditions businessmen needed every weapon they could muster. Good transportation, sound banking, and a stable political climate were all important, but no less so was complete and accurate information about customers and clients. This data was provided by the Mercantile Agency. In 1848 the business writer William Ross wrote feelingly of the problem.

The wholesale merchants of the eastern cities were more or less at the mercy of their country debtors, or, at best, had to depend for their knowledge of the country trader's business character and condition, on such references or letters of recommendation as he was able to furnish them, or, on what was still more uncertain— the testimony of clerks or travelling agents, who each house was in the habit of sending annually on collecting tours throughout the country—testimony too often obtained from any but reliable sources . . . . As the population of the country and the number of traders increased, it became a matter of the greatest importance to the merchants of the importing and jobbing cities to acquire, in some way, information respecting the conditions of the country traders, which should be complete, reliable, and constantly *fresh*.

# 6/THE BUSINESS OF BANKING

ON MARCH 1, 1836, THE CHARTER OF THE BANK OF the United States expired, thus ending the life of that powerful institution. Its president, Nicholas Biddle, had a month before obtained a charter for the Bank of the United States of Pennsylvania, and hoped to maintain both his power and central bank functions through that institution. But this attempt failed, as the result of bad investments, the 1837 panic, the growth of major rivals in New York, and the withdrawal of federal support. Three quarters of a century later the Federal Reserve System would be established to perform central bank functions, but until then the nation stumbled along without such an institution, utilizing makeshift organizations, private banks, and Treasury alternatives. The lack of a strong central bank was one of the weak spots in the nation's financial fabric, one that would be torn asunder many times in the years that followed. A preview of what was to come could be seen in the 1837 panic. The first chapter of the new dispensation was unrolled in the 1840s.

Through its many branches in all parts of the nation the Bank of the United States had served to maintain liquidity, providing funds for farmers and businessmen, discounting notes, and insuring a stable currency. The owner of a BUS note in New Hampshire knew it would be accepted by a citizen of Georgia; a farmer in Ohio received BUS notes drawn on the New York branch as though they were gold, for he had confidence in the institution, even as he distrusted its politics. Now he was obliged to find other institutions, other currencies, and alternative methods of settling debts, transferring funds, and receiving payments for goods and services, and these were hard to come by. The history of commercial banking in the 1840s was one of adaptation to the post-BUS era. The states tried various makeshifts and adaptations of existing institutions to fill the needs of businessmen, and although some were moderately successful, no single institution or program was able to take up the slack. Not until the early 1860s would national banking achieve some kind of rationale; only with the coming of the Federal Reserve System would a new central bank of substance make its appearance, and even then, the Federal Reserve would lack the powers of the old BUS. The end of that central bank led to increased needs for clearing houses and credit investigation agencies, but its first impact was felt in the area of commercial banking.

There were two strains in commercial banking in the 1840s. The first and by far the more important was state banking, in which state-chartered institutions attempted to carry on central bank functions. When a revulsion against these "monopolies" developed in the mid-1840s, there was a turn to free banking, which as its name implies was the development of banks which functioned without specific charters but under state regulations.

State-chartered banks are as old as the country, but a major step in the direction of establishing a systemized structure occurred in 1824, when a group of Boston banks united to form what was called the Suffolk System. Each member bank agreed to maintain deposits at the Suffolk Bank, and these would act as a reserve against its notes and those of correspondent banks of members of the Suffolk System. Thus, notes drawn on the Mechanics Bank of Boston were quickly and easily redeemed at the Suffolk Bank. In addition, the Mechanics Bank had the right to present notes drawn on the Charleston banks at the Suffolk counters, and have the face amount credited to its account. The Suffolk Bank would then undertake to send the note to Charleston for collection.

In this way, the Suffolk Bank acted as a central bank for its region, a sort of BUS in miniature. All of this presented the Suffolk Bank with troublesome details and additional work. Should the Charleston correspondent bank refuse to honor the note, the Suffolk Bank and the Mechanics Bank would be obliged to work out settlements and terms. At times the Suffolk Bank suffered losses, and its salaried employees had to be increased regularly as its business increased. But since each member of the System had to maintain a minimum of $5,000 in gold on deposit at the Suffolk Bank, and in addition came to consider it a central bank for Massachusetts and later on almost all of New England, the Bank's power and prestige grew, as did the volume of its commercial business.

The Suffolk System and its success led to countermoves

from New York. During his short term as governor in 1829 Martin Van Buren recommended, and the legislature passed, a new banking law that provided for a Safety Fund, under the terms of which any chartered bank had to contribute annually for six years one-half of one percent of its capital to a fund, which was to be used to assist those New York–chartered institutions in danger of insolvency. The law also established a commission to inspect the chartered banks and limited note issues to twice a member bank's capital and loans to two and a half times the capital. The Safety Fund was designed to assure New York businessmen of the solvency of state institutions and encourage them to use the member banks rather than the BUS or those of the Suffolk System. One might say the Jacksonian struggles in the area of banking were also fights between three systems and cities —the BUS of Philadelphia, the Suffolk System of Boston, and the Safety Fund of New York. The crushing of the BUS eliminated Philadelphia in the struggle for banking leadership in America, and during the next decade New York and Boston state banking programs would contend for supremacy, with New York winning by the end of the 1840s.

When Jackson withheld federal funds from the BUS prior to and after the 1832 election and beginning the next September, he deposited them in state banks throughout the nation, also known as "pet banks" for the special relationship they had to the Administration. Thus, state banking grew rapidly in the period prior to the 1837 panic. In 1829 there were 329 state banks with a capital of $110 million, in 1834 the number had risen to 506 capitalized at $200 million, and on the eve of the panic the number was 788 with more than $300 million in capital. State bank note circulation more

*Nicholas Biddle, president of the Second Bank of the United States.*

than doubled in the period from 1830 to 1837, while loans and discounts increased from less than $200 million to over $500 million.

The 1837 panic destroyed many of these chartered

institutions, a good number of which were in shabby condition anyway, controlled by opportunists, political hacks, and individuals who knew little of the business. Others managed to remain open for a few months or even years after the panic, only to close down when rumors as to their solvency were circulated, leading to a rush of customers asking for deposits, followed by a shutting of the doors. The bedrock year for state banking was 1838, when dozens of the shaky institutions closed down each month. On the other hand, the states eagerly chartered new banks, which were often headed by the same men who weeks before had proclaimed their bankruptcy. Thus, the banking statistics offer a paradoxical picture of an increase in the number of state banks in the late 1830s while at the same time loans and discounts declined sharply, deposits evaporated, and circulation stagnated. Bank capital rose, but much of it was in the form of doubtful paper. Gold holding declined, a clear indication of the precarious bank liquidity of the period. Thus, in 1837 there were 788 state banks holding a total of $83 million in gold; by 1840 there were 901 state banks, but the gold reserves were down to $33 million.

By that time, however, a reform wave hit the states, so that new charters were not so easy to come by. The number of state-chartered banks fell to 691 in 1843, and although business continued to be poor in that last of the depression years, the gold reserves increased, solvency seemed restored, and confidence in the chartered institutions was somewhat better. Still, the reputation of state banking would remain poor for years to come. In the recovery year of 1843 U.S. Treasury officials complained of the lack of trustworthy in-

stitutions in which to deposit federal funds. There were
only nineteen worthy of such designation that year. Signifi-
cantly, twelve of these were in the Northeast, with a majority in New York, which by then had won its contest with
Boston and had become the capital center of the nation.

The combination of state bank failures, a continuation
of the Jacksonian reform movement, and the desire on the
part of some financiers to avoid or ignore state regulations
resulted in an upsurge of the Free Banking movement in
the aftermath of the 1837 panic. And this was considered a
suitable alternative not only to the BUS, but to such developments as the Suffolk System. As the reformers saw it,
banking had too long been a preserve of the rich; anyone
should be permitted to open a bank who had "sufficient
capital, reputation, and honor," wrote the New York
*Tribune* in 1845. The writer did not indicate, however,
what this sufficiency might be.

The New York experience with free banking was both
the most important and most typical example of the system.
The state's Safety Fund system had been shattered by the
1837 panic, as eleven banks attempted to draw funds at the
same time when the Fund had insufficient capital to save
four. News of this caused a wave of failures to develop in
late 1837 and early 1838, and resulted in widespread political activity against the chartered banks during the 1838
elections. The result was the Free Banking Act of 1838,
which soon after was accepted as a model by Michigan and
then by other states. Under the terms of the act, anyone who
could raise "sufficient capital" to open a bank could do so,
and would automatically receive a charter that bestowed

upon him "the necessary powers to carry on the business of banking—by discounting bills, notes, and other evidences of debt; by receiving deposits; by buying gold and silver bullion, and foreign coins, by buying and selling bills of exchange, and by issuing bills, notes, and other evidence of debt; . . . and no other powers whatever, except such as are expressly granted by this act."

The charters required the banks to back their notes with mortgages or state bonds, and hold a reserve of 12.5 percent in gold. Other states that copied the New York law varied the reserve requirements, in most cases pegging the gold reserve at a higher percentage. For example, Louisiana's law required a 33⅓ percent reserve against bills. New York claimed its reserves were low because its banks were trusted; Louisiana bankers charged that the New York bankers were too adventuresome, especially when one considered the bad experiences of 1837-1838, and that some New York banks were not to be considered as correspondents.

But such claims had substance. Those banks established under free banking laws were often in shakier shape than the older, chartered institutions. On the other hand, most were established in the early 1840s, and those that held on until 1843 were able to survive the decade, more the result of good times than sound, conservative banking procedures.

The free banking laws usually had provisions for state examination of books. These clauses were inserted in the laws at the insistence of reform elements, and although they gave the appearance of stability to the examined banks, this was more often than not a poorly disguised deception.

In Michigan, for example, the bank examiners would make
known their itinerary weeks before taking to the road. Then
the banks in the area would make plans for making their
reserves appear more solid than they were in fact. The exam-
iner would examine the books and gold of the first bank,
and then, as he rode to the next, a special messenger would
carry the first bank's gold to the second, where it would be
counted as part of that institution's reserves. The Michigan
law, one of the models of its kind, required free banks to
maintain a reserve of 30 percent in gold. The law was believed to have been upheld—until the practice of double,
triple, and quadruple counting was uncovered after a wave
of failures in 1846. An investigation followed, and the
report charged that if the Free Banking Act had been en-
forced as thoroughly as it appeared to be, Michigan would
have been left without a single bank.

In order to avoid pitfalls of free banking, some states,
unwilling to continue complete reliance on chartered institutions, went into the banking business on their own. Such
was the case in Indiana, where the State Bank of Indiana,
with half its capital subscribed by the state, dominated the
banking scene. It had a central office and seventeen branches
throughout the state, in addition to maintaining good correspondent relations with New York, Philadelphia, and
Boston institutions. If the Indiana experience may be taken
as a demonstration of the potential for state banking, we
may judge it an acceptable alternative to the BUS. But like
Nicholas Biddle's bank, the State Bank of Indiana was
assaulted as the home of special privilege. Since it had a
monopoly in Indiana, it earned the ire of every reformer in

*Second Bank of the United States in Philadelphia, built in 1824. An outstanding example of Greek revival architecture, it was designed by William Strickland.*

(ALOIS K. STROBL, PHILADELPHIA CITY PLANNING COMMISSION)

the state. In 1855, after two decades of excellent management, the State Bank of Indiana was liquidated, to be replaced by free banks of dubious quality and poorer reputation.

The early success of the Indiana experiment led other states to imitate it, but none were successful. In Mississippi, for example, the state took control of the BUS branch and transformed it into the Union Bank, which had an initial capital of $15 million, $5 million of which was subscribed to by the state. But the Union Bank was poorly managed from the start, made improper loans and failed to live up to its charter. In the end it failed, and repercussions of its collapse caused widespread suffering in Mississippi for years thereafter. On the other hand, free banking was little better in the state, and the absence of a sound system held back economic growth in Mississippi for decades.

This patchwork of free banks, chartered banks, and state banks could not fill the gap left by the destruction of the BUS, but the nation's businessmen, farmers, and bankers did the best they could with what they had. One of their biggest problems was the assessment of the worth of currency printed by local banks. Thus, bankers in Maine were obliged to judge the value of notes printed by a small bank in Louisiana, often when they knew little of its condition and soundness. Most banks in the Northeast published daily or weekly "note-finders" for their clerks and managers, to enable them to better evaluate the notes that came across the counters. Some bank paper was acceptable without question, while other notes could be taken if presented by prized customers, or in small denominations, or to settle certain claims. Other notes would be accepted, but only at a discount from the face value. Banks would accept notes in settlement for obligations, with the understanding that the customer would pay interest on what amounted to a loan until the note had been presented at the issuing bank for redemption in gold. At times the directors themselves would take a hand in making the determination. In his book, *Banks of New York and the Clearing House,* published in 1858, J. S. Gibbons offers a picture of one such session.

The president of a New York bank, addressing the directors, notes that a draft was presented that day. "Joseph Chambers offers a draft on Green & Davis, of San Francisco, on Thrust & Co. of New York, and accepted—at seventy-five days, for five thousand dollars."

The firm of Thrust & Co. is probably a new account, and the president asks if anyone knows anything about the principals. A director does know something, and says: "They began business a year ago, with thirty thousand dollars capital—are said to have done a profitable trade in the produce line—had shipped heavily to California. The Co. [Company] was a young man who came out of Bacon's—the big packer on West Street. Guess he hadn't much money —say, five thousand dollars; but very smart. Thrust was the capitalist. Put in twenty-five thousand dollars, hard cash— about all he had."

"What age is he?"

"Thirty-five to forty."

"Man of family?"

"Oh, yes; I've known him these twelve years. Got half a dozen children. You must know him, Mr. President! He married Stubble's daughter, wine merchant, there at your corner. Guess he ran away with her, and made the old man mad. But they're all reconciled now, and he's Stubble's principal advisor in them new stores he's building in Murray Street."

"Is that the man?"

"That's the man, sir."

"Well, who married Stubble's other daughter?"

Here the president warns the gentlemen not to wander too far from the subject under discussion, and again notes they are there to discuss business.

Another director asks, "You said he was in the California business?"

"Yes, sir. Made some very successful shipments there last Spring."

"I've got very little confidence in California,—very little."

"It's a good way off, that's a fact. I'd rather do business with people that trade nearby."

Another director voices his opinion. "Wouldn't touch it with a ten-foot pole. Bad line. Let it slide, Mr. President. We can do better with our money." And so Messrs. Thrust & Co. do not get the note discounted.

Bankers and others in the business of accepting or rejecting out-of-town commercial paper had to rely upon such informal information, personal judgments of directors, and catch-as-catch-can assessments in most cases, but at times in the 1840s they would call upon the specialized services of professional credit men, such as those employed by Tappan at the Mercantile Agency (see Chapter 5). Consider the case of Joseph Scott, and the use made by the bank of his credit rating. As before, the president addresses his Board. "Here is Joseph Scott, of Wheeling, four hundred and sixty dollars, seven months to run. What do you know about him?"

A director speaks. "Well, Mr. President, Scott has dealt

with me five years, and never failed to pay promptly. He represents himself as an owner of real estate, worth ten thousand dollars. Besides that, his stock averages some twenty thousand over all his debts. I have a correspondent there who confirms his statement, and The Mercantile Agency here says the same thing. Scott's general character is very fair. Church member—very gentlemanly. I sell him about three thousand dollars a year, and he owes me, running, say two."

In another case the president wants to verify the state-

*The Parker House in San Francisco, site of the first bank in California.*

(COURTESY, GWEN BRISTOW)

ment of a firm in Toronto. Again, according to Gibbons, "he sends an inquiry to the 'Commercial Agency' of Messrs. Paul & Pry [really McKillip & Sprague, a credit agency of the period] and in thirty minutes gets the following answer:

Jonas Marks, Toronto, general hardware. Began business, in 1849, with cash capital, $10,000. Not very successful for the first two years—rather fond of frolics—credit at home not good. In 1852, got run over by a railway car, and lost half a leg. Recovered $5,000 damages. Settled down and began to thrive immediately. In 1853, married a daughter of one of our wealthiest citizens who has since died, leaving an estate of three hundred thousand dollars to be divided among twelve children. M. is one of the executors. His business has been much improved since '52. In '55 he realized a handsome sum by selling off some real estate, and was appointed deacon in the church. Credit is now A-1.

The work of the agencies in assisting the banks of the post-BUS era was invaluable; without them interregional and interstate business would have been difficult, if not impossible. Bank business grew in the 1840s and the early 1850s, as did that of mercantile establishments wanting to know more of the reputation of clients and customers. Indirectly, then, the demise of the Bank of the United States and the financial chaos following the 1837 panic resulted in the growth of the Mercantile Agency and other firms performing the same or similar services.

Support for clearing houses was another result of the disestablishment of the Bank of the United States. While it existed most large banks maintained accounts at the BUS, and so regular clearances were unnecessary: the BUS merely kept a running record of each bank's accounts, and bills and charges were sent out when necessary. The destruction of the BUS changed matters considerably; now each bank was responsible for settling accounts with all of its neighbors, and the work was time-consuming, tedious, and fraught with dangers. In New York, for example, Friday was clearing day, when the week's accounts had to be settled. That morning each bank's treasurer would calculate the amounts owed other institutions in the city. He would then count out the funds — usually in gold or gold certificates — place each pile in its own bag, and then send it by messenger to the bank indicated. Then runners were sent scurrying through the city's streets, often under guard, hoping to reach their destinations unscathed. During this time business all but closed down in the banks, since each sent out large amounts of gold and could not conduct business until the inflow began in the afternoon.

Clearly such a system was wasteful and dangerous. After a while the clerks arranged to meet at one spot, where exchanges were arranged among them. This was somewhat better, but still inefficient. Albert Gallatin, the former secretary of the treasury who later on became president of the National Bank of New York and from there led the fight against Biddle, offered several methods of streamlining the operation. One of these called for the establishment of a municipal clearing house, where the clerks could go with their settlement moneys for exchanges. Later on, in 1841, Gallatin refined the idea so as to have each member maintain reserves at the clearing house, with transfers between banks made in terms of accounting adjustments rather than the actual shipment of gold. In his pamphlet, *Suggestions on the Banks and Currency of the Several United States in*

*Reference Principally to the Suspension of Specie Payments,*
Gallatin wrote:

There is a measure which, though belonging to the administration
of banks, rather than to legal enactments, is suggested on account
of its great importance. Few regulations would be more useful in
preventing dangerous expansions of discounts and issues on the
part of the city banks, than a regular exchange of notes and checks,
and an actual daily or semi-weekly payment of the balances. It
must be recollected, that it is by this process alone that a Bank of
the United States has ever acted or been supposed to act as a
regulator of the currency....

In order to remedy this situation, it has been suggested that a
general cash office might be established, in which each bank would
place a sum in specie, proportionate to its capital, which would be
carried to its credit in the books of the office. Each bank would
be daily debited or credited in those books for the balance of its
account with all the other banks. Each bank might at any time
draw for specie on the office for the excess of its credit beyond
its quota, and each bank should be obliged to replenish its quota,
whenever it was diminished one half, or in any other proportion
agreed upon....

At first Gallatin's idea, though recognized as sound,
was rejected by the New York banks. Who would control
the proposed clearing house? What use would be made of
its gold deposits, which in time might become quite large?
The New York bankers had not fought the BUS so as to
create a new giant central bank in their own city. Despite
Gallatin's good reputation, there were rumors he had helped
depose Biddle only to try to take his place at a new BUS.
George D. Lyman, a financial editor of the *Journal of
Commerce,* recognized this problem, and tried to solve it by

*View of Wall Street from the roof of Trinity Church. The domed building is the Merchants' Exchange.*

(STOKES COLLECTION, NEW YORK PUBLIC LIBRARY)

142

suggesting the creation of a new bank, the Exchange Bank, shares of which would be owned by all those who hoped to use the clearing house. Then the Exchange Bank would become the Clearing House, owned and utilized by all. But this, too, was rejected.

Increased volume and the obvious failure of the old methods of clearance led finally to the establishment of the New York Clearing House in 1853, which was based on the Gallatin proposal of 1841. In time the Clearing House would act not only as a convenient institution through which accounts could be settled, but as an instrument for stability in the city. During periods of financial distress the Clearing House would issue certificates of deposit against its gold reserves, which were used by banks to maintain liquidity. Some scholars have likened its operations in such times to that of the Federal Reserve today, with Clearing House certificates comparable to Federal Reserve notes. This had not been in Gallatin's mind in 1841, although it had been in embryo in the minds of some of his critics. Instead he, like the men at the Mercantile Agency, was concerned with the creation, development, and expansion of the nation's banking and business systems. The great economic expansion that began in 1843 and then took off in 1845 was a testimony to their success.

# 7/THE BUSINESS OF TRANSPORTATION

WHILE NOTING THAT THE RAPID PACE OF AMERICAN
life made the nation's businessmen more brusque than
Europeans, foreign visitors were charmed by the hospitality
they received from western farmers and southern plantation
owners. The farmers and planters would stop their activities
often and open their homes to any friendly stranger who
happened along. In the words of one Englishman, the western farmers appeared "the most generous people on earth,"
while even those Europeans who despised slavery commented favorably on the manners and grace of the slave-
owners.

Like all aspects of American life, this generosity had
its roots in the land, which remolded Europeans into a new
people. Strangers were welcomed for several reasons, one
of which was the diversion they offered from the monotony
of daily life and the news from the outside world they
brought with them. The fact of the matter was that America
was not a unified nation in the early decades of the nine-

teenth century, but more a collection of regions with isolated towns and isolated settlements. Businessmen and
farmers both realized the need for better transportation,
without which their standards of living could not improve
and the wealth of the land could not be fully utilized. This
attitude was also reflected in immigrant guidebooks in the
1830s. One popular work, *A New Guide for Emigrants to
the West,* written by J. M. Peck in 1837, not only described
the life awaiting those who crossed the Appalachians, but
unconsciously explained western hospitality to strangers.

The backwoodsman of the West has many substantial enjoyments.
After the fatigue of the journey west, and a short season of priva-
tion and danger, he finds himself surrounded with plenty. His
cattle, his hogs and poultry, supply his table with meat; the forest
abounds with game; the fertile soil yields abundant crops; he has,
of course, milk and butter; the rivers furnish fish and the woods
honey. For these various articles there is, at first, no market, and
the farmer acquired the generous habit of spreading them pro-
fusely on his table, and giving them freely to a hungry traveler or
indigent neighbor. . . .

Peck went on to write that this isolation was a temporary phenomenon, for even then a railroad was about to be
constructed in that part of the West. It might be said that
in the minds of Americans of that time the East ended at a
line where inadequate transportation began; once goods
and individuals could move eastward with greater ease, the
area ceased to be considered "wild." The Americans of that
era realized the need for better transportation and communication and worked to meet it. Over half the nonagricultural product of the nation was invested in such improve-

ments—a statistic that has remained constant to the present day.

The first important transportation system was, of course, the rivers, lakes, and coastal waterways. Even after Boston and New York were connected by turnpike it was still cheaper to ship goods by water around Cape Cod than to send them overland. The earliest southern plantations were built on the banks of rivers, to facilitate the shipment of cotton and tobacco to market. In fact, rivers helped determine the social structure of the South. As the waterways came down from the Appalachians they encountered "the fall line," where waterfalls made necessary the unloading and reloading of ships and boats. The area east of the fall line was known as the Tidewater, since the river there was influenced by estuarian and tidal forces; that west of the fall line was the Piedmont—literally, foothills. The aristocracy and "old families" tended to live in the Tidewater, and they looked down on the families of the Piedmont. George Washington was of the Tidewater; Patrick Henry of the Piedmont; Thomas Jefferson had familial ties to both regions. Such things were important in the late eighteenth century.

For those living in areas not served by rivers or ports, roads were necessary, and the first of these were carved from the wilderness in the seventeenth century. Later on they became permanent, well-known routes. In almost all cases roads either began or ended at a port or portage; the roads were considered extensions of water transportation, or connections between two bodies of water. As road construction increased in the early nineteenth century, companies were formed to construct turnpikes, and some of these formed connections between cities as well as provided access to water transportation. By 1821 some 4,000 miles of turnpike, much of it plank road, had been constructed, and another 2,500 miles had been authorized. Those who could afford to pay tolls traveled on these routes, while those who could not were obliged to use the "shunpikes," or dirt roads that ran alongside turnpikes in some parts of the country.

Turnpike construction stimulated the development of corporations in America, for individual businessmen lacked the capital needed for such large-scale construction. In most cases road promoters would seek to sell shares to fellow-businessmen, but in time they learned that farmers and shippers along the proposed route were also ready customers for shares, especially when they were told that without their purchases the pike could not be constructed. In New England alone some $6.5 million was raised and invested prior to 1840, and more than $7.5 million in Pennsylvania. Such investments seemed wise in the early nineteenth century: the turnpike was often a monopoly, serving a growing area, providing a needed service. But turnpikes were rarely successful financially. Freight business was seasonal, poorer farmers continued to use shunpikes, and many of the roads were located in undesirable areas by over-optimistic promoters. Only half a dozen of the more than two hundred Massachusetts turnpikes ever showed profits, and the most successful of these, the Salem Turnpike, paid an average dividend of only 3 percent per annum. It was a rare turnpike—or canal or railroad, for that matter—that would enrich its original shareholders. With a few shining

*The Old Newburg Toll Road in New York State.*

exceptions, all were forced into bankruptcy at one time or another. America's transportation systems of the nineteenth century helped their users, provided jobs for workers, stimulated economic growth in the West, became bonanzas for construction companies, and provided large fees for law-yers. But little accrued to the purchasers of their stock.

The turnpikes set another pattern. In those instances where road construction was desirable but private capital unavailable, governments offered assistance. This was par-ticularly true in the South and West, less so in New Eng-land and the middle states. In some cases—most notably the South Carolina and Indiana turnpikes—the states themselves owned and operated the pikes, but in others the state merely purchased stock in private companies.

The canal-building mania appeared as it became evi-dent that turnpikes were financial failures, and it was sparked by the construction of one of the few spectacularly successful ditches, the Erie Canal, which was completed in 1825. Financed by the state, running 364 miles, and con-necting the cities of New York's northern tier with the Hudson, it was a financial and economic success, which at the time was hailed as a wonder of the world, proof that Americans were capable of great feats of engineering. It also made possible shipping between the West and New York City, and helped make that port the largest in the hemisphere.

Like the turnpikes, many canals were financed by stock sales to customers and a closed group of businessmen. Since more capital was needed for a canal than a pike, more stock was sold, and much of it found its way to Wall Street. In the 1830s canals were the "glamour stocks" of the day, and the fever reached London, where canal stocks—especially new issues—were snapped up as soon as they appeared. For example, Rhode Island's Blackstone Canal, capitalized at

$500,000, received more than $1.5 million in bids. But, even more amazing, when the Morris Canal running across New Jersey to the Delaware River tried to raise the unheard-of sum of one million dollars, it received bids for twenty times that amount. It immediately became the "in stock" on Wall Street and sparked the bull market of the early 1830s. But unfortunately, canal construction also felt the pinch of hard times; it led the way down in the panic of 1837.

Just as states financed turnpikes, they also gave land grants to canal companies or constructed them as state projects. Since canals required larger sums of money for construction than did pikes, the need for state and eventually federal aid was more pressing. And where states did not actually purchase stock, they made low-interest loans to promoters. States assisted in the construction of almost all the 3,326 miles of canals that were built in the United States before the great canal era ended in 1840.

Canals failed to provide a satisfactory answer to the country's pressing transportation needs for a variety of reasons. First of all, they were often costly to build. The best stone turnpikes cost from $5,000 to $10,000 a mile to construct; the average for a canal was close to $25,000 a mile, and the Chesapeake & Ohio cost $60,000 a mile. Also, it was expensive to maintain a canal. No sooner was the Erie completed than it was widened, and almost constant dredging was needed, since most canals were no more than a few feet deep. In times of drought many turned into muddy quagmires, while they were unusable during flood season, and after both periods they had to be repaired.

Then there was the problem of overbuilding. Before

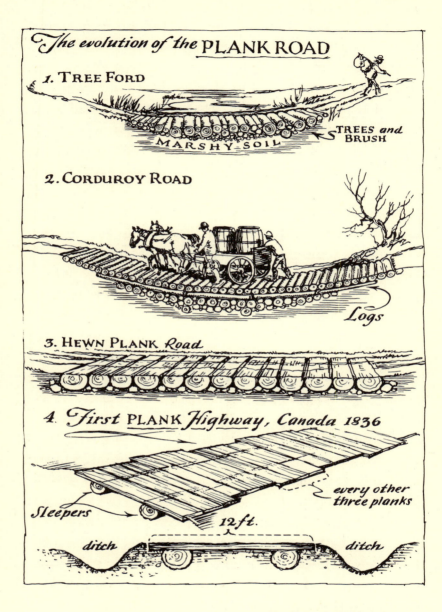

The evolution of the PLANK ROAD

*1.* TREE FORD

MARSHY SOIL

TREES *and* BRUSH

*2.* CORDUROY ROAD

*Logs*

*3.* HEWN PLANK *Road*

*4. First* PLANK *Highway, Canada 1836*

*every other three planks*

*Sleepers*

*12 ft.*

*ditch* *ditch*

(FROM ERIC SLOAN'S "OUR VANISHING LANDSCAPE," PUBLISHED BY FUNK & WAGNALLS)

152

the Erie was completed, canal promoters would find an area that needed a canal for sound economic reasons, and then try to organize a company to construct it. After the success of the Erie, when canal stocks were the darlings of Wall and Lombard streets, the same promoters would construct a canal in almost any location—even if it meant duplicating lines—so as to cash in on the boom. Thus the canals were overbuilt, under-utilized, and also poorly managed. Like the turnpikes, the canals on the whole filled an important need, but they were never as profitable as expected. Moreover, canals declined because they could not compete with the railroads, which provided similar services at lower costs, or more rapidly, or more reliably—and at times all three.

In 1830 the nation had 1,277 miles of canals and 73 miles of railroads; ten years later the figure for canals was 3,326, and for railroads, 3,328. By 1850 the canal mileage had stabilized at 3,698, while that of railroads soared to 8,879. Not a single major canal was begun after 1840, at a time when the age of the railroad was just beginning. The iron horse would dominate the American transportation scene for the rest of the century, and in the process tie the nation closer together, opening markets to the back country, providing jobs for immigrants, and even changing the nation's view of time itself. Henry Thoreau, seeking a self-contained life at Walden pond, realized this before most Americans. "They come and go," he wrote, "with such regularity and precision, and their whistle can be heard so far, that the farmers set their clocks by them, and thus one well-regulated institution regulates a whole country. Have not men improved somewhat in punctuality since the railroad was invented? Do they not talk and think faster in the depot than they did in the stage-office?" For almost a century the railroad would be the romantic symbol of the outside world to young men and women, opening their visions to horizons wider than those of their small towns.

The railroad did not burst on the scene suddenly. As early as the fourth century B.C. men in Alexandria had dreamed of steam-driven cars, but not until the eighteenth century did experiments with such vehicles take place. During the American Revolution, Oliver Evans, a pioneer in the development of industrial machinery, tinkered with the steam-driven carriage. Financing his work with funds obtained from his other inventions, Evans constructed a workable model in 1804. He argued that steam-driven carriages, traveling over rails, would be less costly than canals, more reliable and swift than turnpike travel, and safer than both. But the nation's businessmen in the early decades of the nineteenth century were convinced that turnpikes, and later canals, would serve their purposes. Shortly before his death in 1819, Evans wrote:

I do verily believe that carriages propelled by steam will come into general use, and travel at the rate of 300 miles a day. But one step in a generation is all we can hope for. If the present generation shall adopt canals, the next may try the railway with horses, and the third generation use the steam carriage.

It did not take long for the railroads to be accepted. The first horse-drawn line, the Granite Railroad, was completed in 1826, and others followed. Used to transport bulky materials such as coal and stone, the early lines were short and makeshift, with crude roadbeds and cruder cars. The

154

initial railroad lines were so primitive that when the Delaware & Hudson Canal Company tried to use an imported British locomotive, the *Stourbridge Lion*, it soon discovered it was far too heavy for the tracks, and the locomotive had to be abandoned. But the experiments continued, and in 1830 the *Best Friend of Charleston* pulled a train successfully along the tracks of the Charleston & Hamburg. That same year the Baltimore & Ohio, the first true railroad, was completed, organized by a group of businessmen who thought it could compete successfully with the Chesapeake & Ohio Canal. On a trial trip during the railroad's first year of operation Peter Cooper's engine, *Tom Thumb*, raced a horse. The locomotive covered thirteen miles of the line in one hour but was unable to beat the horse.

Before 1830 many northeastern states granted charters to railroads, and in the 1830s many key lines were constructed in the East and the first tentative moves across the Appalachians were made. By 1840 Pennsylvania had the most mileage—576 miles of track—and New York was in second place, with 453. That year Delaware had only 16 miles of track, and Maine had 10, while there were no railroads at all in Tennessee, Missouri, Vermont, or Arkansas.

Even more important than the demonstrations of the railroad's feasibility and economic potential were the solving of major technological problems and the creation of an operational framework for the lines. At first railroaders ignored technological advances and treated their lines as a new version of the turnpike. Utilizing turnpike construction methods, they constructed roadbeds of crushed rock on which were set concrete or granite blocks. These were quickly abandoned and replaced by wooden rails, which also proved unacceptable. Then the railroaders experimented with iron bars or strips affixed to wooden rails, but these worked loose, curled into "snakeheads," and had to be repaired or replaced regularly. In 1831 Robert Stevens of the Camden & Amboy Railroad found the English T rails satisfactory. But most other lines rejected them, and until the early 1870s wooden and iron strap rails could be found in some parts of the country.

American railroads were slow to adopt a standard gauge. In New England most lines spaced their tracks 4 feet, 8½ inches apart, while in the South 5 feet was more common. The Erie Railroad used a 6-foot gauge, so as to prevent diversion of its traffic to other lines. Some lines frequently changed gauges to meet new advances in cars and locomotives; the line between Philadelphia and Charleston did so at least eight times from 1834 to 1870. Not until the post–Civil War period did the 4-foot-8½-inch gauge become the American standard.

The first cars resembled stagecoaches. They even had elevated seats in the rear for nonexistent coachmen, although some lines actually hired a few to sit there, an early example of featherbedding. The cars themselves were constructed of wood, often by prominent stagecoach firms, but in the early 1840s new companies, not tied to the old ways, appeared. The first coaches could carry only a dozen or so passengers each; by the mid-1840s, coaches that could accommodate forty or more were in service. There were even a few sleeping cars, which through accident or design resembled the interiors of canalboats.

*View of the upper village of Lockport, Niagara County, New York, showing the ten combined locks on the Erie Canal.*

(THE GRANGER COLLECTION)

The cars were tied together with chains, so that when sudden stops were made the passengers were jarred against each other. There were no toilet or dining facilities; since most journeys were short, they were not deemed necessary.

Passenger charges and track utilization were also problems. In the 1830s individuals would book passage on railroads in much the same way as they would for steamships. Meanwhile, rail managers attempted to get the maximum returns from their investment. At first some roads were run like turnpikes; that is, any individual who paid a fee could take his vehicle on the rails. A series of bad accidents ended this experiment, and by the late 1830s the companies allowed only their own rolling stock on the rails.

The trains tried to run on schedule, and their records in the late 1830s were fairly good. They made short runs on under-utilized track, and there were few complications insofar as schedulings were concerned. But their safety records were not as good: the cars often ran off the tracks, and locomotive explosions were not uncommon. One such accident took place on the New York & Harlem in July 1839.

About 10 o'clock in the morning the steam engine which comes into the city with the cars ran off the track opposite Union Park. The steam was already generated to excess, but, unfortunately, the engineer neglected to blow it off. It is also supposed that the water had not been taken in properly at the stopping place. When the engine had thus run off the track, a number of passengers, mostly mechanics, lent their services to get it on again. While thus surrounded, the boiler burst. The chief engineer was blown to pieces —his legs went into Union Park, his arms on a pile of lumber on the other side of the avenue....

Railroad passengers of the day also rode in constant fear of fire. The engines burned wood, which let off huge sparks and cinders that often ignited the dry wooden cars. While traveling through the East Coast, the European visitor Harriet Martineau complained that locomotives were a public menace; she saw several gowns ruined on the lines. George Combe, the phrenologist, was involved in several accidents, and at one time he was called upon to help push a train into a station. He wrote that the exertion was really unnecessary, for soon after they had begun a farmer appeared with a team of horses, and the ease with which they pulled the train led him to conclude that the locomotive would have to undergo great improvements before bettering the horse. Combe also noted that the trains' inability to navigate easily around bends in the road was "most dangerous."

Many of these problems were corrected in the 1840s, a decade of great technological advance in railroading. Safety devices such as regular ties and spark catchers made their appearances, and Matthias Baldwin, a locomotive manufacturer who turned out his first engines in the late 1830s, made several major breakthroughs. The most outstanding of Baldwin's innovations were boilers that seemed accident-proof. Baldwin engines could tolerate 120 pounds of steam, whereas English locomotives reached their limit at little more than half that amount. Baldwin's products were so well constructed that some were still in service and doing a creditable job forty years after they pulled their first cars. They were also heavier than the spindly engines of the 1830s. Indeed, Baldwin's engines were equipped with "cow-catchers," for they could easily kill any animals that wandered on the tracks. Grading and banking of curves was also perfected in the 1840s, so that engines would not have to slow to a crawl around turns.

Now passengers purchased tickets for trips, and they traveled on large cars, which were not only safer but which provided some comforts, such as padded benches. Also, as railroad use became more common during the decade, rates began to fall, leaving comparable canal tolls far behind. By the late 1840s passenger fares ranged from 1.5 cents a mile in New York to 5.35 cents in Mississippi, while freight charges varied from 4 cents per ton-mile in Vermont to 24.39 cents in Mississippi. By 1850 a passenger could travel from New York to Cincinnati, a distance of 857 miles, for $15.50, and from Baltimore to Cincinnati for $13. Prior to the coming of the railroad, such trips would have been impossible for all but the hardy and desperate. By 1850, however, farmers were able to send their grain from the Northwest to New York at charges that at the time seemed reasonable. The same farmer, fifteen years before, would probably have turned his surplus wheat into whisky and sold it to a trader going east.

Express services also multiplied in the 1840s. In 1839

*River traffic on the Mississippi at St. Louis.*
(COURTESY, KENNETH M. NEWMAN, OLD PRINT SHOP, NEW YORK CITY)

160

William Harnden established a runner system between New York and Boston. As business picked up in the mid-1840s, he expanded to other cities, and imitators began similar enterprises. By the end of the decade, express services were in existence between most of the large cities, forming a kind of private postal system.

There is no way of knowing exactly how much money was expended on railroad construction and rolling stock in the 1840s; the best estimate for the 1830–1850 period is $348 million. If we take into consideration such factors as the growth of the economy and inflation, an equivalent figure today would be approximately a trillion dollars.

Raising such huge sums presented difficulties in the aftermath of the 1837 panic, although ingenious promoters usually found ways. The most obvious sources were the states and cities that badly wanted lines. Maryland and Baltimore, for example, took half the stock of the Baltimore & Ohio Railroad, setting a precedent for others to follow. Some $60 million in state aid went into railroads in the 1840s, which came on top of the more than $44 million spent by the states during the 1830s. Local and municipal governments more than matched these sums, so that approximately half the construction costs of the major lines were paid with public funds. Massachusetts loaned $4 million to the Western Railroad in the early 1840s, and purchased an additional $600,000 worth of its stock; when the line was connected to Albany, that city raised $1 million to provide for construction costs. New York State subsidized the Erie to the tune of $3 million, and added $9 million more for other lines from 1840 to 1846.

Pennsylvania, proud of its leadership in rail transportation, invested $10 million in railroads during the 1840s, and the pattern was much the same throughout the East. However, after the 1840s such immense grants became politically impossible and towns and cities were forced to take up the slack left by the state.

The federal government made its contributions to railroad development in the 1840s, though not in the form of outright investments, loans, or grants. First there were the surveys: federal agencies cooperated with builders by providing technical assistance free of charge. Then the government made available to the states federal lands within their boundaries, with the understanding that these acreages would be given to specified railroads. Finally, Congress reduced the tariff on iron used in railroad construction, forcing domestic producers to lower their prices, and in this way causing construction costs to fall and profits to rise. Although the tariff was increased somewhat in 1843, it remained low throughout the remainder of the decade, in large part due to the efforts of railroad lobbyists in Washington. One of the opponents of the railroad lobby, Senator James Buchanan of Pennsylvania, was considered the "farmer's friend"; he protested the benefits enjoyed by railroaders, and more particularly, the power of their lobby.

If you defeat them at this session, they will be here in greater force than ever at the commencement of the next. Their importunity will never cease whilst the least hope of success shall remain, and we have learned from our experience that they have both the ability and the will to select shrewd and skillful agents to accomplish their purposes before Congress.

A large part of the money needed for railroad construction and operation was raised from private investors. Prior to the 1837 panic a good deal of this came from Europe; during the six years after the crash, domestic lenders and investors provided the funds. Some of the nation's large banks, especially those in Boston and New York, also participated in the financings.

When the national economy recovered in the mid-1840s, speculative fever once again rose, and the desire for rapid fortunes infected the middle class. Grandiose tales of the potential of the Michigan Central attracted Boston investors, while New Yorkers took much of the stock of the newly formed Michigan Southern in 1846. The Illinois Central was financed by New York banks, as were other large lines in the trans-Appalachian region. But the American money markets alone could not supply the vast sums

*Cincinnati, key jobbing center of the 1840s.*
(COURTESY, KENNETH M. NEWMAN, OLD PRINT SHOP, NEW YORK CITY)

necessary for railroad construction. Fortunately foreign assistance was available, and London investors were particularly eager to play a role.

By the mid-1840s London investors had forgotten the panic of 1837. A new group of speculators had made their appearance in the British capital, and they made it their business to learn of business opportunities in America. England was still expanding, to be sure, but the real growth seemed to be in the United States, and particularly in American railroads. Starting in 1847 American promoters were able to sell bonds and stocks with ease in London. Within six years Englishmen owned 26 percent of American railroad bonds and slightly less than 3 percent of the stock. Such major lines as the Philadelphia & Reading and the Illinois Central were on their way to becoming English-controlled, while foreign investors came to look upon the Erie and other eastern lines as blue chips.

By the end of the 1840s many of the American lines had excellent rolling stock and covered considerable mileage. Non-English railroaders considered American cars and locomotives the best in the world, and American rolling stock could be found in every European country. By that time the Erie had more than 450 miles of track, making it one of the longest in the world, and the Baltimore & Ohio, the South Carolina, and the Georgia Central all extended more than 200 miles. The Illinois Central, although still in the planning stages, estimated that by the mid-1850s it would have more than 750 miles of track. As the country grew, the railroads would expand, for the great distances of the United States required major carriers. Turnpikes and canals were insufficient to meet the demand for cheap, dependable transportation; only the railroads filled the bill.

All of this notwithstanding, railroad stocks and bonds were one of the worst long-term investments to be found in the 1840s and 1850s. One could speculate successfully in these securities, for their prices rose spectacularly, always on the promise of increased earnings and large dividends. But these increased profits rarely materialized, and when they did, it was for a small, select, group of railroads, the best managed ones in the prime locations. The others paid dividends, to be sure, but more often than not the funds were obtained through the sale of additional securities. A few statistics will illustrate this dilemma. In 1849, a boom year economically, London investors could have purchased high-grade bonds returning 8 to 9 percent. That same year the Illinois railroads, the most profitable in the nation, showed a return on capital invested of 8.7 percent. The Michigan lines returned only 4.2 percent, and the figure for the western states as a whole was 5.6 percent; that for the East was even lower.

Despite all the financial and other help given the American railroads, most were unable to show more than mediocre profits in good years, and losses mounted in the bad. Factors beyond the control of the lines produced this situation. Necessarily, a large part of their business was the carrying of agricultural products, an operation that was highly seasonal. For a few weeks out of the year the lines ran at full capacity, and in these periods their profits were enormous. For the rest of the year most lines ran at a loss, but the heavy capital investment in rolling stock and track

**PREFERRED STOCK**

## Great Falls and Conway Rail Road.

$ N° 65    3 SHARES

370 to 372 inclusive

### Be it Known,

That *Luther D. Sawyer* of *Ossipee*

is *Proprietor* of *Three* Shares of the Preferred Stock of the

**GREAT FALLS AND CONWAY RAIL ROAD,**

on which One Hundred Dollars per Share has been paid in, and the holder is entitled to receive of the Treasurer a semi-annual dividend of Four Dollars per Share on the first days of January and July in each year, until the same be redeemed; and the Corporation and its Assigns may, at any time after the first day of July, 1855, redeem this Preferred Stock by paying the holder thereof the original cost of the same, and the dividends aforesaid up to the time of such redemption. This Stock is transferrable by an assignment thereof on the Books of the said Corporation, or by any conveyance in writing recorded on said Books.

In Witness Whereof, the President and Treasurer have hereunto set their Hands, and affixed the Seal of the Corporation, this 27th day of January A.D. 1851

*Nath. Wells* President.

*D. G. Rollins* Treasurer.

GREAT FALLS & CONWAY RAILROAD G&CRR 1844

C. O. P. Moody, Printer.

The early history of this railroad, which was chartered in 1844, is obscure. Apparently the line was opened for operation in 1849 and comprised 26 miles of road from Great Falls, Maine, to Union Village, New Hampshire. In 1865 a consolidation was effected with the Great Falls & South Berwick Railroad, the new company operating 73 miles of trackage under the name of Portsmouth, Great Falls & Conway Railroad Company. This company was leased in 1873 to the Eastern Railroad and was consolidated in 1890 into the Boston & Maine Railroad Company.

*A typical railroad stock certificate of the era.*

still had to be serviced. Thus arose the expedient of floating more and more bonds each year, causing the lines to develop top-heavy capital structures, increasing interest charges, and making managements frantic. Some of the lines experimented with variable charges, increasing prices during busy periods and lowering them to attract traffic in the slack seasons. These lines were accused of trying to bleed the farmers white, and state legislatures soon put an end to the practice. Henry Varnum Poor, the best-informed student of the railroads of the period, implied as much in 1855, when he wrote:

There is no fallacy in the assumption upon which our railroads have been built—that they are adapted to the commercial needs of the country, and that, economically constructed and managed, they can earn a satisfactory income upon their costs. If they prove unproductive, it must be due, consequently, to their excessive costs or bad management. It is owing to *one* of these causes that the holders of unproductive property are without dividends.

But there was another way to obtain dividend funds, and that was to bribe legislatures. Railroaders were often successful in this, and their lines survived, but at the price of tarnishing the industry's reputation.

The problem of overbuilding, which had haunted the canals in the 1830s, plagued the railroads in the 1840s. Early in the next decade some observers began to take note of the practice. A reporter for the *American Railroad Journal* wrote in 1853:

By a well contrived and well managed plan a road may be built, that is not wanted, and will never pay, and capitalists saddled with securities that are not better than the road. Certainly great caution is necessary, or the result I have foreshadowed will be realized in more instances than one, in Ohio and Indiana.

As though to fulfill the prediction, the officers of the Little Miami of Ohio, in their 1856 annual report, said:

The number of competing routes, and the eagerness of those who control them to procure business, have reduced the prices both of freight and travel below the point of just remuneration, and have obliged us to perform a large amount of service without a corresponding profit.

Great profits could be made in railroad building, and some lines, realizing this, formed construction affiliates with separate corporate identities. The public was permitted to purchase shares in the railroad; those in the construction company were held by the line's officers. Thus, it behooved the railroad's leaders to expand continually, even when it hurt the line. Moreover, there was no check on the quality of the construction, which was often poor as a result of shaving costs. An English visitor, Douglass Galton, noted the shoddy quality of American roads, and not knowing the financial arrangements, concluded it was due to the needs of the country.

The character of American railways, so different in its prominent features from that of railways in this country, is the result of the want which they have been called upon to supply. A means of communication was required which could be laid cheaply and rapidly through forests and cultivated and uncultivated districts .... The practice of constructing the railways in a hasty and imperfect manner has led to the adoption of a form of rolling stock capable of adapting itself to the inequalities of the road; it is also constructed on the principle of diminishing the useless weight carried in a train.

The situation on Wall and Lombard streets, where the demand for railroad securities continued to grow in the late 1840s, encouraged the formation of companies that planned to construct roads where none were needed. When speculators were willing to purchase securities of any American company with the word "railroad" in it, why refuse to supply them with the paper? Thus, shaky lines, poorly located, without hope of success, did not lack sponsors. But this practice, too, was noted toward the end of the 1840s and in the early 1850s. The *Indianapolis State Journal,* writing in 1852, said:

The Jeffersonville Road will be completed to Columbus early next season—the branch of the New Albany road from Jasper to this city is certain to be made within a short time—and the road . . . to Cincinnati, by way of Lawrenceburg, is also certain to be completed at any early day. All these roads will come in competition with the Madison Road, and, in our opinion will render its stock of very little value . . . .

Of course, there would be a day of reckoning. In 1857 such lines as the Delaware, Lackawanna & Western, the Fond du Lac, the Fort Wayne & Chicago, and even the prestigious Erie and Illinois Central, went into bankruptcy, victims of their own mistakes and the panic of that year. A pattern was set that would continue into the first years of the twentieth century; scarcely an economic panic would occur that was not set off, directly or indirectly, by the railroads.

America could not have developed as rapidly as it did without the railroads, canals, and turnpikes, all of which were important in the 1840s. Not only did they tie the country together economically, making possible a large internal market and the development of the West, but they encouraged the growth of other industries—iron, coal, construction, and textiles.

Fortunately for the country, those who paid the bills for the railroads did not know that they were, in a fashion, subsidizing the nation's development. Vigor, glamour, optimism, and increased revenues do not necessarily translate into profits. In such terms railroading was a sick industry during its first period of great growth in the 1840s.

# 8/THE BUSINESS OF SLAVERY

MUCH HAS BEEN WRITTEN ABOUT SLAVERY CONCERN-
ing its moral and political aspects, and in the 1840s the
written and oral debates were approaching an intensity that
clouded the nation's future. But there was another aspect
of slavery, at times overlooked in that public dialogue.
Slavery was a business, an investment in human chattel, a
way of economic life. In its own way, the effect of slavery
on the economy of the country was as significant as was
the issue of the morality of the institution on the nation's
history.

The southern states were agricultural, and despite the
flourishing commercial business in some ports and the early
attempts to plant a factory system in the interior, seemed
destined to remain so. American cotton was in great demand
in Europe and provided by far the largest single American export and earner of foreign currencies. The slave
states by and large favored low tariffs, so as to put pressure
on domestic manufacturers to keep the prices of their goods

as low as possible. They favored a decentralized banking system in order to avoid control from New York, Philadelphia or Boston. Finally, the southern states were dubious as to the value of federally funded internal improvements, which would favor the river-poor and railroad-hungry northerners, but would be paid for in large part by southern taxes.

Agriculture still dominated life in the North and Midwest, but the commercial interests in these sections were important and fast-growing after the effects of the 1837 panic had been corrected. Although manufacturing was still a secondary enterprise, it, too, was growing, and both merchant and manufacturer demanded legislation favorable to their interests. This meant high tariffs to protect young American industries from foreign competition, a strong banking system to facilitate commerce, and federally sponsored internal improvements to create a large market for goods and services. In all three areas the northern businessman usually clashed with the southern planter. Each viewed the growing power of the other with anxiety. To most northern businessmen additional slave states meant more senators and congressmen opposed to the high tariffs and internal improvements. Thus many northerners became anti-slavery on political grounds, and in the late 1830s and early 1840s the debate was centered on such issues.

Of all the arguments mustered by the pro-slavery forces to defend the institution, none was as strong as the claim that slavery was vital to the economic well-being of the United States. Without slavery, the argument went, cotton could not be produced economically, and if cotton declined, so would the South, and ultimately the nation. What substance was there to this view? Were the plantations flourishing economic units? Was the huge investment in slaves wise and sound? In essence, did it pay?

The pro-slavery writers approached this kind of discussion with great care, to avoid appearing crass and heartless. But in fact most discussed the slave as though he were simply an object of economic value, such as a wagon or machine. Some viewed the slave as a racehorse or a dog, good not only for service, but also for breeding. Statistical presentations in support of pro-slavery arguments were crude, a fact that is not surprising, since economic analysis was still in its infancy in the antebellum era. Furthermore, then as now it was possible to present data in such a way as to show a profit or loss depending on the desires of the accountant.

*Cartoon of slave auction in Richmond, Virginia.*
(THE GRANGER COLLECTION)

The raw data, however, has remained, and modern economists have used it to answer the economic questions.

The slave census of 1860 was far more detailed and accurate than those preceding it, and may provide more complete answers than the 1850 statistics. Since the institutional and economic base of slavery did not change materially during the pre–Civil War generation, the conclusions drawn from the 1860 data would also be applicable to the period of the 1840s.

In 1860 there were 3,950,513 slaves in the United States, and 383,637 slaveholders. The slaveholder of 1860 owned an average of ten slaves, two more than his 1850 counterpart. But this figure is somewhat deceiving, as the 1860 breakdown indicates (see Table 1).

Thus, 275,681 of the 383,637 slaveholders owned fewer than ten slaves, and almost a million slaves lived on small plantations or farms.

Most blacks were employed in a variety of tasks, from field work to household chores; they served as midwives and blacksmiths, and in some cases were considered friends of the master. There is no accurate method of computing their economic worth, their productivity, or their value. The farmer who owned one or two slaves may be compared to the one-car owner of today, who uses his vehicle for a variety of tasks, and so finds it difficult to estimate just how much it adds to his income. The situation was different on the large plantation, which could be compared to a large firm with many delivery trucks and special vehicles, whose worth would be far easier to determine. Generally speaking, the smaller the number of slaves per farm, the more difficult it is to uncover economic costs and rewards.

The most important price determinant was the value of cotton. Most slaves were employed, directly or indirectly, in its cultivation. As the cotton price rose or declined, so did the price of slaves. However, the relationship was not exact. For example, a plantation owner expecting a good crop and a high cotton price might purchase additional slaves months

TABLE 1 / SLAVES AND SLAVEHOLDERS, 1860*

| Number of Slaves | Slaveholders |
| --- | --- |
| 1 | 76,670 |
| 2 | 45,934 |
| 3 | 34,747 |
| 4 | 28,907 |
| 5 | 24,225 |
| 6 | 20,600 |
| 7 | 17,235 |
| 8 | 14,852 |
| 9 | 12,511 |
| 10–14 | 40,367 |
| 15–19 | 21,315 |
| 20–29 | 20,789 |
| 30–39 | 9,648 |
| 40–49 | 5,179 |
| 50–69 | 5,217 |
| 70–99 | 3,149 |
| 100–199 | 1,980 |
| 200–299 | 224 |
| 300–499 | 74 |
| 500–999 | 13 |
| 1,000 and over | 1 |

*SOURCE: U.S. Bureau of the Census, *Agriculture in the United States in 1860,* p. 247.

before the harvest, and if others followed his lead, the price of slaves would rise before that of cotton. The reverse held true when expectations were poor; then slave prices would decline months before the cotton income arrived. Indeed, cotton and slaves provided excellent lead indicators for one another (see Table 2).

Prior to 1837 slaveholders insisted slavery was a profitable enterprise. Little was said of the matter during the next seven years, but then the argument reappeared. Some planters—especially those of Mississippi and Louisiana—offered statistics to prove their claims, but these were incomplete and often biased. Antislavery writers were quick to show the flaws in such arguments. They also noted that these planters owned some of the best cotton land in the world and that this land, more than slavery, was the source

TABLE 2 / PRICES OF COTTON AND SLAVES, 1835–1853*

| Year | Average Price of Prime Field Hands | Average New York Price of Upland Cotton |
|------|------|------|
| 1835 | $   900 | 17½¢ per pound |
| 1837 | 1,300 | 13½¢ per pound |
| 1839 | 1,000 | 13½¢ per pound |
| 1840 | 700 | 9   ¢ per pound |
| 1844 | 600 | 7½¢ per pound |
| 1845 | 600 | 5½¢ per pound |
| 1848 | 900 | 9½¢ per pound |
| 1851 | 1,050 | 12   ¢ per pound |
| 1853 | 1,200 | 11   ¢ per pound |

*SOURCE: Ulrich B. Phillips, "The Economic Cost of Slaveholding in the Cotton Belt," *Political Science Quarterly*, XX (June 1905), pp. 257–275.

of their prosperity. Nor did the planters spend much time discussing whether or not they would have been better off with free labor.

Frederick Law Olmsted, writing in the mid-1850s, said that in his home district in New York native American farm laborers were paid $10 a month plus board and lodging; immigrants were paid still less. In eastern Virginia at the same time, able-bodied slaves were hired from their owners at $120 a year, plus board, clothes, and medical service. From the point of view of the renter, it appears that he would have been better off with free laborers, who could be fired if they did not perform their duties well. The slave, on the other hand, could work slowly and still remain in his employ. One visitor, writing of plantation slaves, noted: "Nothing can be conceived more inert than a slave; his unwilling labour is discovered in every step that he takes; he moves not if he can avoid it; if the eyes of the overseer be off him, he sleeps; the ox and the horse, driven by the slave, appear to sleep also; all is listless inactivity."

Thomas Cooper, a British economist who resided in South Carolina in the mid-1820s, came to the same conclusion, as did most other writers of the antebellum period.

The usual work of a field hand is barely two thirds what a white day labourer at usual wages would perform; this is the outside . . . . Nothing will justify slave labour in point of economy but the nature of the soil and climate which incapacitates a white man from labouring in the summer time, as on the rich lands of Carolina and Georgia, extending one hundred miles from the seaboard. In places merely agricultural, as New York, Pennsylvania, Illinois, Indiana, Missouri, slave labour is entirely unprofitable. It is so even in Maryland and Virginia.

BY

# HEWLETT & BRIGHT.

## SALE OF

# VALUABLE
# SLAVES,

## *(On account of departure)*

The Owner of the following named and valuable Slaves, being on the eve of departure for Europe, will cause the same to be offered for sale, at the NEW EXCHANGE, corner of St. Louis and Chartres streets, on *Saturday,* May 16, at Twelve o'Clock, *viz.*

1. **SARAH**, a mulatress, aged 45 years, a good cook and accustomed to house work in general, is an excellent and faithful nurse for sick persons, and in every respect a first rate character.

2. **DENNIS**, her son, a mulatto, aged 24 years, a first rate cook and steward for a vessel, having been in that capacity for many years on board one of the Mobile packets; is strictly honest, temperate, and a first rate subject.

3. **CHOLE**, a mulatress, aged 36 years, she is, without execption, one of the most competent servants in the country, a first rate washer and ironer, does up lace, a good cook, and for a bachelor who wishes a house-keeper she would be invaluable; she is also a good ladies' maid, having travelled to the North in that capacity.

4. **FANNY**, her daughter, a mulatress, aged 16 years, speaks French and English, is a superior hair-dresser, (pupil of Guilliac,) a good seamstress and ladies' maid, is smart, intelligent, and a first rate character.

5. **DANDRIDGE**, a mulatoo, aged 26 years, a first rate dining-room servant, a good painter and rough carpenter, and has but few equals for honesty and sobriety.

6. **NANCY**, his wife, aged about 24 years, a confidential house servant, good seamstress, mantuamaker and tailoress, a good cook, washer and ironer, etc.

7. **MARY ANN**, her child, a creole, aged 7 years, speaks French and English, is smart, active and intelligent.

8. **FANNY or FRANCES**, a mulatress, aged 22 years, is a first rate washer and ironer, good cook and house servant, and has an excellent character.

9. **EMMA**, an orphan, aged 10 or 11 years, speaks French and English, has been in the country 7 years, has been accustomed to waiting on table, sewing etc.; is intelligent and active.

10. **FRANK**, a mulatto, aged about 32 years speaks French and English, is a first rate hostler and coachman, understands perfectly well the management of horses, and is, in every respect, a first rate character, with the exception that he will occasionally drink, though not an habitual drunkard.

☞ All the above named Slaves are acclimated and excellent subjects; they were purchased by their present vendor many years ago, and will, therefore, be severally warranted against all vices and maladies prescribed by law, save and except FRANK, who is fully guaranteed in every other respect but the one above mentioned.

TERMS:—One-half Cash, and the other half in notes at Six months, drawn and endorsed to the satisfaction of the Vendor, with special mortgage on the Slaves until final payment. The Acts of Sale to be passed before WILLIAM BOSWELL, *Notary Public*, at the expense of the Purchaser.

*New-Orleans, May 13, 1835.*

PRINTED BY BENJAMIN LEVY.

*Poster advertising slave auction in New Orleans.*
(COURTESY, THE NEW YORK HISTORICAL SOCIETY, NEW YORK CITY)

At one time historians assumed that since slavery was unprofitable—and demonstrations of the truth existed even in the 1840s and 1850s—southern planters must have been blind, stupid, or ignorant. Most were none of these; a people that produced a George Washington, a Thomas Jefferson, and a James Madison, and in the next generation a John C. Calhoun, a Robert Toombs, and an Andrew Jackson, did not suddenly choose a foolish leadership. In 1846 the South was represented in Congress by John Berrien and Alexander Stephens of Georgia, Pierre Soulé and John Slidell of Louisiana, Robert Walker and Jefferson Davis of Mississippi, Willie Mangum and Asa Biggs of North Carolina, and R. Barnwell Rhett of South Carolina; Calhoun was the South's leader in the Senate, and its most formidable intellect. These were men of keen intelligences, among the best the South ever sent to Washington. But they were not businessmen in the nineteenth-century sense of the term. Unlike the merchants and bankers of New York, Boston, and Philadelphia, they did not judge a civilization or a society in terms of profits and assets. Their forays into economic proofs of the value of slavery were logically satisfying but economically deceiving. In the 1840s it was possible to make a plausible case for railroad profitability; such could not be done for slavery, not even in the best of times on the most fruitful plantations. Southern writers adopted the words and phrases of modern capitalism, but they never acquired its spirit. America was becoming a business civilization in the early nineteenth century, and in such a civilization the southern view was doomed to failure.

But what could be done about such a situation? Abolitionists in the North, Midwest and Europe spoke bluntly of the immorality of slavery, to which the southern apologists replied that it was simple to criticize others and advocate sweeping changes elsewhere, but at the same time refuse to make reforms at home. The southerners offered a variety of justifications for the institution, but the key to the problem was really demographic. What would happen if the slaves were suddenly freed, or freed even over a long period of time? As they saw it, the South would be destroyed by a rising tide of color.

The white South did indeed have a tiger by the tail in

TABLE 3 / POPULATION OF SLAVE STATES, 1850*

| State | Whites | Free Negroes | Total Free | Slaves |
|---|---|---|---|---|
| Alabama | 426,515 | 2,250 | 428,765 | 342,894 |
| Florida | 47,120 | 926 | 48,046 | 39,341 |
| Georgia | 513,083 | 2,586 | 515,669 | 362,966 |
| Kentucky | 770,061 | 9,667 | 779,728 | 221,768 |
| Louisiana | 254,271 | 15,685 | 269,956 | 230,807 |
| Maryland | 418,763 | 73,943 | 492,706 | 89,800 |
| Mississippi | 291,536 | 898 | 292,434 | 300,419 |
| Missouri | 592,176 | 2,667 | 594,843 | 89,289 |
| North Carolina | 552,477 | 27,271 | 580,458 | 288,412 |
| South Carolina | 274,775 | 8,769 | 283,544 | 384,925 |
| Tennessee | 767,319 | 6,280 | 773,599 | 249,519 |
| Texas | 133,131 | 926 | 134,057 | 53,346 |
| Virginia | 894,149 | 53,906 | 948,055 | 473,026 |

*SOURCE: J. D. B. De Bow, *The Industrial Resources of the United States,* Vol. III, p. 419.

the 1840s. In 1850 there were approximately 3.5 million Negroes in the United States and 19.2 million whites; but most of the Negroes were residents of the South and the population of that region was 3.35 million whites and 3.11 million Negroes. Already, in the 1840s Negroes were in the majority in Mississippi and South Carolina.

Few slaveholders of the period speculated on what would happen if the long-enslaved blacks—who in the past had given evidence of a desire for and ability to carry out insurrection—were not kept permanently in bondage. And Frederick Douglass, himself a slave in the 1830s, implied that the white South would never permit an alteration of the status quo. In 1833 Douglass was sent to a farm owned by Edward Covey, who "enjoyed the reputation of being a first rate hand at breaking young negroes."

If at any one time in my life, more than any other, I was made to drink the bitterest dregs of slavery, that time was during the first six months of my stay with this man Covey. We were worked all weathers. It was never too hot, or too cold; it could never rain, blow, snow, or hail too hard for us to work in the field. Work, work, work, was scarcely more the order of the day than of the night. The longest days were too short for him, and the shortest nights too long for him. I was somewhat unmanageable at the first, but a few months of the discipline tamed me—in body, soul, and spirit. My natural elasticity was crushed; my intellect languished; the disposition to read departed, the cheerful spark that lingered about my eye died out; the dark night of slavery closed in upon me, and behold a man transformed to a brute!

Southern slaveholders told themselves, in books and articles, and at parties and conventions, that the slave was content—that blacks like Douglass, who desired freedom, were rare. But the more honest of them realized such was not the case. Under the rhetoric and pseudoscience, under the thin veneer of the slave civilization, lay the problem that could not be faced and that would not go away. And so arose the expedient of increased brutality, such as that experienced by Douglass. Like others who went through the same ordeal, Douglass was crushed, and in the process he learned a valuable lesson.

To make a contented slave, you must make a thoughtless one. It is necessary to darken his moral and mental vision, and, so far as possible, to annihilate his power of reason. He must be able to detect no inconsistencies in slavery. The man who takes his earnings must be able to convince him that he has a perfect right to do so. It must not depend upon mere force: the slave must know no higher law than his master's will. The whole relationship must not only demonstrate to his mind its necessity, but its absolute rightfulness. If there be one crevice through which a single drop can fall, it will certainly rust off the slave's chains.

The most dramatic protests against slavery in the 1840s came from groups and individuals known collectively as abolitionists, but who in practice had little in common except their antipathy for slavery. The antislavery spectrum included such people as editor Richard Henry Dana, who believed an aroused public opinion could convince the slaveholders to end the institution, and William Lloyd Garrison, who by 1840 was convinced that violent revolution was necessary. Garrison thought Dana a simple fool; Dana criticized the "wildness and fanaticism" of the radicals. Other abolitionists included New York ministers, who preached sermons against slavery and asked for God's intervention to stop the owning of human chattels; former slaves, who helped run the underground railroad; former president and then congressman John Quincy Adams, who fought for an end to slavery until his death in 1848, at the age of eighty-one; and the students in Hartford, Connecticut, some as young as ten years old, who circulated petitions in 1841 to encourage writing letters against slavery to congressmen.

Arthur and Lewis Tappan were anomalies in the abolitionist movement. Radical abolitionists tended to view businessmen as being in league with the slaveholders; the Tappans were successful businessmen. Foreign visitors usually pictured businessmen as interested only in the pursuit of the dollar; the Tappans were involved in a myriad of social causes: abolitionism, the rights of labor, feminism, and utopian communities. Businessmen generally considered the abolitionists demagogues; the Tappans were not only reasonable and calm, but also effective, which could not be said of most of their group. Radical abolitionists considered the moderates dupes of the slaveocracy, while the moderates claimed the radicals were setting back the cause of freedom by their excesses; the Tappans had friends in both camps. They were moderates who paid the fine for William Lloyd Garrison when the fiery editor was jailed for libel. The *Liberator,* Garrison's radical antislavery newspaper, could not have survived without Arthur Tappan's funds. Yet the brothers never lost faith in the political system and the law, and for this the radicals criticized them. The Tappans might be considered the purse of abolitionism, but they were far more.

The antislavery struggle eventually resolved itself into a contest between the approach of moderates such as the Tappans and that of radicals like Garrison. The former believed that the institutions of America could be made to work, and through them slavery could be done away with, while Garrison felt that extralegal methods and violence would be needed before the slaves could attain their freedom. Arthur and Lewis Tappan were not dreamers; as businessmen they understood both the northern merchant and the southern plantation owner. They did not expect to win the war against slavery in a single season, but they thought triumph would come after long, patient effort. The alternative, as they saw it, was a bloody war, the worst in American history, and one the nation might not survive. Garrison would not wait; manumission to him was not a process but a condition. If the slaveholders would not free their chattels, he was prepared to take up arms. He believed that his cause was just and transcended all other considerations. In the end the Garrisonians won control of the abolitionist movement. And as slavery increasingly appeared to be a moral issue incapable of compromise, the nation took a giant step toward the Civil War.

In 1831, the same year that the Tappans helped organize the New York Committee for a National Anti-Slavery Society, Garrison published the first number of the *Liberator,* which he promised would break up "the conspiracy of silence" with which the moderates and the slaveholders protected the "peculiar institution."

I *will be* as harsh as truth, and as uncompromising as justice. On this subject, I do not wish to think, to speak, or write, with moderation . . . . I am in earnest—I will not equivocate—I will not excuse—I will not retreat a single inch—AND I WILL BE HEARD.

For the next nine years the fortunes of the moderates and the radicals would be determined in large part by events neither could control, but which turned public sentiment one way or another. Each time a peaceful advance was made in the direction of abolition, the Tappans' influence increased; each act of violence against the abolitionists strengthened Garrison's hand. In some cases acts of violence strengthened neither. For example, Nat Turner's insurrection, which came shortly after both the *Liberator* and the New York Committee had been formed, temporarily shook the abolitionist movement. Garrison considered the rebellion a foretaste of the future, while the Tappans warned that unless peaceful means were found to channel abolitionism, more violence could be expected.

In 1833, slavery was abolished peacefully in the British Empire, and this gave heart to the American moderates. The same year the New York Committee reformed itself into the American Anti-Slavery Society, and it applauded British manumission. Garrison approved the British action but warned that slavery in the United States could not be ended merely by a legislative enactment. Arthur Tappan, then president of the New York City Anti-Slavery Society, roundly condemned Garrison, who he said would destroy constructive work toward emancipation, while Garrison characterized Tappan as a well-meaning but ineffectual figure.

The next struggle to muster strength for the moderate

*William Lloyd Garrison.*

and radical positions took place on the college campuses. Abolitionism was a major issue in the antebellum period, and it divided faculties and student bodies across the country. Abolitionist-minded students in southern schools demonstrated, and when they were silenced left for northern institutions. There were no major college riots until the 1850s, but pressures began to build as early as 1834. In that year the students at Lane theological seminary in Cincinnati, which had been heavily endowed by the Tappans and was known as an abolitionist stronghold, held a series of debates on the subject that lasted eighteen nights and that were sparked by Theodore Dwight Weld, a Tappan agent. In the end the students decided to work for the cause of "immediate emancipation gradually carried out." This sounded like a compromise between the Tappan and Garrison positions, and the Tappans were willing to accept it. Not so President Lyman Beecher, who felt that the students had gone too far. As a result most of the students left Lane and transferred to Oberlin College near Elyria, Ohio, which now became the center of student abolitionist thought. Oberlin also received generous help from the Tappans, even though many of its students would eventually embrace Garrison's position.

By 1838 Lewis Tappan realized that the two brands of abolitionism could not coexist, and he ceased aiding the radical groups. But he might have curtailed his assistance in any case, since the Tappans were so severely hit by the 1837 panic that they could scarcely afford to assist even their own organizations. Seeking other allies, Garrison came out in favor of women's rights, thus forging a union with the feminists. At the New England Anti-Slavery Convention of May 1838, the Garrisonians backed a proposal to receive women into the organization on equal terms. When the motion passed several important figures resigned, but Garrison won feminist support that proved useful in coming battles against the Tappans. In September 1838, Garrison supported attempts on the part of peace crusaders to form a more active organization, and they, too, became his allies. Garrison brought all his allies together in a new coalition, the Massachusetts Abolition Society, which was larger and more influential than the New York Anti-Slavery Society. His careful planning bore fruit in 1840, when he won control of the national abolitionist organization. By making certain that his supporters attended all meetings at the convention that year, and by ferrying delegates to the convention when necessary, Garrison won appointments for his followers to key positions on the board. With this, the Tappans and their group withdrew from the national organization, leaving the field to the radicals. As they saw it, Garrison had watered down the abolitionist drive with his diversionary, though important, moves in the direction of feminism and peace crusading. For his part, Garrison now dreamed of an alliance of all major protest groups in a massive assault on the slaveocracy.

The Garrisonians and the Tappanites went their separate ways in 1840. When Garrison attended the World Anti-Slavery Conference in Britain, he found himself the center of attraction. Lewis Tappan remained active in the abolitionist movement, but not as a member of the American delegation; instead, operating on his own, he maintained contact with foreign correspondents and gave them his views of the anti-slavery struggle. Increasingly, however, his attention was drawn to business matters; the Mercantile

Agency, in particular, demanded a great deal of his attention. Still, he did join with Gerrit Smith and others to found the Liberty party, which was to test both abolitionist strength and the political institutions of the United States. The party's first convention, held in Albany in April 1840, nominated James G. Birney for the presidency and Thomas Earle of Pennsylvania for the vice-presidency, but the Liberty campaign proved a dismal failure. Birney received only 7,000 votes, failing to capture a single county, and even in New York, the center of the party's strength, he drew only 3,000 votes. Altogether, the abolitionists' first experiments at the polls proved disastrous.

After the election the Tappans indicated a willingness to explore new means of cooperation, but only if the moderates were accepted as equals. Lewis Tappan even offered to use money in the "Martyr Fund," established to aid families of imprisoned abolitionists, to help Garrisonians. The offer was rejected; it was not made again. Each group in its own way assisted the underground railroad, which aided a number of fugitive slaves in the mid-1840s, but in most other activities they remained distinct.

The Democratic party of Andrew Jackson, strong and united in the 1830s, split at the seams in the 1840s. The Baptist and Methodist churches divided into northern and southern wings. Southern matrons who had gone to Newport, Rhode Island, with their marriageable daughters in the 1830s began to seek sons-in-law in Charleston, South Carolina, in the 1840s, while northern families avoided southern resorts for winter vacations. The division of the abolitionist movement was not an isolated phenomenon, but only the most striking and obvious result of the tensions that were beginning to divide the nation.

One might say that many northern leaders of the antebellum period had decided that in one way or another slavery had to be limited, contained, or done away with. The Tappans offered a peaceful method of accomplishing the last of these ends; Garrison thought violence was the only solution. Those who desired nonviolent political action to achieve abolition maintained influence in the years to come, but the drift of the times was toward confrontation. This would come in 1860 and 1861.

# 9 / THE DISTAFF REVOLT

MOST EUROPEAN VISITORS TO AMERICA IN THE LATE 1830s and 1840s were fascinated by the American women they met. Frederick Marryat, the English novelist, thought them "the prettiest in the whole world," and considered those he saw in Cincinnati the handsomest of the nation. J. B. Buckingham was also charmed by the women of Cincinnati, but thought Baltimore had more attractive females: "few if any cities in Europe could produce so many handsome women." Others preferred the Creoles of New Orleans, but there were few partisans for those of New York and Philadelphia, and Boston's females were considered intelligent but not very attractive physically. Some foreigners had complaints. The German writer Fritz Lieber thought "their busts not sufficiently developed," while another German complained of their "Devilish Big Feet." Others noted their poor health, general delicacy, and pale complexions. Some attributed these conditions to the great courtesies shown the women by men, who waited upon them with greater care than their European counterparts would have; others thought the undue courtesy the result of the sickness of the females.

The Englishwoman Harriet Martineau believed American women more moral than Europeans and attributed this to early marriage; she also thought that the high place women had in American society was due to their shortage in a land where men seemed to outnumber women. In 1850 there were 8.8 million native white males and 8.5 million native white females; the foreign-born population was 1.2 males and 1.0 females. The slave population was more equally balanced, with 1.2 million of each sex. Yet in America a woman of twenty was believed to be beyond hope of winning a bachelor to marry, and by twenty-five she sought a husband among the widower population. Foreigners criticized American women for their extravagances, but noted that the men didn't seem to mind. They also found fault with the way they raised children, who were far more independent in America than in Europe. Some natives agreed: "I am afraid that the next generation . . . will be a poor, weak, inefficient and selfish race, as parents will listen to all their whims & indulge them in sloth & petulance," wrote a Boston clergyman.

Much of this was untrue, exaggerated, distorted, or oversimplified, and reflected more the limited vision and perspective of the observers than the defects of the people they met. Whether or not American women were more beautiful than Europeans would be hard to say, but European visitors tended to meet middle and upper class ladies in the cities, and not frontier wives or slaves. The former were expected to work less than their poorer sisters, and had more time for, and interest in, beauty care. Should a typical upper-class woman be told she was going to meet an English gentleman at a dinner party the next evening, she would spend the day preparing for the event. She would take care to charm the visitor; since all Europeans were assumed to be more cultured and refined than Americans, the task would not be onerous. Such a woman would swoon, act faint, and give the appearance of delicacy, since this was the style in Europe at that time. Perhaps the American woman overdid it, and so impressed the visitors as being weak.

In all probability the Europeans who commented upon the American woman's morals were referring to adultery, which was rare. The American birthrate was high, childbed deaths were commonplace, and women were needed to work alongside their men. On the other hand, prostitution was more common in America than in Europe, due largely to the shortage of females; unwed mothers were not unknown, and if the newspapers of the time are to be believed, rape was frequent. Yet little or nothing of this is to be found in the journals and letters of foreigners visiting America. Consider, for example, two statements on the nature of American women. The first is from the German visitor Francis Grund, who admired them as he did all things American.

There is, in the great majority of American ladies, that calm subjection of passion and temper, which they deem indispensable to female dignity or grace; but it does not follow that, on this account, they must be devoid of imagination and feeling. Their eyes are, perhaps, less expressive of what, in Italy, would be called *passion;* but they are beaming with intelligence and kindness; and the great number of Europeans annually married in the United States proves at least, that they are capable of kindling love and permanent attachment. But the strongest argument in favor of their sentiments is the almost universal practice of marrying for love, to which only few of the fashionable coteries in the large cities seem to make an exception . . . . As regards the morality and virtue of American ladies, it will suffice to say that they are not inferior to the English, who are universally acknowledged to be the best wives and mothers in Europe. The slightest suspicion against the character of a lady, is, in America, as in England, sufficient to exclude her from society; but, in America, public opinion is equally severe on men, and this is certainly a considerable improvement. Actually, there is no country in which scandal, even amongst the most fashionable circles, is so rare as in the United States, or where the term *"intrigue"* is less known and understood.

Of course, Grund was talking about "ladies"—meaning the upper and middle class females—as distinguished from common "women." The women of the frontier, the lower and immigrant classes, and most importantly, the slaves, would have elicited quite a different observation from Grund. Sojourner Truth, a former slave who worked in the underground railroad, spoke of her life at a women's rights meeting in 1851:

Well, children, where there is so much racket there must be something out of kilter. I think that twixt the niggers of the South and the women of the North, all talking about rights, the white man will be in a fix pretty soon. But what's all this here talking about? That man over there says that women needs to be helped into carriages and lifted over ditches, and to have the best place everywhere. Nobody ever helps me into carriages, or over mud-puddles, or gives me any best place! And ain't I a woman? Look at my arm! I have ploughed, and planted and gathered into barns, and no man could head me! And ain't I a woman? I could work as much and eat as much as a man—when I could get it—and bear the lash as well! And ain't I a woman? I have borne thirteen children, and seen them most all sold off to slavery, and when I cried out with my mother's grief, none but Jesus heard me! And ain't I a woman? . . . Then that little man in black there, he say women can't have as much rights as men, because Christ wasn't a woman! Where did your Christ come from? Where did your Christ come from? From God and a woman. Man had nothing to do with Him!

Tocqueville sensed that American women were quite different from their European counterparts, but this man who understood America better than any visitor or native of his time, and whose predictions as to the nation's future conflicts were in all other respects so accurate, believed they were content with their lot. European women, he said, were in a clearly subordinate position, while the Americans were considered by men as equal but different. Each sex was charged with a different sphere of activity, and each was expected to assume authority and exercise judgments. "You will never find American women in charge of the external relations of the family, managing a business or interfering in politics," he noted. "But they are also never obliged to undertake rough laborer's work or any task requiring hard physical exertion. No family is so poor that it makes an exception to this rule." Clearly Tocqueville was not thinking of the frontier wife, who worked as hard as, if not harder than, her husband. Farm wives throughout the nation helped in the fields while taking care of the home, and in the process often wore themselves out or literally worked themselves to death. Nor did Tocqueville consider the barriers to female education when he wrote, "while they have allowed the social inferiority of women to continue, they have done everything to raise her morally and intellectually to the level of man. In this I think they have wonderfully understood the true conception of democratic progress." Tocqueville truly admired American women and praised their accomplishments: "If anyone asks me what I think the chief cause of the extraordinary prosperity and growing power of this nation, I should answer that it is due to the superiority of their women." Both sexes understood this, he thought, and accepted it.

To sum up, the Americans do not think that man and woman have the duty or right to do the same things, but they show an equal regard for the part played by both and think them as beings of equal worth, though their fates are different. They do not expect courage of the same sort or for the same purposes from woman as from man, but they never question her courage. They do not think a man and his wife should always use their intelligence and understanding in the same way, but they do at least consider that the one has as firm an understanding as the other and a mind as clear.

But what if a woman chose to use her mind and talents in a way that transgressed the parallel paths described by Tocqueville? In such a case she could expect ridicule, abuse, and even physical violence. Feminists were shouted off their platforms in the late 1820s and early 1830s, and their lives were threatened afterward. Female teachers in New England in the 1830s had to remain single; if they married, they would certainly be fired. Their salaries were often a quarter or less those paid males, and they could not expect to advance to administrative posts. The Lowell textile mills, which all foreigners tried to visit, hired farm girls to work the looms not because they were superior at the tasks but because they would work for a fraction of the salary paid men. The cotton-fabric manufacturers assumed that women would work for a few years, amass a dowry, and then marry. To do otherwise was abnormal.

It was also considered abnormal for a woman to be interested in sex. Such an interest, it was said, was unlady-like and vulgar. For a woman to admit pleasure from inter-course was unthinkable; it immediately branded her as im-moral and suspect. Contraception was also taboo. At a time when the infant mortality rate in the state of Massachusetts was approximately 130 in a thousand, and a woman could expect to see only three of her four children live to the age of eighteen, family planning was not tolerated. Childbirth was also a common cause of death, a fact attested to by the large number of widowers with children throughout the nation.

When Robert Dale Owen, in his 1830 book, *Moral Physiology*, recommended and described contraception, his life was threatened. Charles Knowlton's *Fruits of Philos-ophy, or, the private companion of young married people,* appeared two years later, and like Owen he recommended contraception for the health of the mother and the preven-tion of overpopulation. Knowlton went further than Owen; he described the sex organs and their functions, and conse-quently went to jail. Ten years later the *Boston Medical*

*Journal,* in commenting on the Knowlton book—which by then had become an underground "best seller"—said, "We think . . . the less that is known about it by the public at large, the better it will be for the morals of the community." Yet men not only were free to read such works, but were expected to do so.

Given the national climate of the 1830s and 1840s, it is little wonder that a movement for women's rights took root. One would scarcely have expected it to happen in a country like France, where women were told from childhood to expect nothing from life other than the adoration of a man. It was different in America. The Declaration of Independence, though speaking of all *men* being created equal, seemed to apply to women too. The great rush of reformism in the 1830s and the leveling philosophy of Jacksonian Democracy added fuel to the fires. Women were permitted to join the abolitionist, temperance, peace, and related crusades, and although they were not allowed to hold leadership positions they did yeoman work in the field. Democratically inclined men were willing to listen to women in such movements, and this must have encouraged them in their activities. Such women as Lucretia Mott, Elizabeth Cady Stanton, Lucy Stone, and Susan B. Anthony began their careers as workers in such reform movements and only later transferred their whole attentions to the crusade for women's rights. Their early work allowed them to capitalize upon a logical weakness in the male reformer's camp. How could one claim to advocate democracy while denying women full rights? How could the Transcendentalists preach individualism without defending the rights of women to be individuals? How could the abolitionists support the right of the slave to full freedom without granting the same right to women? Those who opposed abolitionism, Transcendentalism, and other reforms had no difficulty in opposing women's rights, but the reformers did. They were the first antagonists the crusade would engage.

The mood engendered by abolitionist radicals had its effect. The extravagant oratory, the predictions of Armageddon, the exaggerations of the radicals, came to be believed even by those who knew empirically they were not completely true. The feminists portrayed American women, probably the most liberated of the era, as being treated like insects at worst and lapdogs at best. Women who had attained importance and celebrity primarily because they were in America, not Europe, claimed to have suffered the worst persecutions imaginable. The fact that so many feminists began as abolitionists was partly responsible for this. In time the feminists seemed to confuse their lot with that of the slaves, and in their minds the two movements intermingled and became one. Lucy Stone, a prominent abolitionist and feminist, led a campaign against female colleges, which, she said, "I do abhor with an abhorrence I cannot express." When asked why, she replied that they reminded her of the slave galleries in southern churches. In the early days of the Civil War Elizabeth Cady Stanton and Susan B. Anthony put forth a plan in all seriousness that called for sending every male white southerner to Liberia after the North's victory.

The path from sweet submission to militancy was marked by frustration, caused more often by allies than

*Angelina E. Grimké.*
(THE GRANGER COLLECTION)

enemies. Female reformers only came in contact with unfriendly critics when they spoke at open meetings or read
opposition newspapers, and they expected what they re-

ceived from that quarter. Throughout the 1830s and 1840s, however, feminine abolitionists, temperance workers, and members of other reform movements were snubbed and placed in minor positions by their male fellow-members. The Sons of Temperance, the leading anti-alcohol movement in the 1830s, allowed women to circulate petitions and obtain pledges, but they could not join. Not until the 1840s did the organization consent to the formation of an auxiliary, the Daughters of Temperance, which was established with separate but equal rights. The two groups met in convention in 1852, but from the first women were excluded from the platform. As a protest against this treatment, Mrs. Stanton and Susan B. Anthony organized the Woman's State Temperance Society of New York, which permitted males to join but not to hold office. The males were shocked, and at the Men's Temperance Society meeting late in 1852 a delegation of clergymen told Samuel J. May, the president, that "we will withdraw from the convention if it seats women." May tried to find a compromise, but failed. Throughout the rest of the 1850s, the male and female temperance workers snarled at each other almost as much as they did at "demon rum."

Women had similar difficulties in the abolitionist movement. The first women's association with a political objective, the Philadelphia Female Anti-Slavery Society, was formed in 1833, with Esther Moore its president and Lucretia Mott corresponding secretary. The Society was always small, however, since most women worked through abolitionist groups headed by men. The Grimké sisters, Angelina and Sarah, were particularly active in the American Anti-Slavery Society in the mid-1830s and were the first major figures to attempt to unite the abolitionist and feminist movements. They were encouraged in this by radical abolitionists and discouraged by moderates. Both factions believed in equal rights, but while the radicals thought to end all bigotries in one fell swoop, the moderates hoped to deal with the pressing problem of abolition first and then turn to other matters. Theodore Weld, Angelina's husband and himself a moderate, urged her to concentrate on the slavery issue:

Let us all *first* wake up the nation to lift millions of slaves of both sexes from the dust, and turn them into MEN and then when we all have our hand in, it will be an easy matter to take millions of females from their knees and set them on their feet, or in other words transform them from *babies* into *women*.

Weld's point of view was shared by a majority of abolitionists, perhaps not always for disinterested reasons. Slavery was a more obnoxious and obvious target than the suppression of women. As a movement, abolitionism was able to attract a far wider audience than feminism, obtain more funds, and receive a greater national hearing. Although they rarely said so openly, the male abolitionists often implied that women had no right to compare their plight with that of the slaves, and moderate feminists themselves agreed with this point of view. Time after time the feminists would present their demands to the abolitionists, only to be rebuffed when faced with an appeal for unity. Almost all feminists belonged to abolitionist organizations; the reverse could not be said for the abolitionists.

Feminists were told that once slavery was ended the reformers would join with them to end the oppression of women. But when emancipation finally came, few men

*Signing the pledge to abstain from alcohol.*
(THE GRANGER COLLECTION)

joined in the new crusade. It has been suggested, with good reason, that the abolitionists were never committed, singly or as a group, to the fight for equal treatment of the sexes. The end of slavery shattered the fabric of white southern life but had little effect on the day-to-day existence of Transcendentalist circles in Boston. In effect, the abolitionists, who owned no slaves and who lived in areas where there were few Negroes, advocated radical changes for a region far from their homes. Feminism was another matter. Should the women's rights brigades win their battles, Boston as well as Charleston would feel the impact. And the abolitionist males were not certain they wanted such a change in their own backyard.

Although barred from positions of leadership in the abolitionist movement, women's rights advocates remained wedded to it throughout the late 1830s and until the mid-1840s. This was evident at the first National Convention of American Anti-Slavery Women, held in 1837, when the majority of delegates agreed to concentrate their attentions on abolitionism. In part this was due to a recognition of priorities, but it was also a result of the opposition they aroused. As the women arrived at the convention they were surrounded, insulted, and threatened by anti-abolition mobs. Although references were made to their sex, it was clear that the crowd hated them more for their ideas than for their gender. Some of the feminists took this as a compliment and gloried in this kind of opposition.

The situation was even worse at the 1838 convention. This time the mob forced its way into the hall and threatened to destroy it if the women would not leave. Some started to move to the doors, but Angelina Grimké rallied them, and they remained. An abolitionist newspaperman present called the mob "infuriated southern slave holders and cowardly northern tradesmen," but most were actually lower-class workers. The next day, as the mob chanted, "Burn the building," antislavery men pleaded with the women to leave, but they again refused. That night, after the meeting had ended and the delegates had retired to their hotels and homes, the hall was burned to the ground.

The next day the convention continued its work in a school-room, and remained in session until all business had been considered. The delegates returned home, more attached to abolitionism than they had been prior to the convention, and less reluctant to see feminism take a secondary role in the reform movement.

This attitude made it all the easier for Garrison to win feminist support against the Tappan moderates at the 1840 convention of the American Anti-Slavery Society. Garrison had consistently promised to work for equal rights for women and dedicate himself to the task once slavery was ended, while Tappan and the moderates were still unsure of their feelings regarding feminism. The Garrison news-papers had roundly condemned the mobs at the 1838 convention; the moderates had said little of the matter. In effect, Garrison had wooed the women successfully, and they responded by giving him the votes needed to make him victorious over the moderates.

The Garrisonians repaid the favor at the World Anti-Slavery Conference that was held in London in 1840. Lucretia Mott and Elizabeth Pease, both leading feminists and abolitionists, had been named as delegates by the Garrison-controlled American Anti-Slavery Society, but James Birney and other moderates were also delegates, and they joined with a majority of the foreign spokesmen who opposed female representation. Henry B. Stanton, a moderate, was one of the American delegates, and he brought with him his new bride, Elizabeth Cady Stanton. All realized that on the first day, when credentials were presented, the British delegates would challenge the right of American women to sit in the hall. Thus, before the conference could discuss slavery it would have to deal with feminism.

The first speaker was an old English abolitionist, Thomas Clarkson. The delegates listened to his rambling address out of respect but they were more curious to hear what the next speaker, Wendell Phillips of the United States, had to say. Phillips was an ally of Garrison, but his views on the seating of delegates were not fully known. Phillips ended doubts by proposing the formation of a committee whose task it would be to draw up a correct list of convention members, which would automatically include all those who bore proper credentials from their national organizations. If Phillips' proposal was approved, the female members of the American contingent would be seated without further question. Immediately there was movement on the floor, as delegates rose to shout their disapproval of the plan. Dr. J. Bowring, a member of the House of Commons, rose in dismay. "What, are American women coming to England as representatives . . . not to be welcomed with honor? Not to be put in seats of dignity?" The answer, in a roar, was "No, Never!" With this the convention dissolved into a chaotic jumble of shouted arguments: ministers quoted Scripture to prove women were inferior to men, feminist-minded male delegates called for equality for all, and members of both camps threatened to walk out unless they were satisfied with the resolution of the issue. Joseph Sturge, a lifelong abolitionist who prided himself on his dedication to justice, pleaded with the feminists to be "reasonable," or as Lucretia Mott put it, "begged submission of us to the

*Lucretia Mott.*
(THE NEW YORK PUBLIC LIBRARY)

London Committee." There is little evidence that more than a handful of the delegates changed their minds as a result of these shouted conversations. One of them, however, was

207

Henry Stanton. His wife convinced him of the right of women to sit equally with men; indeed, she was so impressed by the coolness and eloquence of Lucretia Mott that she became increasingly active in the women's rights movement.

As expected, the conference voted to reject the Phillips proposal. Women were permitted to attend, but not as delegates. Instead they were to sit in a special section, behind a screen, to listen but not talk.

Garrison arrived after this decision had been made. He was fresh from his victory over the moderate abolitionists at the American Anti-Slavery Society meeting in New York, which made him the most famous American abolitionist, and his speech had been long anticipated by the delegates. But when he learned that the female American representatives had not been permitted to take their places, he refused to deliver his speech, and for the rest of the convention he sat with the women in the screened portion of the hall. The women appreciated Garrison's gesture, realizing it was the greatest act of good faith he could offer.

But the London convention effected great changes in the women's rights movement. It showed the feminists that with few exceptions the male abolitionists could not be trusted to support the cause of equal rights for the sexes— not in 1840, and probably not if slavery were to end. Feminist abolitionists would continue their efforts to end slavery, but they no longer considered their two interests as parallel. Instead, some began to view the male abolitionists not only as hypocrites, but as their future enemies.

The World Anti-Slavery Conference was also important in that it brought together Lucretia Mott and Elizabeth Cady Stanton, who would provide the motive force for feminism in the 1840s. "So entirely one are we," wrote Mrs. Stanton, "that . . . to the world we always seem to agree and uniformly reflect each other. Like husband and wife, each has the feeling that we must have no differences in public."

During the next seven years the two women, in common with most female abolitionists, devoted themselves to the cause of freeing the slaves. And all the time they continued to be treated as second-class citizens by most male abolitionists, and as harlots by the pro-slavery forces. By 1847 both women were prepared to act independently of their male supporters to secure their rights. "My experience at the World's Anti-Slavery Convention," wrote Mrs. Stanton, "all I had read about the legal status of women, and the oppression I saw everywhere, together swept across my soul, intensified now by many personal experiences. It seemed as if all the elements had conspired to impel me to some onward step. I could not see what to do or where to begin—my only thought was a public meeting for protest and discussion."

Lucretia Mott was undergoing a similar period of reflection. She wrote to Mrs. Stanton, saying that she was visiting in the upstate New York area and that she would like to spend a day with her. For the past few weeks she had been meeting with feminists. "I poured out the torrents of my long-accumulating discontent with such vehemence and indignation that I stirred myself, as well as the rest of the party, to do and dare anything." Together with Martha

Wright and Mary Ann McClintock, they decided to hold a Woman's Rights Convention at Seneca Falls on July 19, 1848.

The convention itself was a small affair. Most of the delegates lived in the vicinity of Seneca Falls and a few men were also in attendance. Since no woman had ever presided over a meeting of this nature, James Mott assumed the chair on the first day. Mrs. Mott delivered a speech the second day, but the most important piece of business transacted by the convention was the drafting and ratification of a Declaration of Sentiments, which was based on the Declaration of Independence.

We hold these truths to be self-evident; that all men and women are created equal; that they are endowed by their Creator with certain inalienable rights; that among these are life, liberty, and the pursuit of happiness; that to secure these rights, governments are instituted, deriving their just powers from the consent of the governed.

The history of mankind is a history of repeated injuries on the part of man towards woman, having in direct object the establishment of an absolute tyranny over her. To prove this, let facts be submitted to a candid world.

The Declaration went on to enumerate the grievances of the feminists. Just as the original Declaration of Independence had listed eighteen, so did the 1848 Declaration. Among the more important of these were:

He has never permitted her to exercise her inalienable right to the elective franchise.

He has compelled her to submit to laws, in the formation of which she had no voice . . . .

He has made her, if married, in the eye of the law, civilly dead.

He has taken from her all right in property, even to the wages she earns . . . .

He has so framed the laws of divorce, as to what shall be the proper causes, and in case of separation, to whom the guardianship of the children shall be given, as to be wholly regardless of the happiness of women—the law, in all cases, going upon the false supposition of the supremacy of man, and giving all power into his hands . . . .

He has monopolized nearly all the profitable employments, and from those she is permitted to follow, she receives but a scanty remuneration.

He closes against her all the avenues to wealth and distinction which he considers most honorable to himself. As a teacher of theology, medicine, or law, she is not known . . . .

He has created a false public sentiment by giving to the world a different code of morals for men and women, by which moral delinquencies which exclude women from society, are not only tolerated, but deemed of little account in man . . . .

Mrs. Stanton, who wrote most of the Declaration of Sentiments, did not expect legislation upon all points, but they were the goals of the movement in 1848.

The convention received wide publicity in the press, and for the rest of the year it was debated with the kind of zeal that had previously been reserved for abolitionism and temperance. Most editors, led by James Gordon Bennett of the New York *Herald,* thought the women radicals were crackpots and frustrated old maids. Horace Greeley took the movement more seriously, and he commended the women in the New York *Tribune.* Several leading male abolitionists now realized that they had treated the feminists too

Yᴱ MAY SESSION OF Yᴱ WOMAN'S RIGHTS CONVENTION—Yᴱ ORATOR OF Yᴱ DAY DENOUNCING Yᴱ LORDS OF CREATION.

(THE GRANGER COLLECTION)

cavalierly in the past, and they hastened to rectify snubs real and imagined. When the Woman's Rights party was formed soon afterward, they hastened to join. Garrison was its first vice-president, and William Henry Channing, John Pierpont, and other male reformers also held office—always serving under a woman president.

Still, the women's rights movement and party withered. In 1849 gold discoveries in California captured the public imagination and women's rights was relegated to the back pages of most newspapers. Moreover, as the slavery controversy became heated, those men and women who might have fought for feminist goals were drawn to the struggle for abolition.

The first phase of the feminist movement ended with little accomplished. The time was right for a movement of this nature, but, paradoxically, the timing was wrong. The egalitarian atmosphere of the 1830s and 1840s nurtured feminism, brought it to bloom, and provided the women's rights advocates not only with converts but with an audience. Increasingly, however, the nation's attention was drawn to the single issue of slavery in all its political, economic, and social ramifications. Had abolitionism not been so obviously a more pressing issue, Elizabeth Cady Stanton, Lucretia Mott, and their co-workers might have won at least some of their eighteen points. But the issue of slavery preoccupied men's attention in the antebellum period, and consequently feminism as a movement faded swiftly after the early 1850s.

# 10 / SECTIONALISM: THE POLITICAL DILEMMA

PRESIDENTIAL ELECTIONS RARELY RESOLVE ISSUES, BUT they often serve to focus discontent, thus eliminating discussion of obsolete problems and affording new ones a national forum. Questions that appear vital in one election will oftentimes have given way to others four years later. In election years politicians attempt to gauge the national mood and to present programs and slogans that will attract sufficient votes to elect a president. Few movements begun in an election year have ever been completely successful, and few issues have been resolved satisfactorily. Ideas that appeal to the public one year may bore it the next, and politicians who stay too long with such ideas may find they have lost their constituencies. Successful leaders and parties recognize this, and continually remold and revamp their approaches according to public desires. Should a leader succeed in this strategy, he is called pragmatic and adaptable; should he fail, he is labeled unprincipled.

Such a transformation of issues was taking place within Jacksonian Democracy in the late 1830s and early 1840s. It was a complicated and often confused movement, revolving around a man who himself was an enigma. More often than not Andrew Jackson acted out of impulse and emotion rather than from ideological commitment. But he had a keen sense of politics, and he forged a coalition of farmers, workers, and small businessmen into a powerful organization.

Just before his death Jackson was asked if there was anything he regretted. He replied there was; he wished he had shot Henry Clay and hanged John C. Calhoun. Clay and Calhoun opposed many of Jackson's programs, but equally important, the president disliked them for personal reasons. Jackson considered Clay's American System—a nationalistic program to unite western farmers, southern planters, and northern manufacturers—a blueprint to turn the nation over to the upper class, and he was equally opposed to Calhoun's developing sectionalism. But it is far easier to isolate what Jackson opposed than to say what he favored, for at different times in his political career he was on both sides of most issues.

Even taking this into consideration, it is still possible to set forth some generalizations about Jacksonian Democracy. The keynote of Jacksonian Democracy was its belief in a government *by* the common man, and not only *for* him. A man such as John Adams believed in rule by an aristocracy of talents; Jackson thought the national government uncomplicated enough to be administered by anyone of reasonable intelligence. Jacksonians feared great concentrations of economic power, advocating instead small business and farming. They were opposed to sectionalism and on the face of it were intensely nationalistic, but at the same time Jackson was unwilling to see a strong federal government assume responsibilities for activities which he considered were those of state and local governments. Jackson was strongly anti-European; he believed that the United States was not only a new nation, but a new civilization as well—one that had nothing to do with Europe.

Jackson symbolized the movement of the 1830s but he did not create it. Nor did the so-called Jacksonian Democracy die when he left office, or when his protégé and successor, Martin Van Buren, retired from the presidency four years later. Even his opponents came to accept many of the Jacksonian ideas and ideals, and when they did not, they fashioned political careers from this opposition. All of the ingredients that went into the political stewpot of the 1840s were present in the 1830s; only the recipe was different. Jacksonian Democracy built upon the foundations of Jeffersonian politics and in turn provided the base for Manifest Destiny and related movements in the 1840s.

The transformation from the old Jacksonianism to the new came between 1837 and 1841. The 1837 panic shook the confidence of many Americans and shattered the political hopes of President Van Buren. During the last three years of his presidency the Whig opposition used the depression to depict him as a bungler and a fool. But the Whigs were unable to present an acceptable alternative to Van Buren. Thus, in the congressional elections of 1838 the Democrats maintained control of the Senate and increased their House margin; it appeared that the Jacksonian coalition of farmers, workers, and small businessmen was still intact. The Whig leaders were faced with a problem. Van Buren would run for reelection. Although the nation's voters had soured on him, there was no Whig capable of defeating the president. Henry Clay had too many enemies. The anti-Masons knew Clay to be a Mason, and the abolitionists and other opponents of slavery saw him as a slaveholding politician who had defended the institution in Congress. Daniel Webster, another possible Whig nominee, had little support outside of New England, and similarly other Whig hopefuls could only claim regional popularity. The Whigs could win, it seemed, only if they nominated a man who did not appear to be a Whig.

The same dilemma held true for the issues. If the Whigs came out in favor of slavery, they would lose the North; to criticize the institution meant losing the votes of Calhoun's southern Democrats, who were strongly opposed to Van Buren and might accept a Whig. The Whigs also had to take ambiguous stands on economic issues. Generally speaking, the North favored a high tariff and the South desired a lowering of the rates. Similarly, agrarian America opposed a strong central bank, while mercantile interests thought one necessary to preserve what remained of the national credit. Clearly, the party had to proceed with great care, making certain that any position taken would win more votes than it would lose. Furthermore, the Whigs had to find a candidate who appeared strong and determined, but who actually stood for little and said less.

The Whig convention was held in Harrisburg, Pennsylvania, in early December 1839. At the beginning of the convention Clay had most of the delegates, but the majority of these were from states the Whigs could not hope to win in the general election. Then two new candidates emerged. The first was General Winfield Scott, the commander of American forces along the Canadian border who had attracted favorable notice when he acted to preserve American honor and prevent war during the Anglo-American crisis of 1837. The second was General William Henry Harrison, the hero of the War of 1812, who had done well as one of the four Whig candidates for the presidency in 1836. Scott was an unknown; Harrison had the appearance of being a Whig Jackson. He had strong support in the West and in Pennsylvania, two areas the Whigs needed if they were to win. Harrison seemed to be the ideal Whig candidate and he won the nomination.

Since Harrison had served in Congress from Ohio and was considered a northerner, the convention chose a southerner, John Tyler of Virginia, for the vice-presidency. Tyler was a former Democrat who left the party when Jackson attacked the Bank of the United States. He had supported Clay during the opening days of the convention, and so his selection placated that faction of the party. The ticket seemed perfectly balanced; Harrison had support in the North and West, Tyler in the South. And what of the issues? The Whigs found an imaginative solution to that problem. Since any platform would only lose them votes, they adjourned without writing one.

As expected, the Democrats renominated Van Buren at their convention in Baltimore in early May 1840. Unlike the Whigs, the Democrats wrote a platform—one that stressed the importance of internal improvements, opposed a national bank, and favored assumption of state debts by the federal government. The 1840 platform reaffirmed Jacksonian policies, and so alienated the Calhoun Democrats that many of them gave their support to Harrison.

The campaign was a lively and interesting one. As per orders, Harrison remained quiet, or if pressed to speak, did so in generalities. His managers, among whom were Thurlow Weed and Nicholas Biddle, concentrated on constructing a myth of his prowess, simplicity, and democracy. If elected, they said, Harrison would clean up the mess in Washington. The day of his inauguration, March 4, 1841, would be a great day, wrote a Whig newspaper, the Springfield *Republican*. "Then will the farmer of North Bend strike his plough into the soil of corruption at Washington and turn it to the light of the sun." When the Democrats attacked the sixty-seven-year-old Harrison as an ancient misanthrope and stated that he would be happy to have a pension of $2,000 a year, a barrel of hard cider, and a log cabin to live in, the Whigs turned the comment to their advantage. Although Harrison by birth was a Virginia aristocrat, the Whigs didn't deny that their candidate was a rustic; instead they publicized the fact. Harrison parades, featuring log cabins, were held in many cities. Van Buren, they said, lived in Washington like a king, drinking champagne and eating French foods, while their man was content with the good simple life and old-fashioned American alcohol. The party even bottled Old Cabin Whisky in miniature glass cabins. The product was made by the E. C. Booz

*Henry Clay.*
(THE NEW YORK PUBLIC LIBRARY)

Company of Philadelphia and the company's name on the bottle's side added a new word to the lexicon. Thus, the candidate of Jackson's party was made to seem an aristocrat, while the Whigs took on the appearance of the party of the common man.

The popular vote was close. Harrison received 1.3

221

million votes to Van Buren's 1.1 million. But Harrison won a sweeping victory in the electoral college, capturing all of New England except New Hampshire, and all the middle states. Harrison won states in the South where the Calhoun–Van Buren clash had wrecked the chances of the Democrats, and where Tyler's name on the ballot worked magic. "We took Harrison," said Hugh Legaré of South Carolina, "because Tyler was his endorser—and it was known we would take him under no other condition." Harrison received 234 electoral votes to Van Buren's 60, and the Whigs won control of Congress as well.

In the aftermath of the balloting it appeared that Calhoun and Clay, and not Harrison, were the true victors. With Van Buren defeated, Calhoun returned to the Democratic party and immediately began his campaign to remake it in his own image. Since no one believed that Harrison had an idea of his own, it was expected that he would take orders from Clay; Webster was named secretary of state, but most of the other cabinet appointments went to Clay supporters.

Clay's influence could be seen in one part of Harrison's inaugural address, in which he deplored the growth of executive power and stated his desire to follow legislative leadership. The speech itself was remarkable. For one thing, it was the longest inaugural speech in American history—longer than all four of Franklin D. Roosevelt's, with room left over for Lincoln's second inaugural. It was as though having been muzzled during the campaign, Harrison was determined not to relinquish the floor. Then, too, it was unusually bereft of ideas: the new president

*John Tyler.*

(THE GRANGER COLLECTION)

concentrated on Roman history and ignored American problems. Harrison did state his belief that no president

223

should serve more than a single term, and he asked for a constitutional amendment toward that end. "I give my aid to it by renewing the pledge heretofore given that under no circumstances will I consent to serve a second term."

Ironically, Harrison had no difficulty keeping this pledge. Three weeks after his inauguration he fell ill with pneumonia, and he died of the sickness on April 4. John Tyler, former Democrat and friend of Henry Clay, a man who understood politics and issues better than Harrison, became the first vice-president in history to succeed a dead president. And with this event, the politics of the 1840s replaced that of the 1830s.

At first it was believed that Clay would have an easy time influencing Tyler. But within weeks it was clear that Tyler would be his own man, and that his ideas differed greatly from those of Clay. In the first place, Tyler insisted that he was as much a president as if he had been elected in his own right; he dismissed Whig suggestions that he was really the acting president who should defer to the cabinet in all important matters. Tyler also refused to commit himself to a single term, and since Clay planned to run in 1844 this put the two men on a collision course. Finally, Tyler's past politics bothered both the Whigs and Democrats; the former considered him a renegade, and the latter viewed him as a turncoat. The president did reject many Jacksonian methods and many of the former president's programs, but he did not accept Clay's anti-Jacksonian measures.

Of all the figures of the 1830s, Tyler most resembled John C. Calhoun in his politics and programs; that is, Tyler was a southerner who, while serving in a national office, remained intent on pursuing policies that would benefit his section. Like Calhoun, Tyler had been willing to work with the Whigs during the Jacksonian era. But after Van Buren's defeat Calhoun returned to the Democratic party, and Tyler would probably have taken the same course if he had not become vice-president. When Tyler became president his ambitions soared, but he could not prevent the Whigs from nominating Clay in 1844; nor could Tyler return to the Democrats. As early as 1842 he was seriously considering a third alternative: the establishment of a new party, with himself at the head, which would reject the carefully worked out Clay programs, the Jacksonian Democracy of Van Buren, and the obvious southern nationalism of Calhoun. In other words, Tyler planned to present himself in 1844 as the new William Henry Harrison, avoiding issues and refusing to take strong stands.

Tyler's first step toward the creation of a third party was his opposition to Clay's legislative program of 1841. The president vetoed or otherwise opposed bills for a third Bank of the United States, a high tariff, and distribution of the Treasury surplus to the states. Then Tyler broke with his cabinet, an act planned by both sides and not unexpected. After Tyler's veto of the bank bill, all members except Webster offered their resignations, which were accepted. Webster, however, was in the midst of delicate negotiations with the British at the time of the veto, and did not want to leave the talks in mid-air. Furthermore, he liked being secretary of state, especially with a promising social season about to begin. When he learned of the resignations, Webster went to Tyler and asked, "Where am I to go, Mr. President?" Tyler, who would probably have preferred Webster to leave with the other cabinet members, said, "You must decide that for yourself, Mr. Webster," and the secretary replied, "If you leave it to me, Mr. President, I will stay where I am." Realizing that Webster would be a good ally in his coming conflicts with Clay, Tyler grasped his hand in friendship. "Now I will say to you that Henry Clay is a doomed man." The new cabinet members were anti-Clay Whigs; Postmaster General Charles Wickliffe, for example, was leader of the anti-Clay forces in Kentucky.

Tyler felt that his base in the South was as strong as could be expected, and knowing that he could not count on much more support from that region while Calhoun remained politically alive, he sought support in the North. The 1842 tariff, which he supported, raised rates, and this pleased northern businessmen while enraging Calhoun's nullifiers, who once again talked of leaving the Union. Tyler maintained contacts with northern farm leaders, Whig politicians, and businessmen, all the time trying to woo them from Clay. But this approach did not work; the Whig party was solidly for Clay, and Tyler could not hope to gain power by repeating old solutions to the old problems. But there were new issues to excite the voters. The seemingly secondary questions of foreign policy of the late 1830s were prime topics of discussion throughout the nation by 1842, and Tyler moved to capture the issues for himself. It was at this point that he revived the dormant question of Texas and the smoldering issue of Canada. And in so doing, he brought the major social movements of the time—slavery, abolitionism, westward expansion, the Young America movement, the anti-British sentiments of the Irish immigrants, and the growth of transportation—to the center of the political arena, where they quickly made the bank and tariff struggles appear antiquated.

By 1840 it seemed that the Canadian rebellion, which had almost destroyed Canada and led to an Anglo-American confrontation, was over. Those United States citizens and dissident Canadians who had raided Canada from "hunters' lodges" along the border were stilled, as were threats of retaliation from Ontario and Quebec. Then, in November 1840, a Canadian citizen named Alexander McLeod visited a saloon in New York State, where he bragged that he had killed an American on board the *Caroline,* an insurgent ship that had been seized by the Canadians in 1837 and burned. Memories of the *Caroline* affair were still fresh in upper New York; the residents hadn't forgotten that the incident had almost sparked a war. After the incident in the saloon McLeod was arrested and charged with murder. The British demanded his release, intimating that if he were executed it would mean war against the United States. As it happened, McLeod was acquitted, and the incident smoothed over. But it served to reopen the entire issue of British-American relations in the St. Lawrence Valley, and beyond that, the question of the border line in the Far West.

In 1841 many Americans felt hemmed in by the British Empire. The British presence in Canada was only one aspect of the problem. American settlers in Oregon and California constantly encountered British pioneers and fur trappers, and clashes between nationals of the two countries had already been reported. By 1841 it was also common knowledge that the British were supporting the independent nation of Texas, hoping to use it as a counterweight against the United States. Finally, the first of the wave of British visitors to the United States in the late 1830s and early 1840s had just published their travel accounts, and some Americans did not like what they read. They thought the praise condescending, the criticisms boorish. It was to deal with these problems of Anglo-American relations, as well as for reasons of personal pleasure, that Webster wanted to stay on as secretary of state.

Webster had no desire for war, especially since any territory acquired from Great Britain would not benefit New England. The belligerent Lord Palmerston had just been replaced at the British foreign office by Lord Aberdeen, who, like Webster, saw nothing to be gained from a war. Aberdeen dispatched Alexander Baring, Lord Ashburton, to Washington to negotiate a settlement of all outstanding differences. Ashburton had a personal reason for wanting peace with the United States. As a leading figure in London's most prestigious banking firm, Baring Brothers—a firm that had many investments in the United States and was constantly considering new ones—Ashburton naturally wanted to protect his firm's interests. They would hardly be safe if war should come. Ashburton and Webster were both willing to compromise on the major issues, and in August 1842 they concluded the Webster-Ashburton treaty, under the terms of which the Canadian-American boundary between the Rockies and the Atlantic was agreed upon, and London made a carefully worded "apology" for the *Caroline* affair. But the treaty said nothing of the boundary between the Rockies and the Pacific, and this issue remained to provide politicians with ammunition for the coming national elections.

By 1843 Tyler realized that he could not expect to receive much support from Whigs and so he began to woo Democrats, in particular the Calhoun wing of the party. He believed that if he could become the favorite of that faction he might win its support in 1844. In such a situation Van Buren would be obliged to leave the party he had once headed, and Tyler could enter the field at the vanguard of a unified southern Democracy. With this in mind, Tyler formulated his southern strategy, the key to which would be Texas. Should Texas be admitted to the Union, it would add one of the finest cotton-growing areas in the world to the nation, help balance the expanding industry of the North, and fortify southern control of the Democratic party. Moreover, since it was widely believed that Texas might be divided into no less than three states, its admission would mean six additional senators to vote with the South on economic questions like the tariff and bank and to help fight the coming battle with northern abolitionists. For Tyler, Texas was the key not only to the nation's destiny, but to his chances of winning a presidential term of his own.

Soon after concluding his work on the treaty with Britain, Webster left the cabinet and was replaced by Abel Upshur of Virginia, a clever politician whose task it would be to annex Texas without stirring up Northern opposition. Upshur did his job well, and for a time it seemed annexation might be accomplished without provoking a national debate. Although northern abolitionists and some congressmen (including John Quincy Adams) opposed the admission of a new slave area, the recent clash with Britain over the Canadian boundary had reawakened expansionist feelings in the North. Westerners and southerners had long desired annexation, and by 1843 the time appeared ripe. Upshur entered into secret negotiations with Isaac Van Zandt, the Texas emmissary to Washington, and by early February 1844 the Texas annexation treaty was ready for submission to the Senate. At the time only a few abolitionist congressmen considered the slavery issue of major importance.

On February 28 Tyler and Upshur were cruising aboard the U.S.S. *Princeton* when a cannon exploded, killing the secretary of state. It was a freakish accident and one with momentous political significance, for a week later Tyler sealed his union with the southern Democrats by nominating Calhoun as Upshur's replacement.

On two previous occasions Tyler had attempted to place Calhoun in the cabinet, and the South Carolinian had refused the offers. To accept would have been to tacitly support Tyler's bid for the presidency in 1844, and Calhoun had his own ambitions for that year. But Van Buren defeated Calhoun's bids to win the support of New York and Massachusetts Democrats, and in 1843 the Van Buren forces, and not the Calhounites, controlled the House caucus. Calhoun realized that his hopes for the presidency were thwarted and he accepted the cabinet post, thereby implying a willingness to use Tyler to stop Van Buren. His objective was to forge a South-West alliance against the North. According to his plan, the South would support western desires for Oregon, and in return western congressmen would vote for the annexation of Texas. In this way Calhoun broadened Upshur's limited objective of Texas annexation into a full-fledged endorsement of Manifest Destiny.

Furthermore, while Upshur had presented annexation as only a political question, desirable since it would increase the size of the nation as a whole, Calhoun thought it had moral overtones as well. He wanted Texas in the Union as much to fortify southern power within the nation as to benefit the nation itself. Finally, Upshur had carefully avoided becoming identified with one faction or another, while Calhoun was the embodiment of the South in all its ramifications. His selection as secretary of state and all that it implied combined with his rhetoric and politics to make slavery, and not annexation, the primary question in the Texas treaty. During the debates on the subject, Calhoun vigorously defended the "peculiar institution" and the rights of the South, thus provoking northern responses and the inevitable polarization that followed. In the end the Senate passed the treaty and Texas became part of the nation, but not before Calhoun had provided an important issue for the election of 1844 and the politics of the decade and a half that followed.

Henry Clay had begun his campaign for the presidency in 1844, shortly after the 1840 election. His break with Tyler only served to increase his activity and determination. In 1844 there was no doubt that he was the strong-

man of the Whig party. He came to the Baltimore convention of late April with the support of more than two
hundred Whig newspapers and Whig conventions in seventeen states. Feeble attempts by Webster, Scott, and others
were quickly brushed aside, as Clay won the nomination
with near-unanimous support.

The situation was far more complicated in the Democratic party. By 1844 Tyler had abandoned his hopes of
establishing a third party, and he expected to receive the
Democratic nomination. Now that Calhoun was out of the
race, the possibility of his taking leadership of the southern
Democrats was seriously considered. But there were others
hoping for Calhoun's mantle and southern support. Lewis
Cass of Michigan and Richard Johnson of Kentucky, both
moderates, appealed to the same constituencies as did Tyler,
and so did James Buchanan of Pennsylvania, widely heralded as a compromise candidate. In the first months of
1844 the southern Democrats were divided between these
men and other, less important hopefuls.

Meanwhile, Van Buren worked diligently to organize
his wing of the party. Since he had no serious rivals on the
left, he was free to seek support among the party's moderates. Thus, in 1843 and 1844, it appeared that Van Buren
was swinging to the middle so as to obtain convention votes
and possibly the election in November. If he were to succeed, the Democrats would have to ignore the question of
slavery, and possibly that of Texas itself. Only in this way
could the party unify and Van Buren return to the White
House.

Henry Clay assumed that Van Buren would be the

Democratic nominee; indeed all signs indicated that he would sweep the field at the Baltimore convention in May. But unlike Van Buren, Clay was convinced the Democrats were so divided that no candidate of theirs could win in November. Because of this, Clay began thinking of his problems as president before actually winning the election. Above all, he wanted to be a peace president, so that he would be able to carry out his domestic programs. He believed that annexation of Texas would lead to war with Mexico. On April 27, 1844, he published a letter opposing annexation, which he claimed was supported only by politicians, New York owners of Texas bonds, and southern fanatics. The nation did not need a war, he said, but rather "union, peace, and patience." He hoped the United States would remain on good terms with Texas, Canada, and Mexico, all of which were destined to share the continent with the United States. Since Van Buren was of the same mind, Clay hoped to keep the Texas question out of 1844 presidential politics.

Van Buren also published a letter, on April 27, in which he said substantially the same things as Clay. But Van Buren had not yet won the Democratic nomination, and unlike Clay, he had to worry about party unity. Therefore, he hedged somewhat on the issue. In his letter he claimed to oppose annexation, but said he would favor it if Mexico recognized Texan independence and American public opinion supported such a policy. In this way, the Whig candidate and the man expected to win the Democratic nomination seemingly agreed to remain quiet on the most pressing issue of the day.

233

Neither Clay nor Van Buren reckoned on John Calhoun. Soon after the two letters were published Calhoun sent a note to Sir Richard Packenham, the British envoy in Washington. In the note, which was released to the public, Calhoun replied to a British inquiry as to American interest in abolishing slavery throughout the world. Calhoun declared that wherever the Negro had been freed he had fallen to barbarism, and claimed that American Negro slaves were better off than black people anywhere else in the world. "What is called slavery is in reality a political institution, essential to the peace, safety, and prosperity of those States of the Union in which it exists." He then went on to assert that the annexation of Texas was inextricably linked to the expansion of slavery.

Whether by design or not, Calhoun made it impossible for the Democrats to ignore Texas and slavery at their convention. Van Buren's carefully organized program to woo the South collapsed, since that section would have nothing to do with a man who in the past had been identified with antislavery sentiment, and whose maneuverings were not taken seriously. Jackson, who had at first supported Van Buren, announced himself in favor of annexing Texas and then, just before the convention met, called for the nomination of a Democrat who would bring Texas into the Union. Van Buren led on early balloting, but the party had previously agreed that a candidate would have to receive two thirds of the votes to become the nominee, and Van Buren fell far short of that number. Boomlets for other candidates appeared and then fizzled. Then, on the ninth ballot, James K. Polk of Tennessee began to receive a large number of votes. By the time the delegates finished switching their ballots, he had won the necessary two thirds, and the Democrats had nominated the first dark-horse candidate in history.

Polk was by no means unknown; Jackson had supported him for the vice-presidency in 1840, and Polk had already won the name "Young Hickory." As governor, congressman, and speaker of the House he had supported all the major Democratic programs set forth by Jackson and later by Van Buren. On the other hand, he favored annexation, although he was not identified with the Calhoun wing of the party. He was, in essence, the perfect man to bring about whatever party unity was possible in 1844.

The "Tylerites" also met in Baltimore, in a badly attended and dispirited convention. Tyler was nominated without opposition, but it was clear that the designation was not worth much, and so the president withdrew from the race, his political plans of the past four years having failed.

Polk's nomination meant that the Democrats would favor annexation and, by implication, the spread of slavery, while Clay and the Whigs would try to straddle the fence on both issues. Like Tyler, Clay had planned long and carefully for the 1844 elections, certain he could defeat Van Buren and a divided Democracy. Polk, and unity among the Democrats, were another matter, and Clay knew he was in for trouble.

Meanwhile, the moribund Liberty party received a new lease on life. Since annexation and slavery were to be the major issues of the campaign, and since neither major party opposed them, there was no place for antislavery forces in the North and West to go but to the third party. In 1844, the Liberty party nominated James Birney and mounted a major campaign in New England and other antislavery centers.

Clay's campaign was uninspired and poorly handled. As befitted his reputation as a cautious man and compromiser, Clay attempted to skirt the issues, and at the same time moved slowly to Van Buren's preconvention position on Texas; he would accept annexation if and when it appeared feasible. Clay's other ideas, calling for a sound currency and internal improvements, appeared somewhat old-fashioned, and even the candidate himself realized it would be difficult to win the election of 1844 with the programs of 1836. In attempting to take the middle ground, Clay failed to win votes in either the North or the South, and he alienated people in both sections. Polk, on the other hand, thought that the United States was destined to control the entire West, not only Texas. Whether this included Canada was not made clear, but Polk did support a platform that called for the "reoccupation of Oregon." His slogan, "Fifty-four forty or Fight," referred to the United States' boundary demands in the Far North and to his intent should they be rebuffed by the British. To this Polk wedded his pledge to annex Texas if elected. Finally, Polk continually referred to his past connections with Jacksonian Democracy, and Jackson spoke out in favor of him during the campaign.

In this way, Polk transformed the Jacksonian Democracy of the 1830s into the party of Manifest Destiny in the mid-1840s, and he did so by appealing to the same

236

constituency as had his mentor. Workers in the North were promised the same kind of domestic programs offered by Jackson and Van Buren, and to these was added Oregon, the symbol of the Irish laborers' anti-British sentiments. Southern planters were assured that there would be no new Bank of the United States, and were promised Texas. Thus, the party of reform became the party of expansion, not because it led the public, but because it was able to respond to the new issues of the time.

Polk was only partially successful in his campaign. He won the election by a narrow margin, receiving only 38,000 more votes than Clay. In the electoral college he obtained 170 votes to Clay's 105. Polk divided the northern states with his opponent but won solidly in the South, thus becoming indebted to that section. By appearing to be the southern candidate and accepting Calhoun's expansionist politics, Polk signaled a victory for the South Carolinian over Jacksonian ideas, but even Jackson himself seemed content with the outcome.

The real surprise of the election was Birney's winning of more than 62,000 votes, almost half of which were concentrated in New York and Massachusetts. Indeed, it may be said that the Birney candidacy cost Clay the election, since without Birney antislavery voters would probably have cast their ballots for the Whig. As early as 1844 it seemed that a union of Clay's economic programs with the antislavery votes of the Liberty party might result in an effective counterweight to the pro-slavery Democrats. But this union would not be effected for another sixteen years, and in the interim the South would remain in control of national affairs. In politics and in other fields, the reformers showed a lack of organizing ability, a penchant for factionalism, and an unwillingness to accept compromise. Slavery and abolitionism were politicized in 1844, but not by one of the reformers; rather, it was the work of John Calhoun, and in that year he won a signal victory for his cause.

# 11/ONWARD TO MEXICO

DURING THE 1844 ELECTION CAMPAIGN, MEXICAN newspapers warned America that the annexation of Texas would be a signal for war. Clay and Van Buren both believed that if Polk were elected annexation would soon follow and Mexico would fulfill its pledge. Birney and other abolitionists asked whether Americans were prepared to die for Texas and slavery. During the campaign Polk promised the "reoccupation of Oregon and the reannexation of Mexico," implying a willingness to fight not only Mexico, but Britain. It would appear clear, then, that Polk's election was in fact a mandate to risk war. But what would be the shape of such a war, and which of America's two continental rivals would be the co-belligerent? This was not clear when Polk entered office; nor were most Americans aware of the problems that might arise from a conflict over Texas or Oregon. In the end the Polk administration was more successful in its war than had been considered possible in 1845, but that success contained the seeds of future, far graver problems than those of Texas and Oregon.

239

Americans of the 1840s had two attitudes toward the abstract idea of war. They had fought well in the colonial and early national struggles, but each war had produced a vocal antiwar group that condemned the incumbent government. During the American Revolution approximately one third of the population opposed the Continental Congress, and the quasi-wars and threats of war during the Adams and Jefferson administrations divided the nation. Toward the end of the War of 1812 an influential group of New Englanders was even prepared to secede from the Union. Indeed, every American war witnessed the emergence of a usually small, but vigorous, antiwar faction.

These protests cannot be categorized, for each war had its own special circumstances, but in most cases, the leaders of dissent could be found in the intellectual community, especially among writers and artists. They were vocal—often eloquent—spoke in moralistic terms, and had access to newspapers and magazines, all of which magnified their influence beyond their numbers. Prior to the Mexican War, many of them could be found in the American Peace Society, which was devoted to the prevention of war at all costs, and many of those influential in the abolitionist and women's rights movements joined the Society and allied groups. Thomas Grimké and his feminist kin were members; Grimké said in 1832, "Cost what it may, we will return good for evil." William Lloyd Garrison considered himself a peace advocate, saying in 1837:

If a nation may not redress its wrongs by physical force—if it may not repel or punish a foreign enemy who comes to plunder, enslave or murder its inhabitants—then it may not resort to arms to quell an insurrection, or send to prison or suspend upon a gibbet any transgressors upon its soil . . . . In no case can physical resistance be allowable, either in an individual or collective capacity . . . .

To which Angelina Grimké added:

If I have no right to *resist evil* myself, I have no right to call upon another to resist it for me, and if I *must not* call upon the Magistrate to redress my grievances, if I have no right to do so, then he can have no right to render me any such aid.

In 1838 Garrison, the Grimkés, Adin Ballou, Bronson Alcott, and other reformers organized the New England Non-Resistance Society. Its message was clear and forthright.

We register our testimony, not only against all wars, whether offensive or defensive, but all preparations for war; against every naval ship, every arsenal, every fortification; against the militia system and a standing army; against all military chieftains and soldiers; against any monuments commemorative of victory over a fallen foe, all trophies won in battle, all celebrations in honor of military or naval exploits; against all appropriations for the defense of a nation by force of arms, on the part of any legislative body; against every edict of government requiring of its subjects military service.

Yet many of those who joined the Non-Resistance Society favored the use of any and all means, including violence, to free the slaves. Even in 1838 Garrison did not rule out violence to accomplish such an end. In the late 1840s he urged armed insurrection against slaveholders, and later on he would praise John Brown, the most violent of the abolitionists. In 1856 Garrison would write, in the

*Liberator,* that while it was all well and good to foment war in Kansas, where free farmers clashed with slaveholders, the same should be done in the South. "If every border ruffian invading Kansas deserves to be shot, much more does every slaveholder, by the same rule; for the former is guilty only of attempting political subjugation to his will, while the latter is the destroyer of human rights, and there is none to deliver. Who will go for arming our slave population?" Joshua Giddings, another peace advocate of the mid-1840s, added that he looked forward to the day when the slaves would revolt, "when the torch of the incendiary shall light up the towns and cities of the South, and blot out the last vestiges of slavery."

Some peace crusaders remained consistent in their beliefs, condemning violence for the sake of abolition as much as violence for Manifest Destiny; Adin Ballou, for example, criticized Garrison's approval of armed resistance to slavery. But most peace crusaders of the 1840s were not so much opposed to war as they were to those wars and conflicts they didn't like. Garrison fought bitterly against a war with Mexico. Such moral stands were to be expected of those who drank deeply from Transcendentalist wells, for the doctrine preached the kind of extreme individualism that made them possible. Some pacifists recognized this. Thomas Wentworth Higginson, who opposed the Mexican War on moral grounds and then approved of slave insurrections on the same basis, was chided for his apparent hypocrisy. His answer was simple and direct: "I am a Non-Resistant, but not a fool."

Yet Polk was correct in believing that the majority

242

of Americans approved taking risks of war to annex Texas, and outgoing President Tyler agreed. In the period between the election and Polk's inauguration, Tyler asked Congress to approve annexation by joint resolution. By a vote in the House of 120 to 98, and 27 to 25 in the Senate, Texas was invited into the Union. The closeness of the vote was due to three factors. Some legislators believed Texas should be annexed through treaty, others wanted Polk to receive the credit for annexation, and a third group was totally opposed to annexation. They were the ones who would condemn the Mexican War when it came.

Polk realized that Mexico would not passively submit to the annexation, for that country still had not recognized the independent Texan government, and it considered Texas part of Mexico. Mexican President José Herrera had told his Congress that he would ask for a declaration of war against the United States as soon as annexation was concluded, or at least when American troops "invaded" Texas. Not wanting to fight Mexico and Britain simultaneously, Polk immediately set about concluding an acceptable treaty with Britain regarding the Oregon boundary.

The Oregon question was complicated by domestic considerations in America, the impending conflict with Mexico, and Britain's awareness of both. Polk insisted that the entire region bounded on the north by the parallel of 54° 40′ belonged to the United States; the British envoy in America, Richard Packenham, observed that by treaty the two nations had agreed to joint occupancy of the territory, and his government would not consider a change. Packenham knew that Polk wanted both Oregon and Mexi-

243

*James K. Polk.*

244

can lands in California, but that Calhoun's supporters in the Democratic party opposed this, since these areas were obviously unsuited for cotton and slavery. To break the deadlock Polk offered a compromise; he would divide Oregon along the forty-ninth parallel and in this way extend the Webster-Ashburton line to the Pacific.

Since Great Britain had little to gain from a quick settlement, Packenham rejected Polk's overture, and the American president in turn stiffened his attitude. In a message to Congress he proclaimed what came to be known as the "Polk Doctrine." He declared that "the people of this continent alone have the right to decide their own destiny." The president rejected any European attempt to play "balance of power" politics on the North American continent. Furthermore, if any European nation wanted to establish a new colony in America it would first have to obtain the consent of the United States. In this way, Polk indicated not only his willingness to fight for Oregon, but his wholehearted acceptance of Manifest Destiny.

The president's belligerent tone was not motivated by shortsighted jingoism, but rather by an understanding of British politics. It was well known that Prime Minister Robert Peel's Tories had little interest in Oregon, where only opposition Whigs had investments. Lord Aberdeen, the foreign secretary, thought Oregon a "pine swamp," not worth the effort and expense of a war with a nation that had become a major customer for British goods. Furthermore, Peel had domestic problems; his recent announcement of a revamping of the tariff had split his own party, and he could not risk further trouble. Opposition leader

245

Lord Palmerston warned Peel that retreat in Oregon would disgrace the Union Jack, and, indeed, the debate on Oregon and the tariff caused the ministry to fall on December 5, 1845. Polk watched London politics with great interest, for if Palmerston came to power it would mean war with Britain, while a return of Peel would mean conciliation and peace. On December 20, 1845, the parliamentary crisis ended, with a Peel victory. Now negotiations between Great Britain and the United States were initiated, and half a year later a treaty was signed establishing the boundary at the forty-ninth parallel with certain minor exceptions. But even before the treaty was signed, Polk shifted his attention to Mexico. By then, too, his horizon had widened. Now he was interested not only in bringing Texas into the Union but also in securing California, where in 1845 anti-Mexican and pro-American revolutions had taken place.

Polk took limited risks in settling the Oregon boundary dispute; even if war should erupt there, the entire Royal Navy would be unable to supply an army in the isolated Oregon region, and there was certain to be opposition to the war in Britain. The case was different in Mexico. Although internally divided and politically weak, the Mexicans were united in their hatred of the United States. The Texas annexation rankled, and Texas' claim that its southern boundary was the Rio Grande angered Mexico City, which insisted that the Nueces, farther to the north, was the true boundary. Furthermore, the Mexican army seemed to be the strongest military force in the hemisphere. It consisted of 32,000 men, trained by European instructors and conversant with the most modern tactics. In contrast, the American army had little more than 7,000 men, and it was ragged by Mexican standards. Also, in case of war Mexico's lines of supply would be much shorter than those of the United States, and her army would be fighting in familiar terrain. Lastly, in mid-1845 it appeared the United States might still become embroiled in a war with Britain. With all these considerations in mind, Polk acted cautiously.

In September 1845, while still struggling with the Oregon question, Polk was informed by his agent in Mexico City, William Parrot, that President Herrera might be willing to sell California to the United States. After conferring with his cabinet, Polk sent John Slidell of New Orleans to Mexico City to bargain with Herrera. Slidell was authorized to offer $5 million for New Mexico and $25 million for California on condition that Herrera would accept the Rio Grande boundary of Texas. If this were done, the United States would also assume the claims of American nationals against Mexico. Slidell's mission was secret, for negotiations might embarrass Herrera.

Polk also used undercover agents to obtain his ends. He knew that the American consul at Monterey, Thomas Larkin, was eager to start a revolt that would end with California's admission to the Union. The president sent a series of letters to Larkin, in which he indicated that he would support a Californian request for annexation, "whenever this can be done, without affording Mexico a cause of complaint."

While Larkin organized his forces, Polk opened a

*Antonio López de Santa Anna (left) and Winfield Scott.*
(CULVER PICTURES, INC.)

"third front" in his maneuverings. He contacted John Frémont and helped him to establish a small military force that camped near Sutter's fort in Sacramento. After clashing with Mexican authorities (and raising the American flag in defiance of them), Frémont withdrew to Oregon, where he awaited future developments and orders from Washington.

The Slidell mission failed. News of his coming preceded him, and the envoy was greeted by a burst of anti-American demonstrations. Fearful of public opinion, Herrera refused to see him, observing that in any case Slidell was not an official American agent, since his appointment had not been ratified by the American Senate. Slidell was humiliated and angry, but he did not leave the

248

capital. Instead, he sent a message to Polk. "Be assured that nothing is to be done with these people, until they have been chastised." He considered the Mexicans "ignorant Indians, debased by three centuries of worse than colonial vassalage." He also told Polk that the Mexican army was overrated. Most soldiers were hill Indians, who had been forced to enlist and were poor in spirit and training.

Herrera was overthrown by a coup on December 31, and replaced by General Mariano Paredes, who was strongly anti-American and eager for war. Paredes immediately reaffirmed Mexico's claims to all of Texas. He professed not to be afraid of the Americans, who, he said, had been roundly defeated by a small British army in the War of 1812, and who in any case had an army inferior to the Mexican force. Paredes also had reason to believe Britain and France would join him in a war against the United States, so as to assure a balance of power in North America.

The Slidell letters and the Mexico coup convinced Polk that war could not be averted, and that it could only benefit the United States. The president sent a dispatch to General Zachary Taylor, ordering him to take his army into the disputed land between the Nueces and the Rio Grande. The wording of one of his messages was guarded, but its meaning clear. "It is not designed in our present relations with Mexico that you should treat her as an enemy; but, should she assume that character by a declaration of war, or any open act of hostility towards us, you will not act merely on the defensive, if your relative means enable you to do otherwise."

On April 11, 1846, a detachment of Mexican troops

arrived at Matamoros, across the Rio Grande from Taylor's army. More arrived the following week, and by April 24 General Mariano Arista had 5,700 men under his command against Taylor's 4,000. On that day Arista sent a detachment across the river into the disputed territory. Taylor ordered his force to meet them the next morning. Arista was obviously hoping for a confrontation, and Taylor was willing to oblige. The two clashed; men on both sides were killed and wounded.

The president learned of the battle on the night of May 9, soon after leaving a cabinet meeting devoted to the Mexican issue. Polk wanted war, but it had been difficult to find a provocation sufficiently serious to merit one. The previous evening Polk had decided to ask for a declaration of war based on Mexico's refusal to pay debts owed American citizens. It was a lame reason, but the best the president could find. Thus, he was delighted to learn of the Arista-Taylor clash. Polk redrafted his war message, which was delivered the following day. "After repeated menaces," he said, "Mexico has passed the boundary of the United States, has invaded our territory and shed American blood upon American soil. . . . As war exists, and, notwithstanding all our efforts to avoid it, exists by act of Mexico itself, we are called upon by every consideration of duty and patriotism to vindicate with decision the honor, the rights, and the interests of our country."

Two days later the war resolution passed the House by a vote of 174 to 14, and the Senate by 40 to 2. The Democrats were unanimously in favor of the war, while the Whigs were split on the issue. This division was a por-

tent of the antiwar sentiment that appeared shortly thereafter.

The war was popular in much of the United States.
"Nine-tenths of our people would rather have a little fighting than not," claimed the New York *Morning News.* The
Richmond *Enquirer* thought the public wanted "a full and
thorough chastisement of Mexican arrogance and folly,"
while the New Orleans *Commercial Bulletin* declared,
"The United States have borne more insult, abuse, insolence
and injury from Mexico, than one nation ever before endured from another . . . . There is now left no alternative
but to extort by arms the respect and justice which Mexico
refuses to any treatment less harsh." Pro-war parades and
demonstrations were held in all parts of the country, but
the belligerency fever was higher in the South than elsewhere. "Onward to Mexico!" became the cry of the hawks
of 1846.

The opposition was even more vocal, especially in the
early days of the war. Congressman Abraham Lincoln demanded that Polk say exactly where on American soil
American blood had been shed. The *National Intelligencer,*
a Whig newspaper, editorialized, "We presume that our
President and his Cabinet are by this time convinced that
they have forfeited the public confidence—the confidence,
that is, of their own party; that of the other they never
possessed." Professor William Kent of Harvard, a leader
in the campus antiwar protests, thought Polk an incom-
petent and believed it was "demoniacal" to make war on
an innocent people. The Whig *Almanac* claimed certain
Democratic politicians were profiting from the war, which

explained their support. Senator Thomas Corwin, one of the most vehement opponents of the conflict, asked:

If there were a Texan population on the east bank of the Rio Grande, why did not General Taylor hear something of those Texans hailing the advent of the American army, coming to protect them from the ravages of the Mexicans, and the more murderous onslaughts on the neighboring savages? Do you hear anything of that? No! On the contrary, the population fled at the approach of your army. In God's name, I wish to know if it has come to this, that when an American army goes to protect American citizens on American territory, they flee from it as from the most barbarous enemy?

Then Corwin went on to make his most extreme statement. Mexicans might well ask, he said, "Have you not room in your own country to bury your dead men? If they come into mine, we will greet you, with bloody hands, and welcome you to hospitable graves." In response, Stephen Douglas of Illinois said: "America wants no friends, acknowledges the fidelity of no citizen, who, after war is declared, condemns the justice of her cause or sympathizes with the enemy. All such are traitors in their hearts; and would to God that they would commit such overt acts for which they could be dealt with according to their deserts." Corwin's Ohio constituents were even more harsh; effigies of the senator were burned throughout the state, and over the "body," often dressed in a Mexican uniform, were such lines as:

Old Tom Corwin is dead and here he lies;
Nobody's sorry and nobody cries;
Where he's gone and how he fares,
Nobody knows and nobody cares.

252

The antiwar forces had their poet, James Russell Lowell, who firmly believed the pro-war forces wanted California for slavery. He wrote:

> They jest want this Californy
> So's to lug new slave-states in
> To abuse ye, and to scorn ye,
> And to plunder ye like sin.

In even blunter words, he said:

> Ez fer war, I call it murder—
> There you hev it plain an' flat;
> I don't want to go no furder
> Than my Testyment fer that;
> God hez sed so plump an' fairly,
> It's ez long ez it is broad,
> An' you've gut to git up airly
> Ef you want to take in God.

Joshua Giddings, a strongly abolitionist antiwar Whig from Ohio who had earned a reputation as a leading reformer in the House, made the most telling speeches against the war.

I regard it as having been put forth to divert public attention from the outrage committed by the President upon our own Constitution, and the exercise of usurped powers, of which he had been guilty in ordering our army to invade a country with which we are at peace, and of provoking and bringing on this war . . . . It is a war of aggression and conquest. Its prosecution will be but an increase of our national guilt. The death of every victim who falls during its progress, will add to the already fearful responsibility of those who, from ambitious motives, have brought this curse upon our nation . . . . But, Sir, I regard this war as but one scene in the drama now being enacted by this administration. Our government is undergoing a revolution no less marked than was that of France in 1792. As yet, it has not been characterized by that amount of bloodshed and cruelty which distinguished the change of government in France. When the Executive and Congress openly and avowedly took upon themselves the responsibility of extending and perpetuating slavery by the annexation of Texas, and by the total overthrow and subversion of the Constitution, and that too, by the aid of northern votes, my confidence in the stability of our institutions was shaken, destroyed. I had hoped that the free States might be aroused in time to save our Union from final overthrow; but that hope has been torn from me.

John Quincy Adams believed the nation might not survive the war, as did others who participated in the antiwar movement. In a July 4 address Charles Sumner of Massachusetts said he thought revolt was imminent: "Blood! Blood! is on the hands of representatives from Boston. Not all great Neptune's ocean can wash them clean." Theodore Parker, speaking that spring, professed not to be surprised that the war had so much support among northern congressmen.

They are no better than southern representatives, scarcely less in favor of slavery and not half so open. They say, Let the North make money and you may do what you please with the nation . . . for though we are descended from the Puritans we have but one article in our creed we never flinch from following, and that is—to make money, honestly if we can, if not, as we can! . . . How tamely the people yield their necks—and say, "Take our sons for the war —we care not, right or wrong."

Henry Thoreau was willing to help start a revolution. "When a sixth of the population of a nation which was undertaken to be a refuge of liberty are slaves, and a whole

*The storming of Chapultepec during the Mexican War.*

(THE GRANGER COLLECTION)

country is unjustly overrun and conquered by our foreign army and subjected to military law, I think it not too soon for honest men to rebel and revolutionize." Thoreau refused to pay that portion of his taxes he felt would help the war effort, and so went to jail. "My friend Mr, Thoreau has gone to jail rather than pay his tax," wrote Emerson. "On him they could not calculate." When Emerson asked Thoreau what he was doing in jail, Thoreau responded by asking his old friend what he was doing outside of jail at such a time.

The antiwar movement of 1846 was not ended by counterarguments and pro-war demonstrations, although there were many of these. Nor was it ended by repression on the part of the government, although such repression was considered. Rather, the antiwar forces were stilled and alienated from potential supporters by a quick, decisive victory in the field.

The United States did not lose a major engagement in the war, but this was due more to Mexican ineptness than to the skill or power of the American army. In the mid-nineteenth century diplomats and generals assumed that wars would end when the enemy's capital had been taken. Thus, the eyes of the United States were on Mexico City, and in turn some Mexican generals hoped to take their troops to Washington. But since Mexico was always on the defensive, it seemed clear that the war would end when Zachary Taylor marched into Mexico City. However, the drive to the capital proved less important than events in the West, where several American armies fought to conquer New Mexico and California. Polk had no desire to annex Mexico, but the Far West was another matter. It might be said that the American objective in the war was California and the Southwest, and the road to annexation led to Mexico City.

Taylor marched to Palo Alto in early May and defeated the enemy garrison in that town. From there he went to Resaca de la Palma, where he crushed a superior Mexican force. He then followed a coastal route and took Matamoros in mid-month. Within two weeks Taylor had established a reputation as a military genius; "Old Rough and Ready" was clearly to be a major hero of the war.

At the same time, the Paredes government began to totter. Realizing this, the United States leaders contacted exiled General Antonio López de Santa Anna and offered to back him in a coup if he would then accept a dictated peace. Santa Anna had long hated the United States, but Washington believed his pledge of cooperation. Santa Anna landed in Mexico in August and within a month was in control at the capital. But he reneged on his promise, rallied the army, and prepared to meet the United States army on the battlefield.

Had Taylor continued to march south he might have ended the war in a few months. But the American army was ragged, enlistments were running out, and Taylor was reluctant to commit his men to battle. After sharp prodding by Polk, he marched to Monterrey and took the city on September 23, 1846. And there he remained, organizing his army and preparing himself for future glories. One of these was the presidency in 1848.

Disgusted by Taylor's inactivity, Polk ordered General

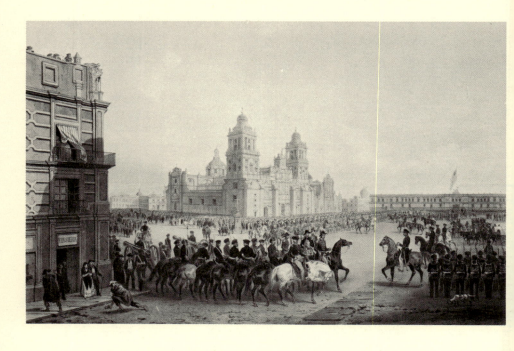

*General Winfield Scott's army entering Mexico City.*
(THE GRANGER COLLECTION)

Winfield Scott to organize an expeditionary force in New Orleans and then take it to Veracruz. He was to assume command of the Mexican expedition; henceforth Taylor would be his subordinate. Before this could happen, however, Taylor marched on Buena Vista, where on February 23, 1847, two days after Scott's Veracruz landing, he defeated a larger Mexican force. This feat made the replacement of Taylor impossible, and thereafter the two generals were co-partners in theory if not in fact.

Like Taylor, Scott had political ambitions, and he realized that the conqueror of Mexico would probably be the next president. For the next two months Scott and

Taylor raced each other to Mexico City, winning regular victories over the Mexicans in the process.

A similar situation developed in California. As soon as the American colony in the Sacramento Valley learned that war had been declared it rose in revolt. By mid-June 1846 the Americans had established an independent republic of California, adopting a flag featuring a grizzly bear and a star. Frémont marched down from Oregon to join the rebels and within a short time he was the leader of the republic. On July 2 Commodore John Sloat arrived at the head of an American flotilla, and five days later he proclaimed California to be part of the United States. Other naval detachments seized the coastal ports and joined with the Bear Flag rebels, who by then had forgotten about independence and accepted annexation. Commodore Robert Stockton arrived in California in late July to relieve Sloat and take command. Stockton met with Frémont, whom he accepted as a subordinate. According to the agreement, Frémont became civil governor of California while Stockton concentrated on naval affairs.

As the Californians were raising the Bear Flag, Colonel Stephen W. Kearny prepared to leave Fort Leavenworth, Kansas, for a march on Santa Fe. He led his column of 1,700 men into the city on August 18 and proclaimed all of New Mexico part of the United States. Then, after sending a detachment southward to join Taylor, he marched to California, where he arrived early in 1847.

Since both men claimed command of the territory, Kearny immediately clashed with Stockton. The commodore suspended Kearny from command and added the territory

259

under his control to California so as to assure Frémont's loyalty. But Kearny refused to accept Stockton's authority and set up a temporary capital of his own. The two forces clashed, and in one encounter Kearny captured Frémont and sent him back to Washington as his prisoner. A subsequent court-martial found Frémont guilty of insubordination, mutiny, disobedience, and prejudicial conduct, and he was sentenced to dismissal from the army. Polk rescinded the sentence, but Frémont left the army anyway; like Taylor and Scott, he hoped for a political career.

In September 1847 Scott and Taylor neared Mexico City. Traveling with Scott was Nicholas Trist, a State Department clerk to whom Polk had entrusted the business of negotiating a peace treaty with Santa Anna. Neither Trist nor Scott was willing to admit the authority of the other, and the two men fought continuously over the conduct of the war and the nature of the peace. This situation was further complicated when Polk, annoyed with Trist's unwillingness to obey orders, suspended his commission. Trist ignored this order, as he did many others, and continued on with Scott. The general took Chapultepec, and on September 14 raised the United States flag in Mexico City.

The American army found the capital in shambles. Santa Anna had fled, and a new provisional government, under President Pedro Anaya, would not take office until November 11. Elevated to power through Trist's connivance and in spite of Polk's repeated statements to the effect that Trist had no authority, Anaya was more than willing to accept a peace treaty, and one was concluded. Under the terms of the Treaty of Guadalupe Hidalgo,

Mexico accepted the Rio Grande boundary and ceded New Mexico and California to the United States; in return the United States agreed to pay Mexico $15 million and to assume all debts owed American citizens by Mexico. The treaty was ratified by a confused Senate in March 1848. In the words of businessman Philip Hone, a strong antiwar Whig, the treaty was "negotiated by an unauthorized agent, with an unacknowledged government, submitted by an accidental President to a dissatisfied Senate, and had, notwithstanding these objections in form, been confirmed. . . ."

The Mexican War was not a costly expedition. Military expenditures were less than $98 million, and fewer than 1,800 American troops were lost in battle. The nation had obtained its glory and had fulfilled most of the hopes of the advocates of Manifest Destiny. There were those, of course, who wanted still more. The New York *Evening Post,* a Democratic paper, said:

Now we ask, whether any man can coolly contemplate the idea of recalling our troops from the territory we at present occupy . . . and . . . resign this beautiful country to the custody of the ignorant cowards and profligate ruffians who have ruled it for the last twenty-five years? Why, humanity cries out against it. Civilization and Christianity protests against this reflux of the tide of barbarism and anarchy.

By this time the antiwar protesters were silent, as the nation celebrated its victory. Almost all the politicians who had voted against the war were either defeated in their next election or resigned voluntarily. Lincoln and Corwin left Congress, as did others of their group, while pro-war Democrats like Douglas were not only vindicated, but obtained national reputations. Without assigning praise or blame to either camp, and avoiding moralizations, one might conclude that the antiwar protesters of the Mexican War era were discredited not for a lack of zeal or argumentation, but because they had opposed a war in which the United States triumphed without much difficulty or cost. Had the war lasted longer, or had the Americans suffered setbacks, Corwin and Lincoln would have appeared prophets. As it was, they had joined the crusade at the wrong time and in the wrong way, and so suffered defeat. In politics, morality is debatable, but what is not, is being on the winning side in a war.

The nation received an added "bonus" as a result of the war; it had trained an army, many of whose members would fight in the Civil War. Ulysses S. Grant and William T. Sherman were lieutenants in the Mexican War, as were George McClellan, George Meade, Joseph Hooker, and John Pope, all of whom would command important Union armies a decade and a half later. Robert E. Lee served as captain in Mexico, and emerged from the war marked for future greatness. Thomas "Stonewall" Jackson, P. G. T. Beauregard, and Braxton Bragg fought in Mexico as lieutenants, while Jefferson Davis and Albert Sidney Johnson were colonels, and Joseph Johnston a lieutenant colonel in the war; all would serve as Confederate leaders. Taylor and Frémont would go on to political careers, and the issues they would discuss would be created from the war's results and their implications. The Mexican War was a small conflict with comic-opera overtones, but it set the stage for a far more serious war, and provided fuel for political debates and elections for the remainder of the antebellum period.

# 12/AN UNCERTAIN PEACE

COMPARISONS BETWEEN PRESIDENTS ARE INVIDIOUS, yet they go on, especially as the executive office grows in power and prominence. Each man who has filled the office has faced different problems, has been limited by his own personality and prejudices, and more often than not has been controlled by contemporary events. From time to time some group, foundation, or individual will conduct surveys and polls to determine which of the presidents were great, near great, average, below average, or mediocre. As might be expected, George Washington, Abraham Lincoln, and Franklin D. Roosevelt have always ranked high in the esteem of historians, while Ulysses S. Grant and Warren Harding alternate as the worst president in American history. These rankings have little meaning and probably do more to confuse the issue than clarify it. We can never know what kind of a president Harding would have been if faced by a Civil War, or how Lincoln would have reacted to Prohibition and the Jazz Age, and yet these two are judged as though such information were available.

What is obvious is that those presidents who served in times of crisis are higher on most historians' lists than those who were in office during calm periods. Historians seem to prefer "strong" leaders to "weak," and it helps if such presidents have been preceded by incompetents and succeeded by fools, for then they seem far superior in comparison. Rankings vary with changes in public sentiment. Liberal eras in American history have brought forth major reconsiderations of men like Franklin D. Roosevelt, Andrew Jackson, and Woodrow Wilson, while during conservative periods there have been revivals of interest in William McKinley, Herbert Hoover, and Grover Cleveland. Reconsideration and revision is the heart of the historical process and meat for the historian, for without it he would be a mere chronicler.

James K. Polk has usually been ranked toward the bottom of the list of great presidents, often a little above Harry Truman and just below Theodore Roosevelt. Part of the reason for this has already been indicated. Polk lived in a period of great change. He was a strong president. He was more comfortable with power and better able to use it than his predecessor or successor. He was largely responsible for leading the nation in a highly successful war, one that ended with one of the largest territorial acquisitions in history. Furthermore, Polk was unique in that he was able to carry out, totally or in large part, every one of his major campaign promises, one of which was a pledge not to run for reelection. At times he has been criticized for his duplicity, half-truths, and brutal seizure of the Southwest, but no serious individual has ever suggested the return of the territory acquired in the Mexican War.

Polk helped focus and resolve the problems that faced the nation when he came to office. In 1845 the balance between North and South was precarious, but it did exist. Polk both tipped the political scales in favor of the South and annexed territories to the Union that would in time ally themselves with the North. Tyler had helped bring to the fore the politics of slavery; Polk made such debates that took place thereafter not mere exercises in logic, but battles for men and land, and in so doing helped set the stage for a conflict far greater than the Mexican War.

For this Polk's party paid a heavy price. "Young Hickory" had been nominated in 1844 as a unity candidate, one who would update Jacksonian Democracy and provide the kind of coalition and issues that would ensure the party power for the foreseeable future. This was not to be. Instead, the Democrat Polk divided his own party over the issue of the war, with one faction, the southern and conservative, backing him, while the other, northern and reformist, opposed him bitterly. By the time the war had ended Polk was more severely criticized by northern Democrats than by most Whigs, and was burned in effigy by many who had voted for him in 1844 and who now claimed to have been betrayed.

The Whigs, who had split on the declaration of war and who early in the fighting were Polk's severest critics, embraced the conflict when it seemed to be going well. As the antiwar Whigs were either dismissed by their constituents or silenced by party leaders, the remainder of the opposition spoke out in favor of Polk's foreign policies. Both Taylor and Scott, the heroes of the war, were Whigs, and many party leaders saw one of them as their passport to the White House in 1848. Paradoxically, many of Polk's successes not only weakened his own party, but strengthened its opposition. Polk had led the nation in a successful war, and in so doing had driven a wedge between the two parts of his own party. After the war the Whigs would widen the split, and they would find allies among the northern Democrats.

In the summer of 1846 Polk asked Congress for an appropriation of $2 million to "facilitate negotiations" with Mexico to end the war. The antiwar Democrats saw this as an opportunity to declare their independence of the president. Most of them were from the North, and they resented not only the war but the growing southern domination of the party. Those who had previously supported the president were now labeled tools of the South by their constituents, and they had to take some action to change this image before the forthcoming congressional elections. One member of this group, David Wilmot of Pennsylvania, introduced an amendment to the appropriations bill specifying that slavery should be prohibited in any territories acquired from Mexico. The "Wilmot Proviso" was of doubtful legality, since it was based on the assumption that Congress had the right to decide such matters. Wilmot's backers argued that the Proviso was based on the Ordinance of 1787, which had forbidden slavery in the Northwest Territory, and that the constitutionality of the Ordinance had never been questioned. Anti-Proviso men, mostly from the South, claimed that each state was guaranteed the right to control its domestic institutions, and that the same held true for territories.

The Proviso was accepted by the House and rejected by the Senate. But it had its desired effect. Wilmot and the other northern Democrats who had supported it were purged of charges of being pro-southern and were reelected to Congress that November.

The Proviso did not die, however; it would remain an issue through the 1850s. It was reintroduced in the new Congress in 1847, and once again it passed the House and was rejected by the Senate. But now the southern Democrats counterattacked. Calhoun took the measure, reworded it in such a way as to favor the South while appearing to be a compromise, and then placed it before the Senate. The territories, he claimed, belonged to all the states, and not to the federal government. Thus, Washington could not pursue policies there that discriminated against any state. Calhoun was referring to the right of slaveholders to bring their chattels into the territories; any attempt to deny this right, he claimed, would be a grave constitutional breach. He then pointed out that his proposal was contrary to the Missouri Compromise of 1820, which had forbidden slavery in the Louisiana Territory north of the line of 36° 30′ but permitted it south of the line. Calhoun said that, however, for practical reasons, he would be willing to support a bill that extended the line to the Pacific. As expected, the Calhoun proposal was rejected, but it added fuel to the sectional fire.

In 1848 William Yancey of Alabama presented a less conciliatory measure. Yancey denounced the Missouri Compromise and repeated Calhoun's argument that Congress had no right to legislate on the question of slavery in the territories. Should it do so by passing the Wilmot Proviso, he said, the South would secede from the Union. The Yancey proposal was endorsed by several southern conventions that year, but most politicians in the South shrank from the word "secession." In time they would change their minds.

The Whigs were delighted with the dissension in the Democratic camp, and they capitalized on it. Senator John Berrien of Georgia, a Jacksonian Democrat turned Whig, applauded the Proviso, an act that at first shocked others of his section in the Senate. Then he went on to explain his actions, and did so in such a way that he won their approval. The Administration, he said, had embarked upon an illegal war against Mexico, and so had no right to take any territory from that nation. On the other hand, the Texas boundaries had to be secured. As he saw it, Polk's maximum demands from Mexico should be the Rio Grande boundary. By this plan, Texas—then the fastest-growing slave state—would be placated, and the annexation of California—which was certain to be a free state—would be blocked. Webster saw the Berrien proposal as a vehicle on which he could ride into the White House in 1848, and he, too, endorsed it.

Henry Clay also saw the merits of the proposal, but, always a better politician than Webster, he took into account the war's popularity with the Whigs. Thus, he did not dismiss the possibility of annexation, but he did add the qualification that no foreign territory would be acquired "for the purpose" of extending slavery. The legal meaning of this was unclear, but in practical terms it was designed to enhance Clay's chances of winning a fourth nomination.

Some Democrats, realizing that their party's divisions would assure a Whig victory, and perhaps even that of the hated Clay, put forth a compromise. Led by former Michigan governor Lewis Cass and Illinois senator Stephen Douglas, this group called for "squatter sovereignty," or, as it was also called, "popular sovereignty." Cass and Douglas argued that the inhabitants of a territory had the right to decide for themselves whether or not slavery would be permitted. Douglas, who came to be closely identified with the popular sovereignty idea, believed that slavery was basically a political issue and therefore susceptible to compromise. Through careful manipulation, he hoped that new states could be brought into the Union in pairs, thereby satisfying moderates in both parties and in both sections of the country.

Cass and Douglas failed to take two problems into account. In the first place, an increasingly large number of people were coming to view slavery as a moral rather than a political question. While politics is the art of compromise, there can be no deals on issues regarded as moral; either one side or the other must be the victor. By the late 1840s the moral dimension had been added to the sectional and political ones, and in time it would become at least as important. Southern, Democratic, pro-slavery forces were advancing to a showdown with northern, Whig, antislavery and abolitionist forces. Yancey and Birney were in a minority in 1847, but their allies and followers were increasing steadily, and as they did, they would crush the moderates between them.

269

The second problem that Cass and Douglas did not consider was time. As they formulated their ideas in 1847, it appeared that the admission of new states could be accomplished in a slow and regular fashion. Such was not the case. In September 1847, just before Scott entered Mexico City, Brigham Young arrived at the Great Salt Lake. Gold was discovered at Sutter's Mill in California in January of the following year. Soon afterward easterners learned of both the gold discoveries and the Treaty of Guadalupe Hidalgo, and to many the former seemed more important. By late summer thousands were on their way to California, and their numbers grew daily. It was clear that California and Deseret would soon ask for admission to the Union as free states. The southern-oriented Administration that had initiated the Mexican War to safeguard the slave state of Texas was now in the position of considering the applications of two new states that would swing the sectional balance in favor of the North. Moderates now realized that they would not have enough time to heal wounds and work compromises. Iowa and Wisconsin had been admitted to the Union in 1846 and 1848, respectively, to balance Texas and Florida. Minnesota and states carved from the Oregon Territory would soon join with California and Deseret to request admission as free states, but there were no areas seeking entry as slave states. No wonder the southerners were alarmed, the moderates disheartened, and northern abolitionists and antislavery forces encouraged, as they looked forward to the presidential election of 1848.

There have been years in history which seem to have a life of their own, and so become bench marks or are con-

*Stephen A. Douglas.*

sidered turning points. Often the meanings and the implications of events are not understood at the time they occur, but participants and observers appear aware that they are living in a time of great change. So it was in 1848, not only in America, but in Europe too. In February, shortly after the conclusion of the Treaty of Guadalupe Hidalgo, King Louis Philippe was forced to abdicate the throne of France, and for the rest of the year that nation was in the grips of revolutionary forces. The revolution spread to Vienna in March, where there were street demonstrations that led to the resignation of Prince Metternich. Then revolutionary groups staged uprisings in Budapest, Venice, Berlin, Milan, and Parma. On March 20 the Sikh aristocracy in India declared war on Britain; four days later Sardinia declared war on Austria. In early April the Chartists—a political and social reform group—marched on London, and although the movement failed, the demonstrators had threatened the fundamental institutions of the land before it ended. In May Prussia invaded Denmark, and in Poland an insurrection was on the verge of success before Prussian troops put it down. This event was followed by new revolutions in France and Vienna, which continued into June. Ireland had its uprising in July, while the Russians invaded the Danubian Principalities (modern Romania) at the invitation of the ruling Turkish government to put down revolts there. August was relatively quiet, but in South Africa the Boers clashed with the British and were defeated at Boomplaats. In September Lajos Kossuth was proclaimed president of a committee for the national defense of Hungary, as that nation continued its struggle for national identity. A third revolution shook Vienna in October; in November the premier of the Papal States, Count

Pellegrino Rossi, was assassinated, a revolution erupted in Rome, and the Pope was forced to flee to Gaeta. Not until December did the revolutionary and violent period end. Emperor Ferdinand I of Austria abdicated in favor of his nephew, Franz Joseph I, who was to rule for fifty-eight years, while in France Louis Napoleon was elected president, thus beginning a career that would last for a quarter of a century. In England James Froude wrote *Nemesis of Faith*—an attack on modern religion, millennialists proclaimed the end of the world, and J. C. Hart swore that Francis Bacon had written all of Shakespeare's works. John Stuart Mill wrote *Principles of Political Economy*—a defense of liberalism, and Karl Marx and Friedrich Engels produced the *Communist Manifesto*.

Although there was no revolution in the United States in 1848, it was the year the Seneca Falls meeting drafted the feminist Declaration of Sentiments and new utopian communities were established, while the Garrisonians, aided by antiwar sentiment, captured control of abolitionism from the Tappan moderates. In Pennsylvania farmers reported seeing blood on the moon; it was widely interpreted as a sign that the world was about to come to an end. Those Whig and Democratic politicians who surveyed .the scene that election year might have wondered if there could be any truth to such signs. Daniel Webster spoke of this in the Senate; the future, he believed, would bring "contention, strife, and agitation." Polk reiterated his pledge not to seek a second term, perhaps thankful for having made it four years earlier.

The Polk administration had done nothing to heal the

Democratic divisions that had been so evident at the 1844 convention, and these divisions had deepened during the Tennessean's four years in office. By 1845 New York Democrats had divided into two factions. The "Barnburners"—so named by their opponents after the habit of Dutch farmers who burned their barns to kill rats—were reformists, an outgrowth of the old Jacksonian working-class coalition of the 1830s. They were accused of being willing to destroy the nation to rid it of their enemies. The Barnburners were strongly in favor of the Wilmot Proviso and by 1847 demanded the nomination of a candidate pledged to enact it into law. Three men would have been acceptable to them: Martin Van Buren, Thomas Hart Benton, and Silas Wright, and of these, Wright had the greatest potential strength. He had served as a reform governor of New York from 1845 to 1847, and then was defeated by his Democratic enemies. But Wright died late in the year, and the Barnburners switched their support to Van Buren, who had made so many enemies by then as to have little chance for the nomination.

The Barnburners were opposed by the "Hunkers," whom they accused of "hunkering" after office and having no discernible principles. The Hunkers were more moderate in their approach, favoring compromise on most issues and the nomination of a candidate who would draw the sections closer together. Whereas the Barnburners usually spoke with moral fervor and had allies among the abolitionists, the Hunkers were politicians to the core and longed for accommodation. They had several candidates, the most notable ones being James Buchanan of Pennsylvania and

Lewis Cass of Michigan. Stephen Douglas of Illinois, the politician supreme, was their ideal, but was not considered seriously in 1848, for he was only thirty-five years old.

The divisions within the New York Democracy were mirrored throughout the North and Midwest, and were evident at the Baltimore convention that met in May. Although Polk would not consider a second term, he did wield great power at the convention, and he threw his support to those who favored accommodation. The first test came over the seating of delegates, since both the Barnburners and the Hunkers had sent delegations to Baltimore. The Polk men tried to compromise the issue by dividing the delegation equally between the two groups. The Hunkers seemed willing to accept this, but the Barnburners called it a betrayal of principle and left the convention, announcing that they would form a party based on the Wilmot Proviso. This act, applauded as a moral victory by the reformers, was greeted by the southern delegates as an unexpected boost to their power. With the Barnburners' departure, there was no reason to seek compromises with the North, and the South took control of the Democratic party. Calhoun's victory was complete.

The Democratic convention then proceeded to write a platform denying the powers of the federal government to interfere with slavery in the states, and on the fourth ballot it nominated Lewis Cass. Perhaps Cass's most attractive attribute was his service as a general in the War of 1812. The nation seemed in the mood for a military man in 1848, but the heroes of the Mexican War were both Whigs. Almost in desperation, the Democrats selected

Cass, and then chose General William Butler of Kentucky as his running-mate.

The Whigs held their convention in Philadelphia in June, and they fully realized that their chances of winning the presidency had never been so good. As had been the case in the past, they hoped to win not so much by their own policies as through Democratic divisions. Zachary Taylor was the leading contender for their nomination. But all who knew him recognized that he had little knowledge of politics and even less interest in the subject. He disliked Polk, and never forgave him for sending Scott to Mexico as his rival, but he also had little love for Scott and less for Cass. In the summer of 1847 Taylor said he would enter politics if only to prevent any of the three from residing in the White House in 1849; as he put it, he was ready to "undergo political martyrdom rather than see Scott or Cass elected." He felt that the people would support him because of his honesty and integrity, and not for his stands on any given issue. Thus, late in 1847, he pledged himself not to say a word about the nation's problems until after he was elected. Representative Caleb Smith of Indiana was shocked; "the man is certainly demented," he said, and others agreed. But even though political astuteness did not guide Taylor's decision, it was a wise one. Whatever he said might have alienated one faction or another, making his nomination difficult and his election problematical. Instead, he appeared as a lonely, tall, handsome figure, a victor in war, a tough commander—in short, the kind of man who could save the nation from chaos. Although few spoke of it, Taylor appeared to have the qualities that made for a dictator or a king, not a president. Still, some thought such a man was what the nation needed in 1848, and he won the support of a group of energetic young Whigs, including Alexander Stephens of Georgia (the future vice-president of the Confederate States of America) and Abraham Lincoln.

Taylor was sixty-four years old in 1848 and a new face in politics; Henry Clay was seventy, and the most familiar face in Washington. Clay would have liked to adopt the stance that had carried Taylor so far, but clearly this was out of the question. Everyone knew where he stood on the issues, just as no one knew Taylor's ideas. Nor was Clay a military hero, although he was reported to have said, bitterly, "I wish I could kill a Mexican," for that seemed the road to political power in 1848. Still, he knew politics as no one else did, and he set out to block Taylor's nomination. Clay could scarcely oppose the war; to do so would be suicidal. Instead, he attacked the way the war had been handled, and repeated earlier pledges not to support the introduction of slavery into territories obtained through conquest. In this way he hoped to attract Wilmot Proviso Whigs while not completely embracing the Proviso, and at the same time to avoid antagonizing moderates in the North and West. He hoped to be, in his own words, "a western man with northern principles." And by spring of 1848 he appeared to have halted the Taylor boom.

Then the Clay drive was stymied, largely because the candidate's own state failed to support him. First John Crittenden, an old Clay ally and his former manager in Kentucky, deserted him for Taylor, and took the state

*Zachary Taylor.*

machinery with him. Then Taylor announced that he was a Whig, but "not an ultra Whig." He would follow Congress in legislative matters, especially in questions involving the tariff, currency, and internal improvements. Taylor went on to say that he favored peace. It was not much of a stand, but it was more than he had offered earlier, and vague though it was, it won Taylor additional support. In the end the general won the nomination on the fourth ballot. Then, to placate the Clay wing, the vice-presidential nomination was given to Millard Fillmore of New York, who was considered a Clay man. The party was disgruntled, but united. The nomination of Taylor indicated that the Whigs had abandoned their negative anti-Jacksonian stance as well as their old leaders. But their new leader was an old man, and even after the convention no one seemed to know what he thought about the important issues of the day. The platform offered no clue, for it concentrated on praising Taylor and avoiding the issues.

The Democrats had nominated a northerner with a program that appealed to the South, while the Whigs chose a southern military man who was known for his Mexican exploits but who lacked a program. Neither party offered much to reformers or to the North. Antiwar protesters, members of the many "Wilmot Proviso Leagues" that sprang up in the 1847–1848 period, abolitionists, and reformers of all political hues now came to believe that only a new party could represent their demands. One already existed: the Liberty party. But the defecting Whigs and Democrats refused to join an organization already controlled by another group, even though they agreed with its goals. The Liberty party's candidate, John Hale, had an excellent record of fighting for abolition while at the same time remaining a moderate, but the defectors had their own candidates and would not accept him.

A group of New England and Ohio Whigs decided to hold a convention in Columbus, and they invited all who believed in "free soil" to come. The Barnburners planned to have their convention in Utica, and they appealed to reform Democrats to abandon Cass and attend their gathering. Realizing that the dissenters were diffusing their strength, Van Buren contacted the free-soilers and Liberty party leaders and pleaded with them to unite in a joint convention, scheduled for Buffalo on August 9. They agreed to come, but made it clear they would not compromise basic principles.

The Buffalo convention was presided over by Charles Francis Adams, the son of the recently deceased John Quincy Adams. Adams was a man of clear antislavery views and a good chairman, with an ability to compromise. The convention, under his direction, adopted a set of resolutions demanding that "there must be no compromise with slavery." However, the main issue was the future of the territories, not abolition of slavery in the South, and this represented a victory for the moderates. In addition, the platform came out in favor of cheap postage, internal improvements, a homestead law, and repayment of the public debt. It pledged the new party, now called the Free Soil party, to "fight on and fight forever for free soil, free speech, free labor, and free men." Van Buren, the old Democrat, received the presidential nomination, while Adams, a young Whig, was selected for the vice-presidency.

*Free Soil party poster, 1848.*

Taylor won the election, with 163 electoral votes to Cass's 127, and a popular vote of 1.36 million to Cass's 1.22 million. The Democrats' southern strategy did not work; Cass won the Midwest and northern New England, and Taylor the middle states and the South. But the vote was close throughout the nation, and the Democrats attributed Taylor's southern strength to approval of his record in the Mexican War, rather than his identification as a Whig. Given a "normal" election, they believed, the South would be solidly Democratic.

Van Buren received no electoral votes, but his 291,000 popular votes were a sharp improvement over the 62,000 Birney had received on the Liberty party ticket in 1844. As expected, Van Buren received almost all his votes from the North and the Midwest. The surprise of the election was his strong showing in New York and Massachusetts, where he outpolled Cass. Had the Democrats managed to hold together in 1848, it is probable they would have won the election. It was the defection of antiwar and pro–civil rights voters from the party that lost the Democrats votes in the northern states and enabled Taylor to win the presidency.

It was equally clear that the nation had just selected a president without a platform. Unwilling to compromise and unable to accept either section's programs for the new territories, Americans had chosen a general who they hoped would prove strong enough to find some way out of the political dilemma of the slavery issue and the heritage of the war. The Democrats controlled the new Senate, but the House was more evenly divided, and the thirteen Free

Soil representatives held the balance of power. The new government was charged with solving some of the most serious problems in the nation's history. Not since Washington's inauguration had the difficulties seemed so obvious; not since Washington had the nation elected a man with fewer commitments.

Taylor took the oath of office on March 5, 1849. He promised to work with the new Congress and to discharge his oath, but said little else. His inaugural was one of the shortest in history. Thus, burdened with maturing problems, disintegrating institutions, and the troublesome aftermath of a war, the nation entered the last year of the 1840s, led by a president who was a political enigma.

A cholera epidemic swept the South during the summer of 1849, killing tens of thousands in that region and then spreading northward. Yet even this did not still the political debates. Wilmot Proviso Leagues grew in number and membership in the North, while Calhoun issued a call for an all-southern convention, to meet in 1850 to decide upon a common course of action against the North. In December 1849 Congress met in an atmosphere of hostility; the lines for future conflict were already drawn. It took an unprecedented three weeks to organize the House of Representatives; sixty-three ballots were required to elect a speaker. In the end Howell Cobb, a moderate Georgian, was selected, but Free Soilers, moderates, and reformist northerners, many of whom had been friendly with Cobb in the past, swore revenge for this "insult" to them.

Meanwhile, the rush to California accelerated, as the

drift of the nation continued westward. As Congress met the New York *Herald* reported:

We are informed that from thirty to fifty thousand dollars' worth of the precious metal is collected daily . . . and this, too, is using only the most common and primitive means, such as willow baskets and tin kettles. The people, it is said, actually pick it up from the crevices in the rocks in lumps of one, two, and three ounces with a jack-knife, and so plentiful is it that an ounce and a half was given for a box of Seidlitz powders . . . . In every direction vessels are being prepared to carry out passengers and merchandise to California. The mania for emigrating to California is spreading in every direction. Adventurers from every street in the city are concerting measures and collecting funds to pay their passages to California . . . . No doubt much disappointment may be encountered, but there is no doubt that this wonderful discovery will soon make San Francisco one of the largest cities on the Pacific, in fact the New York of California.

On December 7 the first passenger ship to California set sail from Boston, and it was followed by others. By the end of the month some six thousand easterners and Europeans had left Boston and New York for what was already being called El Dorado. Now there was talk of a railroad to be constructed to the West Coast, and British and American investors scurried to organize companies, buy shares, and profit from the Gold Rush.

The 1840s ended, then, on a bizarre note. In Washington senators and congressmen pondered whether or not the nation could survive. Young Stephen Douglas and old Henry Clay spent long days and nights hammering out compromises, while other legislators were warning that the time for compromise had ended and preparing for possible

284

—some said probable—civil war. Every report from Washington sent the stock prices in New York down; every scrap of news from California sent them up. The nation was in the midst of a boom: jobs were easy to get, wages were rising, and the economic horizon appeared cloudless. Yet at the same time there was real fear that the country itself could not survive.

Most free Americans had every reason in the world to consider their individual situations satisfactory, but they saw only more trouble ahead for the society. The decade had begun in depression, and it ended on a note of schizophrenia and uncertainty. Few believed that such a situation could last for long; it would be resolved in one way or another. But would the attempt to solve these problems perhaps be worse than the problems themselves? Would it not be preferable to try to live with the tensions rather than accept solutions that would, in all probability, destroy the very fabric of the nation? Some men—Clay, Douglas, the moderate abolitionists, most businessmen, workers, and farmers—believed that the nation could surmount its difficulties without bloodshed, and solve its problems through reason, democracy, and the use of established institutions. But others—an increasing, though still small, number—believed that the time for majority rule, the Constitution, and conventional politics was over. They were prepared to use the sword, if necessary, to obtain their objectives, wage bloody war to implement their moral standards, disregard laws to achieve their idea of justice. In 1849, one of them, Henry Thoreau, wrote *Civil Disobedience,* a book which became a clarion for those of this camp.

Unjust laws exist: shall we be content to obey them, or shall we endeavor to amend them, and obey them until we have succeeded, or shall we transgress them at once? Men generally under such a government as this think that they ought to wait until they have persuaded the majority to alter them. They think that, if they should resist, the remedy would be worse than the evil. But it is the fault of the government itself that the remedy is worse than the evil. It makes it worse. Why is it not more apt to anticipate and provide for reform? Why does it not cherish its wise minority? Why does it cry and resist before it is hurt? Why does it not encourage its citizens to be on the alert to point out faults, and do better than it would have them? Why does it always crucify Christ and excommunicate Copernicus and Luther and pronounce Washington and Franklin rebels? . . . The authority of government can have no pure right over my person and property but what I concede it.

Such thoughts and words are usually found in the writings of saints and tyrants, and most Americans were neither. They, and not the Thoreaus of America, would determine the nation's future. But in 1849 that future was clouded, and the only ones volunteering as guides were the saints and the tyrants.

# CONCLUSION

IT HAS OFTEN BEEN SAID OF ONE MAN OR ANOTHER that he would make an excellent leader in normal times, but not at the present. What such speakers forget is that we have never seen "normal times." Tension and crisis are not unusual; indeed they have been the norm throughout American history.

So it was in the 1840s. This was a decade of great material accomplishment. The 1837 depression gripped the nation at the beginning of the 1840s but ended by 1844. For the next six years the economy performed well. The nation was involved in a war, but even by the standards of the nineteenth century it could not be considered a major conflict. In 1840 the United States was a large nation territorially, but it shared the continent with Canada, Texas, and Mexico, all of which appeared to have shining futures. By 1850 Canada was no longer considered a rival, Texas had been annexed, and the nation had defeated Mexico and taken a large part of its territory. The United

States took in a record number of immigrants in the 1840s, and although there were the expected difficulties of adjustment, by 1850 these did not seem of major importance. Social experimentation flourished in the decade, and this may be considered more a sign of national vitality and freedom than a failure of mainstream Americanism. The same may be said of the drive westward. With the important exception of the Mormons, the new westerners were not escaping America by moving, but were attempting to realize its promise, to spread the kind of civilization they had left in the East. The Mormons, too, were in the American tradition, seeking freedom of religion in a new land. This new nation—so vital, strong, innovative, and complex —fascinated foreign visitors, and even when they criticized Americans they admitted that they possessed freshness and energy.

In 1840 America was in a depression, and yet the national mood remained optimistic. Ten years later, in the midst of prosperity and with news of California gold adding to the material wealth of the nation, the mood had changed to pessimism. This was due to two apparently unresolvable problems, neither of them new, but both of which had come to the fore in the 1840s. The first was slavery. How could a nation "conceived in liberty" accept an institution that enslaved a large number of its people? The second problem was Manifest Destiny, and in particular its manifestation in the Mexican War. How could a just nation instigate such a conflict? By 1848 the two issues were joined, as were the various protest movements they had fathered. Americans, who were considered geniuses at the art of compromise, now faced a situation that would not admit the possibility of compromise. A nation which prided itself on majority rule with safeguards for minority rights now found, in its midst, reformers who rejected both, saying instead that their cause was so right and just that any and all means could be used to accomplish their goals. The heritage of the 1830s was depression, and Americans were capable of solving that crisis, since it involved money, work, and organization—things the nation as a whole understood. The legacy of the 1840s was a moral dilemma, one that was not completely understood.

Echoes of one generation or decade are often heard in others; the problems of the 1840s were not very different from those of today, and they may offer a guide—uncertain and limited—to present conduct and thought. History does not repeat itself, but, at times, useful analogies to the past may be made. In 1933 Franklin D. Roosevelt became president of a country which, like that of 1840, was in the midst of a depression. In his inaugural speech he said, "In such a spirit on my part and on yours we face our common difficulties. They concern, thank God, only material things." In 1969 Richard Nixon, in his inaugural address, referred to Roosevelt's words, and he spoke of the nation's present difficulties in a manner that recalls the problems of 1849.

Standing in this same place a third of a century ago, Franklin Delano Roosevelt addressed a Nation ravaged by depression and gripped in fear. He could say in surveying the Nation's troubles:
"They concern, thank God, only material things."
Our crisis today is the reverse.
We have found ourselves rich in goods, but ragged in spirit;

reaching with magnificent precision for the moon, but falling into raucous discord on earth.

We are caught in war, wanting peace. We are torn by division, wanting unity. We see around us empty lives, wanting fulfillment. We see tasks that need doing, waiting for hands to do them.

To the crisis of the spirit, we need an answer of the spirit. To find that answer, we need only look within ourselves . . . .

Greatness comes in simple trappings.

The simple things are the ones most needed today if we are to surmount what divides us, and cement what unifies us.

To lower our voices would be a simple thing . . . .

# APPENDIX:
## Early Credit Reporting in the United States

CREDIT REPORTING IN THE UNITED STATES BEGAN WITH independent investigators, employed in a variety of relationships and responsibilities. Some were hired by a single company; others, by several enterprises with common interests. Among the pioneers were Thomas Wren Ward, Sheldon P. Church, and Lewis Tappan, men whose vision, personality, and ideas influenced the direction of credit reporting as it evolved in the 1840s.

### TYPICAL CREDIT REPORTS OF THOMAS WREN WARD*

Ward was the American agent of Baring Brothers & Company, the London banking house that risked millions in international trade. It was a company with substantial investments in the United States and its territories. He was

*The original correspondence and reports of Thomas Wren Ward with Baring Brothers & Company are filed in the Office of the Public Archives

a man of action, involved in large risks, especially maritime. His principal commitments were to shipowners and ship operators, financing huge shipments of American cotton to the Far East. He recommended loans to early railroads including a large investment for a steel path across northern Florida. Ward wrote most of his reports between 1833 and 1852, yet his financial vocabulary is modern and direct, with emphasis where necessary for an opinion or decision. The following reports are typical of those sent to the Baring Brothers offices in London.

JAMES MEANS    Boston

*Is guaranty for Means & Sprague of New York. Mr. James Means was formerly a large grocer—now rather retired and concerned in manufacturing. Very safe—prudent—and a capital of $70,000 or more. May want to send orders to you for purchases which you may execute with safety—May 11th, 1833.*

ANDRES DUNLAP    Washington

*District Attorney U. S. Court! ! ! A rank radical and high Jackson man. Has $15,000 and a good income from his profession and other expectations. Safe enough—but I gave him the credit because at the moment he applied there was some talk about the account in London being changed in Washington and he has influence there for good or evil—however I might as well have omitted it.—December 1, 1833.*

---

of Canada at Ottawa. Roy A. Foulke, formerly vice-president and a director of Dun & Bradstreet, Inc., excerpted the Ward reports for publication in *The Sinews of American Commerce* in 1941, a volume celebrating the one-hundredth anniversary of credit reporting by The Mercantile Agency, founded in 1841.

JAMES H. LEVERICH & CO.   New Orleans

*In the grocery business with a capital of $50,000 or $60,000. Mr. L. considered an uncommonly capable and safe sort of man—went from New Jersey and intends to return to New York and live. Oxnard, Remsen, and Howlands and others all say very safe.—October 28, 1835.*

LEE & GOODWIN   Boston

*Are in order. I am surprised that I have not mentioned Mr. Goodwin's capital. He is a steady, prudent, honorable, popular man worth $80,000. W. Lee has $30,000 or $40,000 and his family have large expectations. The collateral branches all rich and honourable—Lee has failed three times and paid up all each time and I think the chances are in favour of not failing again. They have a handsome India commission business—and do not trade largely on their own account. I see no great hazard unless in selling Rupee bills endorsed by them for Palmer, McKillop & Co. of London but I do not know to what extent their bills are sold. I consider Lee & Goodwin as a good account and they are a very popular house—and you should give them particular advice and trust them with attention and confidence.—1835.*

Examples of less detailed reports made in 1833 show Ward's direct reporting language, his wide knowledge, and his ability to interpret credit information concisely:

W. & B. F. SALTER   New York

*Ship owners with a brother in Portsmouth—small property —not uncovered except through me.*

WM. B. REYNOLDS   Boston

*Merchant—owns a packet line to Philadelphia and Real Estate, and owner of the "Duncan" with B. F. Reed and G. D. Carter. Has $70,000. Bold, but supposed safe.*

GRISWOLD & WOOD    Boston

*New importers—no capital or only $10,000 under guaranty of Charles Tappan of Gordon & Stoddard and B. Murry—who is very safe.*

JOHN BERTRAM    Salem

*Merchant—formerly a High Master—safe—fair man with $40,000 capital.*

EDMUND SWETT    Newburyport

*Ship owner with others—not to be uncovered—has some property, but I do not hear much in favour.*

WALTER BAKER    Dorchester

*Chocolate manufacturer. Probably safe himself—I have guaranty of his father—only credit through me.*

Of the foregoing names, the one which has become the most widely known over the intervening years is that of Walter Baker of Dorchester, manufacturer of chocolate. This particular business, when Ward rendered his brief credit report in 1833, was already seventy-eight years old. It had been started in 1765 by one John Hannon, who, in that year, ground the first chocolate in North America. In 1772 Dr. James Baker began to manufacture chocolate, also at Dorchester, and eight years later he acquired full ownership of Hannon's business. In 1791 a son, Edmund, was taken into partnership, and in 1804 Dr. James Baker, now sixty-five years of age, retired, leaving the business entirely in the hands of his son. In 1818 Walter Baker, twenty-six years of age and the grandson of Dr. James Baker, was taken into partnership by his father. Edmund Baker retired in 1824, leaving the enterprise to Walter

Baker, under whose name it became prosperous and widely known. This was the Walter Baker upon whom Ward rendered his report to Baring Brothers & Company, and Edmund Baker was the father whose guaranty Ward most likely held.

That the credit information obtained and interpreted by Ward was unusually sound is amply demonstrated by the manner in which Baring Brothers & Company came through the panic of 1837 and the troublesome years which followed, the worst depression up to that time in the United States. In a recapitulation made in 1843 Ward commented upon these lists, "of 250 pronounced un-doubted in 1835—only 16 have failed, & all the rest now undoubted—and of 245 pronounced as likely to continue good, 22 have failed—and of 280 of the third class, 45 have failed." That record stands as a remarkable tribute to his judgment of men and business enterprises.

The second specialist in gathering credit information, Sheldon P. Church, was a rugged individualist in the pioneer days of credit reporting. We have seen that he served a circle of New York merchandise distributors, whereas Thomas W. Ward served only one client. Church was the author of the second known volume of printed credit reports which were bound in 1847 without the names of the author or the publisher. This volume con-tained credit reports on merchants in the West, the South, and the Southwest for the years 1844-1847. It consisted of 434 pages, each page being 13 x 8 inches.

Sheldon P. Church had a colorful journalistic streak. He was a keen observer and analyst of human nature. Only the initials S.P.C. on two pages of his book of published reports, apparently overlooked when the volume was published, give any inkling of the name of the author.

## TYPICAL CREDIT REPORTS OF SHELDON P. CHURCH

These credit reports are fascinating examples of the free interpretation of information. No words were minced. Unfavorable facts which reflected upon character and honesty were played up with the utmost frankness. Several examples of credit reports from this volume point to Church's acid pen, a colorful vocabulary, and engaging candor:

BINFORD & NIMMO    Richmond, Va.

*A new firm, and doubtless some persons, without analyzing, would call it first rate. Mr. Binford has been many years in trade here under different phases, is worth nothing, never made anything, and never will; he is impulsive, restless, uneasy, of no judgment, prudence, or forecast, and the wonder is that Nimmo ever united with him. The latter by himself would be good; he obtained $25,000 by his wife, in part now badly invested. They are men of good character, for ought I learn.—November, 1844.*

THOMAS J. N. BRIDGES    Memphis, Tenn.

*Will no doubt be doing business in a different name. William Armour, formerly in Jackson, Tenn., is believed to be proprietor of the establishment, and he has lately come to a settlement of his old liabilities in Baltimore, (a large amount) dictating his own terms, and totally refusing to allow any investigation, or to give any satisfactory explanation of his present condition. He merely surrenders his old unavailable assets, mainly suspended debts, scattered through Tennessee and Mississippi.—January 1st 1845.*

Many of Church's reports, like those of Ward, were brief and to the point, but they always carried an unmistakable message. They contained little in the way of ambiguous, side-stepping opinions. Frankly and fearlessly, Church expressed his impressions and convictions without qualifying adjectives. The following examples are typical of his brief, condensed reports:

F. & J. S. JAMES & CO.

HENRY JAMES

KENT, KENDALL & ATWATER

WADSWORTH, TURNER & CO.

BROOKS & HUDSON

LONDON, WILLINGHAM & DREWRY

DANIEL H. LONDON

THOMAS R. PRICE

*Richmond, Va.—These are houses concerning which it is hardly proper to institute an enquiry. They are mostly wholesale dealers, and in their different grades as to amount of business, and demands for credit, all are entitled to rank first rate. K. K. & A. are perhaps too sanguine, and have lost largely by bad debts; but still they have made a good deal, and are considered a rich house.—November 15th, 1844.*

SEAY & SHEPARD    Nashville, Tenn.

*Mr. Seay has been a long time in the auction and commission business—is an industrious, honest man, and has made money. He is regarded as safe for all his engagements.—January 8th, 1845.*

BOND & MURDOCK    Macon, Ga.

*Are going on in their steady, straight, prudent course, and making money; are well off and safe.—May, 1845.*

JOHN WATSON    Detroit, Mich.

> *An old merchant in good standing; owns landed property; is supposed worth $20,000 or more; has had a good share of the Indian trade here; and has made his money in this place. He is safe enough.—July, 1846.*

P. F. VILLIPIGUE    Camden, S. C.

> *A large dealer, capable, and generally successful. He now holds considerable cotton, and is considered safe: buys in Charleston.—July, 1847.*

## LEWIS TAPPAN

The third name to consider, and in many ways the most significant in application to modern business, is Lewis Tappan. As credit manager of his brother's silk house he recognized the costly fallacy of independent credit investigation and the haphazard competitive manner in which credit information was gathered, appraised, and applied to a specific risk. He proposed a central reservoir for credit information which would draw on all sources available. His plan, countrywide in scope, covered the fourteen states, the several territories, and independent Texas. His idea received encouragement from the larger concerns, especially in the port cities of the Atlantic Coast.

The first office of Tappan's Mercantile Agency, which opened in New York in the summer of 1841, offered confidential and impartial credit reports, providing reliable data at a lower expense to participating subscribers. The Tappan idea spread as usage demonstrated its value to buyer and seller alike, broadening the scope of trade and

298

the accessibility and choice of markets. Tappan's basic sources of information were persons active in trade— young bankers, court clerks, lawyers, and sources of supply. Tappan's early correspondents, one of whom was Abraham Lincoln, maintained a periodic flow of intelligence about newcomers in the community and oldtime merchants making steady progress as well as those failing for lack of management talent or capital. Typical of the Lincoln reports is the following:

> *Yours of the 10th received. First of all, he has a wife and baby; together they ought to be worth $500,000 to any man. Secondly, he has an office in which there is a table worth $1.50 and three chairs worth, say $1. Last of all, there is in one corner a large rat-hole, which will bear looking into.*
>
> *Respectfully,*
> *A. Lincoln*

The Tappan-style credit report during the 1840s was, at first, a simple statement of antecedent facts and verification of pertinent details, but it gradually expanded with opinions based on experience in, and observation of, daily business activity.

## TYPICAL CREDIT REPORTS OF LEWIS TAPPAN'S MERCANTILE AGENCY

Tappan's reports were serial stories, unfinished as long as the business existed. The handwritten reports of the 1840s were in use until the 1880s, when the typewriter and chemical methods of reproduction made revolutionary changes in the distribution of credit information.

Many names famous in history began with an entry on a ledger sheet by the Spencerian hand of a staff copyist. For instance, we observe for Aug. 14, 1849, that Samuel Colt is the Manufacturer of "Colt's Pistols." The brief detail in the upper righthand corner tells us that he is the Patentee of "this article." The report indicates progress and profitable operations. Later entries state "Business is Good"; "Enlarging business greatly"; "Involving great outlays of capital, but credit is unquestioned." The report follows the "Colt Pistol," in its phenomenal growth, to England and other European countries.

Jonas Chickering, a maker rather than importer of pianos, had the reputation of building the finest musical instruments in the country, a name retained in the musical world for more than a century. He had factories in Lawrence, Lowell, and Boston, Massachusetts. Lewis Tappan's report on his business, which was first written in 1848, continues with fragmented entries through the next five years.

JONAS CHICKERING     334 Washington St.     Pianos     G.W.C.
Apr 18/48

*An old standard, has the highest reputation as a manufr of superior instruments. Estimated w. 200m.$, wh. he has accumulated in his bus., Now and extens bus. the largest of the kind in the country. May 25/50 A 1 Man. Oct. 19/50. Consid. perf. gd. w. as some say 300m.$. May 29/51 Undoubted. 500 June 17/52 Prime. Feb. 25/53 Upright gd. bus. man, his loss by fire is grt. is about to rebuild. Now estimated at $100m to $125m. Aug. 17/53 Has sold his R. E. in Washington St. for $8 per foot & receives some $80m for it. will have a splendid new establishmt on the neck undoutted. N. Y. Herald. Dec. 10/53. Died suddenly the night on the 9th inst. of appolexy. Dec. 9/53 Repts "Jonas Chickering & Sons" Mr. Jonas Chickering of this firm died last evening. The firm are putting up an immense buildg for a manuf of pianos & his death may embarass them. Still they must have a surplus of 2 or 300m. "Mr. Childs" the financial man has for a long time had full run of the bus. & the yng men have given better attention to bus. than formerly. The loss of Mr. "C" is irreparable both to his fam & the community. Dec. 24/53. The new firm will have 150m.$ Cap in the bus, aside from R. E. "George Child" has power*

*of Attorney and manages the financial department. He had*
*an int. in the bus. and is familiar with his duties. The R. E.*
*will be held in the family. "Mrs. C" and her daughter have*
*a Mortgage on the new Buildings to secure them their int.*
*Concern Continues in good favor and is perfectly safe.*

George W. Simmons of Oak Grove, near Boston, is
described as "one of the shrewdest and smartest Yankees"
in the clothing business in 1847, although he had a failure
chalked against him at an early age. He was the proprietor
of the "far-famed" Oak Hall and was gifted with a keen
sense of personal publicity and original merchandise ideas.
The report tells us that Simmons sent out empty wagons
over distances of 100 miles, carrying banners and slogans
to draw customers to his store. One interesting fact: he sold
for cash or on "very short time." The report is noteworthy
for the financial details on Simmons' operations.

GEORGE W. SIMMONS & CO.          Clothing          Oak Grove

*C.W.G. Aug 26/47. Doing large bus. In good cr. here for*
*2 @ 5 m. $ Aug 27/47 Proprietor of the far famed "Oak*
*Hall" Nos. 32, 34, 36, 38 Ann Street. Age abt 32: fam.*
*Failed 6 or 7 years ago. Soon after commenced present*
*concn, making a great display in the newspapers, advertising*
*at an expense of sevl. m. $ per annum, sending out empty*
*waggons, 100 miles distance covered with placards. One of*
*the shrewdest & smartest Yankees. Good char. Very attent.*
*& has made money. Represents himself w. 30 @ 40 m. $. Is*
*proby w. 25 @ 30 m. $ Stock 30 @ 60 m. $. Sales perhaps*
*200 m. $. Sells mostly for cash on very short time. Antici-*
*pates many of his paymts. Keeps a good act, with handsome*

*balance & generally flush of money. Has not heretofore had a genl. good cr. because of his flashy mode of doing bus. but some houses have trusted him for sevl. years to the amt. of 5 or 10 m. $ & one or two firms to the extent of 15 to 20 m. $. now gaining genl. good cr. which we think he is justly entitled to. Consider his note good for 5 m. $ in his line. Abt. 3 years ago he bought a house in Hamilton St. w. now at least 10 m. $. Abt. a year ago he bought 3 stores & 1 dwelling house for 30 m. $, paying 12 m. $ in goods, being mortgd. for the balance. It is now worth the full amt. paid for it cash proby. more. Apl. 13/48. Mr. Bates his former book-keeper says that his present noml. surplus is 60 m. $. He sells none on cr. excepting what cash customers are in the habit of taking, says 30 days within which to pay their bills.*

Job and publication printers were often poor credit risks, but in the report on White & Potter, Printers, of Boston, written in 1847, interesting information about the nature of power printing at that time is revealed.

WHITE WM. & POTTER R. K.      (Printers) Stoves      13 West St.
(85 State St.)

(See Wright & Potter 5/232)

G.W.G. Aug. 11/47 Publishers of the "Chronotype" & New England Washingtonian

*"W" a smart capable bus. man—excellt printer. "P" shrewd and cautious. They own with "John F. Coles" the Washingtn.*

& 2/3 of the Chrono. ("C" is the editor.) They own an "Adams" express w. $1800, a "Tufts" press $1000 @ $1200, a "Ruggles" power press, one or two hand presses. Good run & doing a successful bus. Pay the very lowest prices for work, ink and tools. "W" owns his presses himself & Accomplishes more than most Journeymen besides attending to outdoor bus. The Boston Type Foundry have a mortg. on the premises but the Agent of the co (Mr Rogers) says the mortg is not near the value of the propr & that he would not hesitate to cr. them $500 & the Agent of the N.E. Type Foundry says he has no hesitation in crediting bills of $40 or $50. Have a store on State St. & ultimately solvency depends very much on the success of their papers. E.P.W. Feb. 29/48 Seen doing abt the same amt of bus. Have recently put in necessary fixtures & now run their presses by steam which they hire. They undoubtedly intend to increase their bus. & make it permanent. Do their bus. very low but as an offset pay the smallest possible prices for labor, etc. Consider them fair at present for mod. amt. Average edition of the Chronotype 4 to 5000 a day. On the day that Hale's speech at Tremont Temple was published they sold 16000.

The clothing industry in New York City was well established in lower Manhattan in the 1840s. Lewis B. Brown started business in 1848 as a clothing jobber. After several years of success as an independent proprietor, he incorporated in 1853. The penmanship of this Mercantile Agency artist is a good example of the material in the New York ledgers.

When the "drummer" of dry goods got off the train in the country town, his first stop was at the livery stable to hire "a rig and a nag," though the horse and buggy were often better styled than the traveler and his sample bag. Silas D. Walbridge maintained a livery stable in Orleans County, New York State.

SILAS D. WALBRIDGE    Orleans County. B. Febr. 10, 44.

*Has again opened a small concern. He has been in the livery business in Rochester and is concerned in a line of "stages on the Ridge Road". He branches out too much, has often been sued within a year, but has paid all thus far. His father has lately failed, and the prop. is moving about from one to another. He has some prop. yet and drives things ahead. I would not think it safe to trust him much of a bill. He may have a fair statement but I don't believe he will be worth much a great while. He traffics too much to be safe in my opinion . . . .*

In 1845 the credit reporter whose initials are C. S. C. called Gershom Broadbent of Baltimore the "self-styled" Stewart of Baltimore, referring of course to A. T. Stewart of lower Broadway, New York City, and known countrywide as the "merchant prince" and founder of the department-store method of merchandising. Several credit reporters, identified by initials and dates, offer varying opinions on Broadbent's business qualifications and credit standing. Broadbent was accused of trickery and, despite his shady devices, succeeded in failing twice. He eventually let the business fall into more capable hands—those of his wife.

The "cloths" business of Crane & Nitchie in New York City started rather precariously in March 1848.

Rufus E. Crane was a clerk whose assets consisted of a recommendation of a former employer, a few dollars of personal savings, and some borrowed capital. More important to his success was some experience in the line. He gradually earned the confidence of suppliers while fighting an adverse tide. Crane started his business career at twenty-six and was fairly well established at thirty-three. He changed partners but never his objective, a fact evident in the report.

On April 4, 1845, credit reporter E. E. D. of the New Orleans office of The Mercantile Agency traced the source of the Louisiana-based Magee, Kneass & Co. investment capital to the Philadelphia office of James Napoleon Michael Magee. Magee and his partner, Kneass, had opened the New Orleans branch about twenty years earlier and had built up a solid credit standing; they were considered "good for $200,000" in the early 1850's.

WESTERN TERRITORY

Tappan's staff of credit reporting correspondents did not confine themselves to just the eastern markets, but were often located in settlements where traders mixed with Indians and half-breeds and engaged in a variety of businesses from dry goods to wet goods, and even cattle droving. Denkla, as a sutler, supplied army garrisons with all their requirements except ammunition.

WM. Y. DENKLA          Fort Gibson          Cherokee Nation
Sutler D G & Geo.

J. T. Oct. 18/46 to July 25/48

*Steady & attent. to bus; young, correct bus. habs. Has consid.*
*cap. in gd standing & gds well; w. 10m clear. Jan 15/49*
*Has lately associated with him a young man "Woodward"*
*are do. well and going ahead in the world, stand well re-*
*garded quite solod.*

Within a few years the Tappan reports took on an
individualistic styling in which the miniscule writing was
also identified with a pattern of abbreviations, the obvious
purpose being to save both space and time of the copyist.

PETER NAYLOR            Iron            65 Broad St., New York City

*June 12/52 Was originally a mftr. of Metal Roofing &c.,*
*by wh. he made a great deal of money: is a cautious shrewd*
*gd. bus. man, has always been successful—Is now entirely*
*engaged in the Cali. trade, has, tis said, 100m/$ invested in*
*the trade, w. 100m/$ more in R. E. &c.—Owns 3 Stores*
*in Stone St., & one in So. William, besides a ho. in Madison*
*Aven. for wh. he gave 20m/$ & has since refused 22½m/$*
*"Thos. Selby" is his Agt. in Cali. & is a 1st rate bus. man in*
*all respects—"N" has been vy. fortunate in his Cali bus.—*
*was rich before he went into it, & has made money at it— He*
*is considd. gd. for anything he wants. Jan. 24/53 In bus.*
*principally in California Trade, said to have made a great deal*

309

*of money, some think him extended so much in that trade, that they dispose of his paper immediately, while others from his shrewd bus. capacity & amt. of means, have great confidence in him. April 13' 54 Rich, w. at least 150m/ $ no better man in the trade. Oct. 28/54 Gd. beyond doubt Is believed to be w. several hundred thousand dolls. Has made, it is sd., a great deal of money in the Calfa. trade. Mar. 28/55. Has done exceedingly well the last 2 years, & has made consid. money Calfa. Oct. 3/55 Is a man of considerab. mes. & in gd. cr.—Feb.26/56 Has a house in San Francisco, Califa, under the firm of "T.H. Selby & Co." "S" is an act. bus. man, of fair char., & gd. for his personal engagements, probably, but is not of much pecuniary responsibility, & the cr. of the house—which is gd. here & in Califa.—is dependent upon "N."s connexion with it. Oct. 4/56. In good stand'g & cr. & consid. good for his contracts. Mar. 28/57 Continues in gd. stdg. & cr. & regardd. reliab. for his contracts. Oct. 27. Continues to sustain his former gd. stand'g & cr. & tho't gd for his contracts. Feb. 58. Is supposed to have gone thro' the crisis, without asking any favors. & is now in his usual gd. standing & cr. & considd. reliable for contracts. April 14/58, Paid, all thro & nothing has transpired to impair his standing & cr: He keeps his bus. within his means & his paper is regarded favorably. He is tho't sound & reliable for his contracts. Oct. 58 Standing & Cr. unimpaired, his California bu. is understood to be profitable & well managed by his son in law, Mc Haclon.*

The collection of handwritten report ledgers of The Mercantile Agency covers the history of business in the United States from 1841 to the late 1880s, when the typewriter with mechanical and chemical reproduction methods provided faster and wider distribution of credit reports. For forty years these reports followed the economic ups and downs of wholesalers, retailers and jobbers, small shops in the metals and clothing industries, and a wide variety of importing-exporting companies which prospered or faded in significance as the nature of trade and industry changed with invention, communication, and transportation. While statistical and economic data are revealed in each report sequence, it is the human factors which are most apparent in the growth and progress, strength and weakness of the management whether it be a large corporation, a medium-sized wholesaler, or a general store in a small community. Methods and techniques have altered with the 130 years of credit reporting, but principles of management are without fundamental change.

# SELECTED BIBLIOGRAPHY

ADAMS, GRACE, and HUTTER, EDWARD. *The Mad Forties.* New York, 1942.

ADAMS, W. F. *Ireland and Irish Emigration to the New World from 1815 to the Famine.* London, 1932.

BAXTER, W. E. *America and the Americans.* London, 1855.

BERGER, MAX. *The British Traveller in America, 1836–1860.* New York, 1964.

BILL, ALEXANDER. *Rehearsal for Conflict: The War with Mexico, 1846–1848.* New York, 1947.

BILLINGTON, RAY. *The Protestant Crusade, 1800–1860.* New York, 1938.

BLAU, JOSEPH, ed. *Social Theories of Jacksonian Democracy.* New York, 1954.

BODE, CARL, ed. *American Life in the 1840s.* New York, 1967.

BOLLES, ALBERT. *Industrial History of the United States.* New York, 1881.

BRANCH, E. DOUGLASS. *The Sentimental Years, 1836–1860.* New York, 1934.

BUCKINGHAM, JAMES SILK. *America: Historical, Statistical, and Descriptive,* 3 vols. London, 1841.

———. *The Slave States of America,* 2 vols. London, 1842.

BULEY, R. CARLYLE. *The Old Northwest: Pioneer Period, 1815–1840.* Bloomington, Ind., 1950.

BURNETT, CONSTANCE. *Five for Freedom.* New York, 1953.

CHEVALIER, MICHAEL. *Society, Manners, and Politics in the United States.* New York, 1839.

CUNNINGHAM, C. WILLETT. *Feminine Attitudes in the Nineteenth Century.* New York, 1936.

DE BOW, J. D. B. *The Industrial Resources, Statistics, Etc. of the United States, and More Particularly of the Southern and Western States,* 3 vols. New York, 1854.

DE VOTO, BERNARD. *The Year of Decision, 1846.* New York, 1943.

DICKENS, CHARLES. *American Notes.* Boston, 1867.

DUBERMAN, MARTIN, ed. *The Anti-Slavery Vanguard.* Princeton, N.J., 1965.

EATON, CLEMENT. *The Freedom of Thought Struggle in the Old South.* New York, 1964.

———, ed. *The Leaven of Democracy.* New York, 1963.

ELKINS, STANLEY. *Slavery: A Problem in American Institutional and Intellectual Life.* New York, 1959.

FILLER, LOUIS. *The Crusade Against Slavery, 1830–1860.* New York, 1960.

FISH, CARL. *The Rise of the Common Man, 1830–1850.* New York, 1927.

FISHLOW, ALBERT. *American Railroads and the Transformation of the Ante-Bellum Economy.* Cambridge, Mass., 1965.

FURNAS, J. C. *The Americans: A Social History of the United States, 1587–1919.* New York, 1969.

GATTEY, CHARLES. *The Bloomer Girls.* New York, 1968.

GENOVESE, EUGENE. *The Political Economy of Slavery.* New York, 1967.

GHENT, WILLIAM. *The Road to Oregon.* New York, 1929.

GIDDINGS, JOSHUA. *Speeches in Congress.* New York, 1853.

GRAEBNER, NORMAN. *Empire on the Pacific.* New York, 1955.

GRATTAN, THOMAS. *Civilized America,* 2 vols. London, 1849.

GRUND, FRANCIS. *The Americans in their Moral, Social, and Political Relations,* 2 vols. New York, 1837.

———. *Aristocracy in America. London,* 1839.

HAMILTON, HOLMAN. *Zachary Taylor,* 2 vols. Indianapolis, 1941–1951.

HANSEN, MARCUS. *The Atlantic Migration, 1607–1860.* New York, 1961.

HENRY, ROBERT. *The Story of the Mexican War.* New York, 1950.

HOLBROOK, STEWART. *Iron Brew.* New York, 1939.

———. *The Story of American Railroads.* New York, 1947.

IRWIN, INEZ. *Angels and Amazons: A Hundred Years of American Women.* New York, 1934.

JAY, WILLIAM. *A Review of the Causes and Consequences of the Mexican War.* New York, 1849.

JENKINS, WILLIAM. *Pro-Slavery Thought in the Old South.* Chapel Hill, N.C., 1935.

LACOUR-GAYET, ROBERT. *Everyday Life in the United States Before the Civil War.* New York, 1969.

LADER, LAWRENCE. *The Bold Brahmins.* New York, 1961.

LITWACK, LEON. *North of Slavery: The Negro in the Free States, 1790–1860.* Chicago, 1961.

LYELL, CHARLES. *Travels in North America,* 2 vols. New York, 1845.

MARRYAT, FREDERICK. *Diary in America,* 3 vols. London, 1839.

MAY, SAMUEL. *Some Recollections of our Anti-Slavery Conflict.* New York, 1968 ed.

MENCKEN, AUGUST. *The Railroad Passenger Car.* Baltimore, 1957.

MERK, FREDERICK. *The Monroe Doctrine and American Expansionism.* New York, 1966.

———. *Manifest Destiny and Mission in American History.* New York, 1963.

MINNEGERODE, MEADE. *The Fabulous Forties, 1840–1850.* New York, 1924.

MORGAN, ROBERT. *A Whig Embattled: The Presidency Under John Tyler*. Lincoln, Neb., 1954.

NEVINS, ALLAN, ed. *The Diary of Philip Hone, 1828–1851,* 2 vols. New York, 1927.

PARKER, ROBERT. *A Yankee Saint: John Humphrey Noyes and the Oneida Community*. New York, 1935.

PARKMAN, FRANCIS. *The Oregon Trail*. New York, 1963 ed.

PAXTON, FREDERIC. *History of the American Frontier, 1763–1893*. New York, 1954.

PHILLIPS, ULRICH. *Life and Labor in the Old South*. Boston, 1935.

PROBST, GEORGE, ed. *The Happy Republic: A Reader in Tocqueville's America*. New York, 1962.

PULSZKY, FRANCIS and THERESA. *White, Red, Black: Sketches of American Society*. New York, 1853.

QUARLES, BENJAMIN. *Black Abolitionists*. New York, 1969.

RAUMER, FREDERICK VON. *America and the American People*. New York, 1846.

RIEGEL, ROBERT. *Young America, 1830–1840*. New York, 1949.

——— and ATHERN, ROBERT. *America, Moves West*. New York, 1964.

SELLERS, CHARLES. *James K. Polk, Jacksonian, 1795–1843*. Princeton, N. J., 1957.

SINCLAIR, ANDREW. *The Better Half: The Emancipation of the American Woman*. New York, 1965.

SMEDES, SUSAN DABNEY. *Memorials of a Southern Planter*. Baltimore, 1887.

SPENCE, CLARK. *The Sinews of American Capitalism*. New York, 1964.

STILL, WILLIAM. *The Underground Railroad*. New York, 1968 ed.

STOVER, JOHN. *American Railroads*. Chicago, 1961.

STURGE, JOSEPH. *A Visit to the United States in 1841*. London, 1842.

SWANK, JAMES. *History of the Manufacture of Iron in All Ages*. Philadelphia, 1892.

TAYLOR, GEORGE. *The Transportation Revolution, 1815–1860.* New York, 1951.

TOCQUEVILLE, ALEXIS DE. *Democracy in America,* 2 vols. New York, 1835.

TRYON, ROLLA. *Household Manufacture in the United States, 1640–1860.* New York, 1966.

WALKER, JAMES. *The Epic of American Industry.* New York, 1949.

WHITE, STEWART. *The Forty-Niners.* New York, 1918.

WILE, FREDERICK. *A Century of Industrial Progress.* New York, 1928.

WOODMAN, HAROLD, ed. *Slavery and the Southern Economy.* New York, 1966.

WORTLEY, LADY EMMELINE. *Travels in the United States, etc. during 1849 and 1850.* New York, 1851.

WRIGHT, CARROLL. *The Industrial Evolution of the United States.* New York, 1895.

# INDEX

(Page numbers in italics denote illustrations)

## DATE DUE

| AP 29 '75 | | | |
|---|---|---|---|
| | | | |
| | | | |
| | | | |
| | | | |
| | | | |
| | | | |
| | | | |
| | | | |
| | | | |
| | | | |
| | | | |
| | | | |
| | | | |
| | | | |
| GAYLORD | | | PRINTED IN U.S.A. |